A GUIDE TO PL/M PROGRAMMING FOR MICROCOMPUTER APPLICATIONS

A GUIDE TO PL/M PROGRAMMING FOR MICROCOMPUTER APPLICATIONS

DANIEL D. McCRACKEN

ADDISON-WESLEY PUBLISHING COMPANY

Reading, Massachusetts • Menlo Park, California • London
Amsterdam • Don Mills, Ontario • Sydney

 Printed in the United States of America. Published simultaneously in Canada. Library of Congress Catalog Card No. 77-90172.

ISBN 0-201-04575-3
ABCDEFGHIJ-MU-798

PREFACE

This book is written for the person who wants to get a rapid grasp of programming for microcomputers, using a modern higher-level language. It assumes no previous experience in programming or in microcomputer applications. Only the most basic background notions of data representation and computer operation are required.

Each of the nine chapters is based on one or more example programs that present the programming concepts in a framework of meaningful microcomputer applications. In fact, over half of the book consists of example programs and discussions of them. All programs have been run on an Intellec Microcomputer Development System, and printed output is displayed for many of them.

The writing of the book has been supported and directed by the Intel Corporation. Several of the programs were adapted from work done by Intel personnel, and their helpful suggestions led to many significant improvements in programs and in the text. I wish it were possible to name all the people who were helpful during the course of the project, but it would take half a page and even then I'd leave some out. All their contributions are gratefully acknowledged.

Ossining, New York
December, 1977

Daniel D. McCracken

CONTENTS

CHAPTER 1

AN OVERVIEW OF PL/M PROGRAMMING

WHAT IS PL/M?

PL/M is a programming language for expressing procedures in a wide variety of systems and applications work with microcomputers. The original design of the language was done by the Intel Corporation in 1973. The presentation in this book is based on a revised PL/M specification issued in 1976 and copyrighted by Intel.

PL/M is a simple language, easy to learn, understand, and use. It is powerful, in that it gives access to the full power of the microcomputer, but uses a compact notation for expressing the desired processing.

PL/M provides a means of programming that:

- often reduces the time and cost of programming,
- increases software reliability,
- improves documentation,
- facilitates software maintenance.

All of these advantages are in part a result of the fact that PL/M permits us to write programs that are easy to understand.

WHAT IS PL/M-80?

PL/M-80 is an implementation of the PL/M language for the Intel 8080 microcomputer. It implements the full PL/M language except for a few relatively minor restrictions.

It is expected that there will be implementations of PL/M for other microcomputers based on the Intel standard. Assuming that these other implementations adhere reasonably closely to the Intel standard, there should be no difficulty in adapting the presentation in this book for use with other implementations.

THE GOALS OF THE BOOK

We shall begin the study of PL/M for microcomputer applications by looking in this chapter at a small but complete PL/M program. In succeeding chapters we shall accumulate knowledge of the elements of the PL/M language as we consider successively larger and more realistic PL/M applications programs. Starting in Chapter 4, after some of the more important fundamentals have been mastered, we shall begin to devote considerable attention to the process by which programs are developed. It is not enough simply to know all of the facts about the PL/M language or to be able to understand a program that some one else has written. It is also necessary to be able to write good programs oneself, given only a specification of what the program must do and perhaps a general indication of how it should do it.

We assume that the reader's purpose in studying this book is just that: to learn how to write good PL/M programs in his or her areas of application.

The way to learn programming is to learn the vocabulary and syntax of the language and what it does, then learn how to read programs that others have written, and then *write lots of programs and run them.* Some of the exercises at the ends of the chapters call for the writing of programs that may in some cases be small by the standards of realistic applications, but which are complete and which should be coded and run on a computer if at all possible. By the time the reader has studied the material in Chapter 5 on procedures, he will have enough knowledge to be writing significant applications programs.

These are the goals and the approaches we shall take to reach them. Now let's get started.

A PL/M PROGRAM

The simple program that we shall study in this chapter is required to read values of two binary variables and produce an output variable that is the "AND" function of the two inputs. For the sake of realism we assume that the inputs describe the status of a door and a switch in some kind of manufacturing process. We assume that these devices have been wired to the inputs of the microcomputer so as to have the following meanings:

For the door:
- 0 means that the door is closed
- 1 means that the door is open

For the switch:
- 0 means that the switch is off
- 1 means that the switch is on

The specifications say that to put the process into operation, the door must be open and the switch must be on. In numeric terms, both values must be one before the process can start.

THE GENERAL CHARACTERISTICS OF A PL/M PROGRAM

Figure 1.1 shows a program that will fulfill these specifications. Let us look first at its overall characteristics before studying the details.

```
 /* A PROGRAM THAT ANDS TWO INPUTS TO PRODUCE AN OUTPUT */

ANDER:
DO;
   DECLARE DOOR$1 BYTE;
   DECLARE SWITCH$1 BYTE;
   DECLARE START$PROCESS BYTE;

   DOOR$1 = INPUT(1);
   SWITCH$1 = INPUT(5);
   START$PROCESS = DOOR$1 AND SWITCH$1;
   OUTPUT(1) = START$PROCESS;
END;
```

Fig. 1.1. A program that ANDs two inputs to produce an output.

We see at the beginning a *comment,* which is any string of characters that begins with /* and ends with */. We have used a comment here to provide a descriptive heading for the program. Actually, comments may be used anywhere that PL/M permits a space. We occasionally use comments within a program to describe what is being done, when the statements themselves are not obvious. A comment is reproduced verbatim in a program listing like that shown in Fig. 1.1 but has no effect on the operation of the program.

We see that the program proper begins with a name followed by a colon and that all of the rest of the program is enclosed between the words DO and END. The fact that the entire program is enclosed in the DO *block* defined by this DO–END pair is signified by indenting all of the statements between the DO–END pair by a consistent amount. This indentation is not required by the language and no meaning is derived from it by the computer. It is a very significant aid to human understanding of the program, however, and strong emphasis will be placed throughout the book on the use of indentation.

Statements

The program consists of a number of *statements*. Every statement terminates with a semicolon. For the sake of clarity we never put more than one statement on a line, although the language specifications do permit it. Statements are sometimes written on more than one line, either for clarity or because they are too long to fit on one line.

The DECLARE Statement

Every variable used in a PL/M program must appear in a DECLARE statement and all the DECLARE statements in a DO block must appear at the beginning of the block. Each of the DECLAREs here contains just one variable and each is specified to be a BYTE variable. This means that the representation of the variable within the computer program will be one byte consisting of eight bits. We shall see in the next chapter that there is a second type of variable, the ADDRESS type, consisting of 16 bits.

In these DECLARE statements we see that the names of variables, more precisely called *identifiers,* may consist of letters, digits, and the dollar sign. The first character of an identifier must be a letter. The dollar sign is used only to improve readability and carries no meaning. Thus DOOR$1 would mean exactly the same thing as DOOR1 and would, in fact, be the same identifier.

The Specification of Processing

After the DECLARE statements we see a blank line, which was inserted to help clarify the structure of the program, separating the declarations from the statements that specify what processing is to be done. We will use blank lines freely to help convey program organization to human readers. Such blank lines, like indentation, carry no meaning.

The Assignment Statement

The statement

```
DOOR$1 = INPUT(1);
```

is an example of an *assignment statement*. The general form of the assignment statement is

```
variable = expression;
```

The statement means:

> "Evaluate the expression on the righthand side of the equal sign, and *assign* that value to the variable written on the lefthand side of the equal sign."

In many cases the expression on the righthand side will be quite simple, as here, but expressions can be rather more complex, as we shall see in due course.

In the assignment statement just shown, the operation specified is to obtain a byte of data from the input port that has been assigned the number 1. The number of ports available and the identifying numbers associated with them are a matter of system hardware architecture. Not every microcomputer system would necessarily have ports with the numbers shown here.

The *input* operation obtains a complete byte of eight bits from the port identified by the number within the parentheses. We assume a problem specification which says that the rightmost bit coming in from this port will be either a zero or a one, depending on the status of the door. It is also specified that all of the other bits of this byte will be zeros.

Similarly, the byte obtained from input port 5 consists of either a zero or a one in the rightmost bit position and zeros in the other seven bit positions. (This use of two separate bytes on two ports to obtain just two bits of information is untypical. It is a simplification to make this first illustrative program manageable.)

The AND Operation

Now we come to the statement that is the primary function of the program: to establish whether the door is open and the switch on. This is done with the *logical operator* AND, which operates on all eight pairs of bits of the two bytes specified on the left and right of the AND. For each pair of bits, the result of the AND is a one if both bits are one, and zero otherwise. Thus in the seven bit-positions in which each bit of the pair is a zero, the result of the AND will also be a zero. In the rightmost bit position, the result will be a one if the door is open *and* the switch is on; it will be zero otherwise.

The result of this operation is therefore either a byte of eight zero bits or a byte of seven zero bits and a one. This value, whichever it is, is assigned to the variable having the identifier START$PROCESS.

Finally we send this byte to the output port having the number 1, where we assume that process-control hardware has been wired to bit zero of that port, which will start the process. Note that output port 1 has no relation to input port 1.

This completes the action required of this extremely simple program, which would halt operation upon reaching the END statement. No realistic applications program would ever stop in just this way, but the language elements required to make the program repeat in a meaningful way would unduly complicate this first program.

Condensing the Program

The variables used in this program serve no other purpose than to improve the human understandability of the program. The last two statements could be condensed to read

```
OUTPUT(1) = DOOR$1 AND SWITCH$1;
```

with exactly the same result. The program could be further condensed to the absolute minimum of

```
ANDER:
DO;
   OUTPUT(1) = INPUT(1) AND INPUT(5);
END;
```

with no DECLARE statements required because there are now no variables.

Realistic programs can rarely be "collapsed" so dramatically. We will frequently use intermediate variables to clarify to ourselves how a program works.

Compilation

The program shown in Fig. 1.1 is a PL/M *source program*. It is not directly executable by a microcomputer, which is controlled by programs in a much more primitive form called *machine language*. The function of the PL/M compiler is to transform a *source program* of PL/M statements into an *object program* of machine instructions that the microcomputer can execute. The compiler is itself a large computer program provided by the microcomputer manufacturer. In earlier implementations the PL/M compiler had to be run on a separate larger computer; the PL/M-80 compiler runs on an Intel Microcomputer Development System, the heart of which is an 8080 microcomputer.

A somewhat more complete, although still abbreviated, description of the Microcomputer Development System and the various systems programs provided with it may be found in Chapter 9.

The Source Program Listing

One of the outputs of compilation is a listing of the program with certain information added. Figure 1.2 shows the listing produced when the program of Fig. 1.1 was compiled. We see that the compiler has added a *statement number* in the leftmost position of each line and a *nesting-level indicator* in the next position. The meaning of the latter will become clear in Chapter 3. If there had been errors in the source program, such as missing semicolons at the ends of statements, references to variables that had not been declared, or any of a wide variety of errors in the syntax of statements, these errors would have been listed with a brief diagnosis. We shall look into this matter in Chapter 9.

```
PL/M-80 COMPILER                                                    PAGE   1

                      /* A PROGRAM THAT ANDS TWO INPUTS TO PRODUCE AN OUTPUT */

   1                  ANDER:
                      DO;
   2    1                DECLARE DOOR$1 BYTE;
   3    1                DECLARE SWITCH$1 BYTE;
   4    1                DECLARE START$PROCESS BYTE;

   5    1                DOOR$1 = INPUT(1);
   6    1                SWITCH$1 = INPUT(5);
   7    1                START$PROCESS = DOOR$1 AND SWITCH$1;
   8    1                OUTPUT(1) = START$PROCESS;
   9    1             END;
```

Fig. 1.2. The listing of the source program shown in Fig. 1.1, as produced by the PL/M compiler.

The Object Program

It is not assumed that the reader of this book is familiar with programming in the machine language of the microcomputers. It is not necessary to have this background to study PL/M or to use it. Just to give a hint of the nature of the microcomputer language, however, we show in Fig. 1.3 the machine-language instructions generated corresponding to each of the four assignment statements.

There is no simple way to demonstrate the functioning of this program exactly as it stands. However, a modified version was written using input and output techniques appropriate to the development process as described in later chapters. This modified program was compiled and run. It produced correct results. This is the normal way to improve one's confidence that a PL/M program is correct.

```
              /* A PROGRAM THAT ANDS TWO INPUTS TO PRODUCE AN OUTPUT */

              $CODE

1             ANDER:
              DO;
2     1         DECLARE DOOR$1 BYTE;
3     1         DECLARE SWITCH$1 BYTE;
4     1         DECLARE START$PROCESS BYTE;

5     1         DOOR$1 = INPUT(1);
                                                   ; STATEMENT # 5
          0000  310000          LXI     SP,@STACK$ORIGIN
          0003  DB01            IN      1H
          0005  320000          STA     DOOR1
6     1         SWITCH$1 = INPUT(5);
                                                   ; STATEMENT # 6
          0008  DB05            IN      5H
          000A  320100          STA     SWITCH1
7     1         START$PROCESS = DOOR$1 AND SWITCH$1;
                                                   ; STATEMENT # 7
          000D  210000          LXI     H,DOOR1
          0010  A6              ANA     M
          0011  320200          STA     STARTPROCESS
8     1         OUTPUT(1) = START$PROCESS;
                                                   ; STATEMENT # 8
          0014  D301            OUT     1H
9     1       END;
                                                   ; STATEMENT # 9
          0016  FB              EI
          0017  76              HLT
```

Fig. 1.3. A listing of the source program of Fig. 1.1 in which the machine instructions generated by the compiler are shown. ***The reader is not expected to be able to understand these instructions.***

CHAPTER 2

PL/M FUNDAMENTALS

INTRODUCTION

In this chapter we shall build a foundation of basic information about PL/M, material that is fundamental to all further study of PL/M programming. This basic material will be sufficient to let us write an interesting and fairly realistic program in the case study at the end of the chapter, to do processing of data in a hypothetical process-control application.

THE PL/M CHARACTER SET

In writing a PL/M program only the following characters may be used:

Upper case letters: ABCDEFGHIJKLMNOPQRSTUVWXYZ
Lower case letters: abcdefghijklmnopqrstuvwxyz
Decimal digits: 0123456789
Dollar sign: $
The character blank:
The apostrophe: '
The special characters: + − * / = : ; . , ( ) < >

Some PL/M implementations may not include the use of lower-case letters. Where lower-case letters are permitted, they are considered to be the same as upper-case letters, for purposes of writing PL/M programs. (Upper- and lower-case letters are still different when considered as data to be processed by a program, however.)

Characters beyond this basic set may be available in some implementations.

VARIABLE NAMES

We shall have much occasion to work with the concept of a *variable*. A variable is a location in memory in which a value is stored and from which it may later be retrieved. Every variable must have a name, also called an *identifier*.

An identifier must begin with a letter, which may be followed by any number of letters, decimal digits, and/or dollar signs. If more than 31 letters and digits are used, the result depends on the particular compiler implementation. Some may simply ignore any characters beyond 31; others may regard such an identifier as an error. The dollar sign may optionally be used to improve readability but carries no significance. Thus, INPUT$4 and INPUT4 are considered to be the same identifier. Any dollar signs are not counted in applying the compiler's rules about identifiers having more than 31 characters. Finally, as noted, upper- and lower-case letters are equivalent in identifiers.

Here are some valid identifiers.

```
A                       CONTROL$INPUT
A1                      CARRIAGE$RETURN$AND$LINE$FEED
A$1                     CRLF
PREVIOUS$LINE           TEMPORARY$BYTE$8
ASTERISK                TEMP8
SOURCE$POINTER          CONTACT$8
QUANTITY$ON$HAND        X1234567890
QUANTITYONHAND          X$$$1234567890
QOH                     POPULATION$COUNT
MASK                    REFERENCE$TEMPERATURE
MESSAGE$1               REF$TEMP
MSG1                    ARRAY$SIZE
DATA$1                  ADDRESS$CONSTANT
```

Here are some invalid identifiers.

12345	Does not begin with a letter
MESSAGE-1	Contains an invalid character
MESSAGE 2	Contains a blank
8$CONTACT	Does not begin with a letter
AND/OR	Contains an invalid character
DATA	Reserved word; see below
MESSAGE&BUFFER	Contains a character not in PL/M character set

REPRESENTATION OF NUMERIC DATA

Data to be processed by a PL/M program must be either a BYTE or ADDRESS quantity. A BYTE variable consists of eight bits and can hold an unsigned integer between 0 and 255, inclusive. An ADDRESS variable is so named because it consists of two bytes, which is 16 bits, the length of an address in the Intel 8080. However, an ADDRESS variable can hold any unsigned integer between 0 and 65535 inclusive, regardless of whether or not a given value corresponds to an actual address in a particular microcomputer system. ADDRESS variables are used for many purposes besides holding machine addresses.

We need both BYTE and ADDRESS variables in order to be able to use memory economically. When we really need more than eight bits, the ADDRESS type is available, but if eight is enough we can use the BYTE type and avoid wasting storage.

There are no fractional numbers or negative numbers in PL/M. The subtraction of a larger number from a smaller number is done with 2's complement arithmetic and produces another positive integer. Likewise, all arithmetic operations on PL/M variables produce integer results.

NUMERIC CONSTANTS

A PL/M numeric constant may be written in any of four number systems, as follows:

1. A *binary number* (base 2) is made up from the binary digits 0 and 1 followed by the letter B.
2. An *octal number* (base 8) is made up from the octal digits 0 through 7 followed by the letter O or the letter Q. The option of using the letter Q is provided to avoid possible confusion between the letter O and the digit zero.
3. A *decimal number* (base 10) is made up from the decimal digits, 0 through 9, optionally followed by the letter D.
4. A *hexadecimal number* (base 16) is made up from the hexadecimal digits 0 through 9 and A through F followed by the letter H. A hexadecimal number must begin with a decimal digit, even if a zero must be used at the beginning when it would otherwise be unnecessary.

In all cases the dollar sign may be inserted as one wishes, to improve readability; it carries no significance.

Here are some examples of PL/M numeric constants. Those in the first column all represent the same quantity and those in the second column all represent the same quantity.

```
      24                  3354
     24D                 3354D
  11000B         110100011010B
     30O     1101$0001$1010B
     30Q                 6432O
     18H                6$432Q
                         0D1AH
```

It is also possible to represent strings of characters in PL/M, each character having a binary-coded representation. Such values can also be stored in BYTE and ADDRESS variables and processed by various PL/M operations. We shall consider such matters in Chapter 4.

RESERVED WORDS

There is a set of words that follow the foregoing rules for forming identifiers but which may be used only in specific ways prescribed by the definition of PL/M language. In particular they may not be used as variable names. These *reserved words,* as they are called, are as follows:

```
ADDRESS     ENABLE       MOD
AND         END          NOT
AT          EOF          OR
BASED       EXTERNAL     PLUS
BY          GO           PROCEDURE
BYTE        GOTO         PUBLIC
CALL        HALT         REENTRANT
CASE        IF           RETURN
DATA        INITIAL      STRUCTURE
DECLARE     INTERRUPT    THEN
DISABLE     LABEL        TO
DO          LITERALLY    WHILE
ELSE        MINUS        XOR
```

THE ARITHMETIC OPERATORS

The four arithmetic operations are specified in PL/M by the following *arithmetic operators:*

+	means to add
−	means to subtract
*	means to multiply
/	means to divide

In addition and subtraction, the result of the operation is of type ADDRESS if either operand is an ADDRESS quantity and of type BYTE only if both operands are BYTE quantities. If one operand is BYTE and the other ADDRESS, the BYTE operand is extended on the left with zeros before the operation is carried out. Multiplication and division always return an ADDRESS result, regardless of whether the operands are BYTE or ADDRESS—even if both are BYTE. In any operation, if the result cannot be contained in the variable to which the result is to be assigned, excess bits at the left are simply dropped, without warning. This could happen, for instance, in adding two BYTE quantities where the sum exceeds 255, or in multiplying two quantities giving a product greater than 65535.

It is important to understand that division in PL/M is always of two integers, with an unrounded integer result. The remainder in the division is simply ignored. Rounding can be achieved, however, by techniques that we shall study later.

Here is an example of the use of addition:

```
TOTAL$CURRENT =  LOOP$1 + LOOP$2;
```

In order for this statement to be meaningful, LOOP$1 and LOOP$2 would have to have been given values by statements executed prior to this one. The effect would be to add the two values and place the sum in the location identified by TOTAL$ CURRENT, replacing whatever may have been in that location previously.

Another example of addition:

```
COUNTER = COUNTER + 1;
```

One is added to the value identified by COUNTER, and the sum placed back in COUNTER. This kind of statement finds frequent use in programming. It demonstrates rather vividly that the assignment statement is not an equation. In fact, it helps clarify meaning if we read such statements as "COUNTER *is replaced by* COUNTER + 1," or "COUNTER *gets* COUNTER + 1," rather than the more obvious but potentially confusing "COUNTER *equals* COUNTER + 1."

Here is an example of subtraction:

```
NET$WEIGHT = GROSS$WEIGHT - TARE;
```

The indicated subtraction is performed and the result is stored in NET$WEIGHT.

Consider this example of multiplication:

```
VOLTAGE = CURRENT * RESISTANCE;
```

It is the programmer's responsibility to be sure that the product will fit in the space allocated for VOLTAGE, whether it has been declared as BYTE or ADDRESS. If VOLTAGE has been declared as BYTE and the product has more than eight bits, i.e., is larger than 255, the storage allocation for VOLTAGE is *not* automatically increased. We shall study the programming techniques necessary to deal with such tasks as we go along.

Finally, here is an example of division:

```
AVERAGE = SUM/3;
```

The value identified by SUM is divided by 3 and the integer quotient—ignoring any remainder—is placed in AVERAGE. The value resulting from a division by zero is "undefined," meaning that although one might discover what happens in a particular computer and particular PL/M implementation, the result is not guaranteed in other machines and implementations. Only by mistake would anyone ever attempt to divide by a constant of zero, but division by a variable may lead to the attempt to do so, depending on data values. If this problem exists, as it frequently does, one must test the divisor in advance, using the IF statement and other techniques to be discussed in the next chapter.

Note that the statement in this example has been written without spaces around the division operator, whereas previous examples had spaces around the operators. This is a matter of taste, to be governed by understandability considerations. We shall ordinarily set operators off by spaces.

THE UNARY MINUS

A minus sign can sometimes be unary, meaning that it applies to only one quantity rather than denoting the subtraction of two quantities. For example, the minus signs in these statements are all unary:

```
A = - 12;
B = -(X + Y);
C = SPEED * (-TIME);
```

The result obtained from a unary minus is the same as if the quantity after the minus sign had been subtracted from zero, and is therefore the 2's complement of the number.

The unary minus is seldom used, and will not appear in any of the programs in this book.

THE MOD OPERATOR

Sometimes it is necessary to obtain the remainder resulting from a division, which we can do using the MOD operator. The name is an abbreviation for *modulo,* the mathematical term for the remainder when two integers are divided. The operator is written between two operands, just like the four familiar arithmetic operators:

```
REMAINDER = SUM MOD 3;
```

This says to divide the value of SUM by 3 and assign the remainder to REMAINDER. If 3 divides SUM exactly, the remainder will be zero; this can also be expressed by saying that SUM is a multiple of 3. If this is not the case, the remainder will be 1 or 2, the only other possibilities on division by 3.

One may not omit the spaces around the MOD without losing its meaning, since if we wrote

```
REMAINDER = SUMMOD3;
```

the compiler would take SUMMOD3 to be an identifier.

PRECEDENCE OF OPERATORS

When an unparenthesized expression contains more than one operator, the precedence of the operators is governed by the following rules:

1. Any unary minus operations are carried out first.
2. Multiplications, divisions, and MOD operations are done next.
3. Additions and subtractions are done next.
4. Operations at the same precedence level are carried out from left to right.

These rules are the same as those underlying ordinary algebraic notation.

For an example of the application of these rules, consider this expression:

```
A + B * C
```

Just as in ordinary mathematical notation, the multiplication takes precedence, so this means to multiply B by C and add the product to A. Again, this expression

```
A / B - C
```

means to divide A by B and subtract C from the quotient. Consider this expression:

```
A / B * C
```

Rule 3 says that this is the same as (A/B)*C. Parentheses must be used to specify A/(B*C), if that is what is meant.

PARENTHESES

Just as in ordinary mathematical notation, parentheses can be used to group operands and thus force the order of evaluation of an expression. Operations within parentheses are carried out before operations outside parentheses. If there are parentheses within parentheses, the innermost operations are done first.

Most PL/M programs will not have complex arithmetic expressions requiring heavy reliance on the precedence rules *or* the use of parentheses for grouping subexpressions. When expressions of even moderate complexity arise, however, a good maxim is: *When in doubt, parenthesize.* There is no penalty for doing so, and it can save the troublesome situation where an expression is legal but does not correctly express our intentions. Such mistakes can be very hard to find, or, worse, may go undetected, leading to wrong results in a running program.

In this expression, the parentheses are required:

```
(A + B) * C
```

Without them, the meaning is different. In the following expression, the parentheses are optional, but do no harm:

```
A + (B * C)
```

THE LOGICAL OPERATORS

There are four *logical operators* in PL/M, for carrying out some of the common logical operations on bits.

The simplest of these is NOT, which is a unary operator (i.e., it takes only one operand). Each bit of its operand is complemented; that is, each result bit is 0 if the operand bit is 1, and 1 if the operand bit is 0. This is often called the *one's complement* operation.

The operator applies both to BYTE and ADDRESS operands:

```
NOT 11001011B yields 00110100B
```

The AND operator operates on pairs of bits. Each bit of the result is 1 if and only if both bits in the corresponding positions of the two operands are 1. For example,

```
       11001011B
   AND 00001111B
yields 00001011B
```

This operator is often used, as we have already seen in the case study in Chapter 1, to determine logical relationships among variables. It can also be used to *mask off* unwanted bits in an operand, as the previous example suggests: The result of the AND operation here is guaranteed to have zeros in the four high-order (leftmost) bit positions. We shall have frequent occasion to use the AND operator for this kind of masking.

The AND operator produces an ADDRESS result if either (or both) operand(s) is (are) ADDRESS, and BYTE otherwise. The same is true of the OR and XOR operators discussed below. As with the arithmetic operators, if one operand is BYTE and the other ADDRESS, the BYTE operand is extended on the left with zeros before the operation is carried out.

The OR operator also works on pairs of bits. The result bit is 1 if either (or both) of the bits in corresponding positions of the operands is 1, and zero only if both operand bits are zero. For example

```
       11001011B
    OR 00001111B
yields 11001111B
```

The OR operator is useful in forming logical functions of actual data variables, and in combining bits from different bytes into one byte. For an example of the latter, suppose one operand always has zeros in its high-order four positions and the other always has zeros in its low-order four positions; it is desired to combine the two into one byte. This OR will do that:

```
       00001101B
    OR 11100000B
yields 11101101B
```

The XOR operator ("exclusive OR") is closely related to the OR, the difference being that it does not accept the "or both" condition. That is, each result bit is 1 if *either* corresponding operand bit *but not both* is 1. The operand bit is thus zero if either both operand bits are zero or both are one. For example:

```
       11001011B
   XOR 00001111B
yields 11000100B
```

If the XOR of two quantities is all zeros, the quantities were the same, bit by bit.

PRECEDENCE OF LOGICAL OPERATORS

It is sometimes useful to write expressions having several logical operators, in which case we need hierarchy rules. In the absence of parentheses, the precedence is as follows:

1. Any NOT operations are carried out first.
2. AND operations are carried out next.
3. OR and XOR operations are carried out last.

Thus the following two expressions are equivalent:

```
A AND NOT B OR C
(A AND (NOT B)) OR C
```

To those readers familiar with logic operations, these rules will be familiar since they embody the usual notation for writing logic expressions. Again, however, complex expressions will be uncommon in PL/M programs, and the free use of parentheses to make meaning unambiguous is encouraged.

ARITHMETIC AND LOGICAL OPERATORS IN SAME EXPRESSION

It occasionally happens that we wish to write expressions containing both arithmetic and logical operators. In the absence of parentheses, there is the same question of precedence: Which operations are done first? The answer is simple: The arithmetic operations are done first. Thus, the following two expressions mean the same thing:

```
CONSOLE$INPUT - 10000000B OR END$SIGNAL
(CONSOLE$INPUT - 10000000B) OR END$SIGNAL
```

(There are also relational operators to go along with the arithmetic and logical operators that we have seen so far. These are considered in Chapter 3 in connection with the IF statement, where they find most frequent use. See page 37 for a discussion of the complete precedence list for all operators.)

SHIFT OPERATIONS

There are many occasions when it is necessary to shift the bits of a BYTE or ADDRESS quantity right or left. For one example of the need for such operations, we shall see, in the case study at the end of the chapter, that bits coming into a microcomputer from an input port are often not in the positions where they are needed for processing. Since additional input ports are relatively expensive, whereas a slight amount of extra processing may have an effective cost of zero, we prefer to move the data by program steps. Other examples will arise in other applications.

The two shifts that we shall consider here move the contents of a BYTE or ADDRESS quantity a specified number of places to the left or right. To specify what is to be done, we have to supply the program three pieces of information: what to shift, how many places, and which direction.

The last item, which direction, is provided when we write the name of the shift procedure that we wish, SHL for Shift Left, or SHR for Shift Right. Following the letters SHL or SHR, we write, within parentheses, first the item to be shifted, then a comma, then the number of places to shift.

For example, we could write this:

```
SHR(BYTE$1, 4)
```

The result would be to shift the value identified by BYTE$1 four places to the right. The four rightmost bits of BYTE$1—those shifted "off the end"—are lost. Zeros are entered at the left. (Note, incidentally, that BYTE$1 is an acceptable identifier even though BYTE by itself is a reserved word.)

Each of the quantities within parentheses can be either a variable or a constant, or, in fact, any expression. We could write, for instance:

```
SHL(00000001B, POSITIONS)
```

The 1 bit in the rightmost position of the first parameter of the shift would be shifted left as many positions as the value of the variable named POSITIONS. If the value of POSITIONS is greater than seven, the result will, of course, be all zeros. If the value of POSITIONS is zero, the result is undefined.

The result of writing one of these shift procedures is to call the procedure into operation and supply the shifted value, wherever the shift is written in an expression. If we want the result assigned to a variable, we can write things like:

```
SHIFTED$ADDRESS = SHR(A, 9);
```

If we want to carry out other operations, more complex expressions can be written. In the case study of this chapter, for instance, we shall see this statement:

```
MAINT$DOOR$1 = SHR(IN$PORT$0, 3) AND 00000001B;
```

This means to shift the value of IN$PORT$0 to the right three places and AND the result with a mask consisting of a 1 in rightmost position. The result is stored in the variable named MAINT$DOOR$1. Since the bits of a byte are numbered from the right, starting with zero, the result of this operation is to place in bit zero of MAINT$DOOR$1 whatever bit is in bit 3 of IN$PORT$0.

Observe that we could have achieved the same result with this statement:

```
MAINT$DOOR$1 = SHR(IN$PORT$0 AND 00001000B, 3);
```

Later in the case study we shall see this statement:

```
OUTPUT(0) = SHL(ALARM$2, 1) OR ALARM$1;
```

This means to shift the contents of ALARM$2 one place to the left and OR the result with ALARM$1, sending the combined result to output port zero.

These shifts return a BYTE result if the operand is a BYTE quantity and an ADDRESS result if the operand is an ADDRESS quantity.

There are four other shift operations that will find occasional use, although not in any of the examples in this book. They are:

ROR	Rotate right
ROL	Rotate left
SCR	Rotate right through the hardware carry flag
SCL	Rotate left through the hardware carry flag

BYTE/ADDRESS COERCION IN AN ASSIGNMENT STATEMENT

We recall from Chapter 1 that the general form of an assignment statement is:

```
variable = expression;
```

This means to evaluate the expression on the right and assign that value to the variable on the left. But what if the expression on the right yields a BYTE value and the variable on the left is of the ADDRESS type, or vice versa? When this occurs, the expression result is *coerced* to match the type of the variable to which it is being assigned. BYTE values being assigned to ADDRESS variables are extended with eight high-order (leftmost) zero bits. ADDRESS values being assigned to BYTE variables are truncated to the eight low-order bits; the eight high-order bits are deleted.

MULTIPLE ASSIGNMENT

Actually, we have so far abbreviated the full form of the assignment statement, which is:

```
variable1, variable2, . . ., variableN = expression;
```

That is, after evaluating the expression on the righthand side of the equal sign, the resulting value can be assigned to any number of variables, the names of which are separated by commas. Thus we can write statements like these:

```
SUM$1, SUM$2, COUNTER = 0;
POINTER$2, POINTER$3 = POINTER$1 + COUNT - 1;
```

When this is done the variables on the left are not required to be all of the same type; BYTE/ADDRESS conversion is carried out as needed.

CASE STUDY: CONTROL OF AN ELECTRICALLY HEATED FURNACE

Let us turn now to a simple application that could be done with a microcomputer, to see how the PL/M techniques that we have studied so far could be used in a realistic application. The example that we shall study is that of an electrically heated furnace. In this chapter we shall work with a very simple version of the application, and then in Chapters 3 and 5—which bring in additional facets of the application—employ additional PL/M features.

We imagine a furnace, perhaps a kiln, that has six doors, each equipped with an interlock switch that indicates whether the door is open or closed. Four of the doors are for maintenance purposes and should all be closed while the furnace is in operation. The other two doors are used in such a way that only one should be open during operation.

The microcomputer is installed in an operator's console, which has a two-position switch indicating whether the furnace is in operation or not. It also has three decimal-digit input devices, often called *thumbwheels,* into which the operator sets the temperature at which he wants the furnace to operate; this is the *reference temperature.*

A thermocouple in the furnace reads the operating temperature; the voltage from the thermocouple drives an analog-to-digital converter (ADC). The operation of the thermocouple and the converter are such that the actual temperature can be approximated by multiplying the ADC output by 1.84. We realize that thermocouples have nonlinear response curves and that, if highly accurate results are required, interpolation methods must be used. The PL/M techniques involved in interpolation will be studied in Chapter 4, and we shall incorporate this more accurate approach in the version of the program shown in Chapter 5. For now, however, we assume that a linear approximation is close enough.

These inputs are supplied to the microcomputer at four input ports. The details of assignment of data items to ports are shown in Fig. 2.1, along with the required outputs. These assignments are also described in an introductory comment in the program.

The program is required to produce three outputs: two alarm bits and a heater current value. One of the alarm bits signals an open maintenance door, and the other signals an illegal status of the two operational doors. The desired heater current is to be computed from the formula:

$$\text{Current} = 0.394 \times (\text{reference temperature} - \text{actual temperature})$$

We assume, for the purposes of this chapter, that the reference temperature is greater than the actual temperature. (In Chapter 3, once we have the necessary PL/M tools, we shall remove this unrealistic assumption.)

The assignment of these output values to output ports is shown in the program and in Fig. 2.1. Readers concerned about the cost of hardware should be assured that, if this were a real-life application, we would be able to combine functions of the ports and get by with one less port. For illustrative purposes here, the additional program complications don't seem worth the effort, but the reader should not assume that we are dismissing hardware-cost considerations out of hand.

A FIRST LOOK AT THE PROGRAM

Before delving into the details of the processing specified by the program shown in Fig. 2.2, note some of its overall characteristics.

We see that, at the beginning of the program, there is a set of comments giving a general description of what the program is required to do and its inputs and outputs (recall that a PL/M comment is any string of text enclosed between the comment brackets /* and */). The use of such a *preamble,* as it is sometimes called, is recommended. PL/M permits a comment anywhere in a program that a space is permitted, so there would be no requirement that the preamble appear exactly where it does here, but this arrangement is conventional.

As in the program of Chapter 1, all statements have been given statement numbers by the compiler. We see that the preamble, since it is a comment and not part

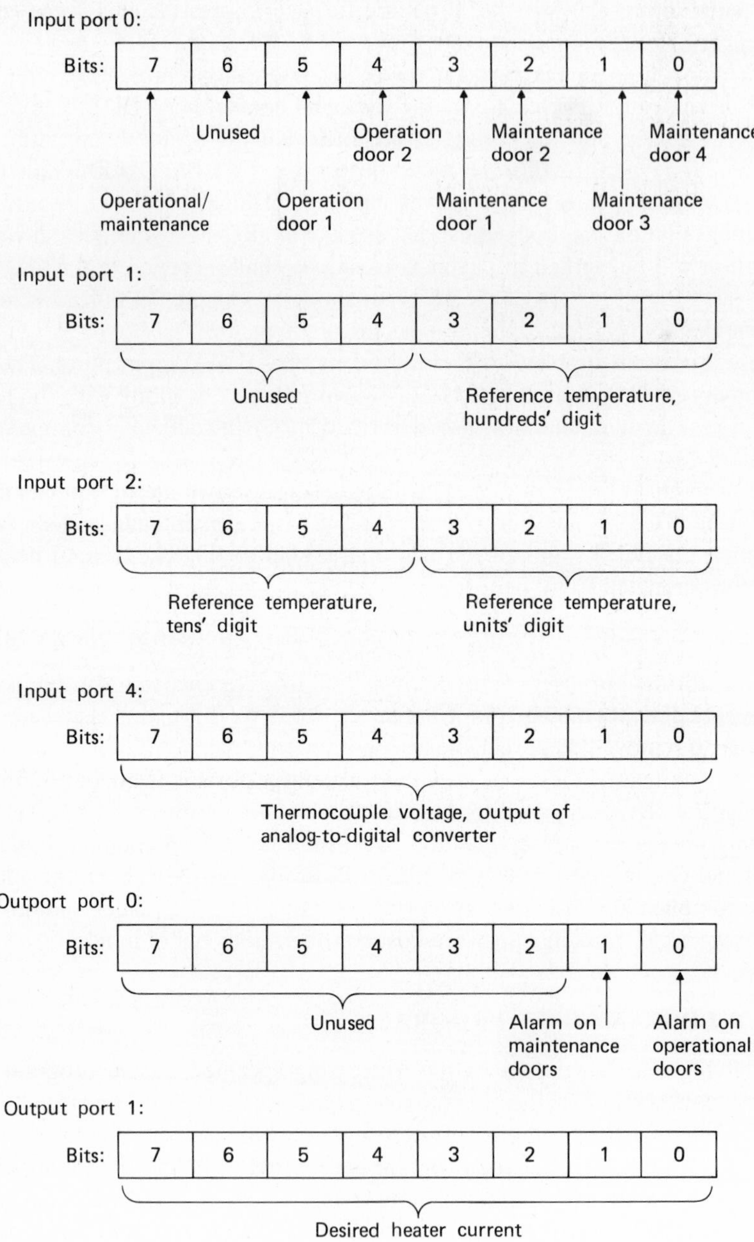

Fig. 2.1. The arrangement of bits in the input and output ports used by the program of Fig. 2.2.

```
PL/M-80 COMPILER    FIG. 2.2                                    PAGE   1

          /****************************************************************************
           *  FIRST VERSION OF A PROGRAM TO CONTROL AN ELECTRICALLY HEATED FURNACE    *
           ****************************************************************************/

          /*
          INPUTS AND OUTPUTS:
          ------ --- -------

          INPUT PORT 0: INDICATOR BITS: BIT 7: 1 = OPERATION, 0 = MAINTENANCE
                                        BIT 6: UNUSED
                                        BIT 5: OPERATIONAL DOOR 1 (0 = CLOSED, 1 = OPEN)
                                        BIT 4: OPERATIONAL DOOR 2
                                        BIT 3: MAINTENANCE DOOR 1
                                        BIT 2: MAINTENANCE DOOR 2
                                        BIT 1: MAINTENANCE DOOR 3
                                        BIT 0: MAINTENANCE DOOR 4

          INPUT PORTS 1 AND 2: THREE BCD DIGITS GIVING A REFERENCE TEMPERATURE:
                                        HUNDRED'S DIGIT: PORT 1, BITS 3-0
                                        TEN'S DIGIT:     PORT 2, BITS 7-4
                                        UNIT'S DIGIT:    PORT 2, BITS 3-0

          INPUT PORT 4: BINARY ADC OUTPUT OF THERMOCOUPLE (8 BITS)

          OUTPUT PORT 0: BIT 0: ALARM (= 1) IF OPERATIONAL AND ANY MAINTENANCE
                                DOOR IS OPEN
                         BIT 1: ALARM IF OPERATIONAL AND ZERO OR TWO OPERATIONAL
                                DOORS OPEN

          OUTPUT PORT 1: BINARY OUTPUT, DESIRED HEATER CURRENT, COMPUTED FROM
                         CURRENT = .394 * (REFERENCE TEMPERATURE - ACTUAL TEMPERATURE)
          AND WHERE ACTUAL TEMPERATURE IS COMPUTED FROM
                         ACTUAL TERMPERATURE = 1.84 * ADC OUTPUT FROM THERMOCOUPLE
          */


 1        FURNACE$CONTROL:
          DO;
 2   1       DECLARE (IN$PORT$0, IN$PORT$1, IN$PORT$2, IN$PORT$4) BYTE;
 3   1       DECLARE (OPERATIONAL,
                      OP$DOOR$1,
                      OP$DOOR$2,
                      MAINT$DOOR$1,
                      MAINT$DOOR$2,
                      MAINT$DOOR$3,
                      MAINT$DOOR$4) BYTE;
 4   1       DECLARE (UNITS, TENS, HUNDREDS) BYTE;
 5   1       DECLARE (TC$OUTPUT, REF$TEMP, ACTUAL$TEMP, TEMP$DIFF, CURRENT) ADDRESS;
 6   1       DECLARE (ALARM$1, ALARM$2) BYTE;
```

```
PL/M-80 COMPILER    FIG. 2.2                                          PAGE   2

  7   1         IN$PORT$0 = INPUT(0);
  8   1         IN$PORT$1 = INPUT(1);
  9   1         IN$PORT$2 = INPUT(2);
 10   1         IN$PORT$4 = INPUT(4);

 11   1         OPERATIONAL = SHR(IN$PORT$0, 7);
 12   1         OP$DOOR$1 = SHR(IN$PORT$0, 5) AND 00000001B;
 13   1         OP$DOOR$2 = SHR(IN$PORT$0, 4) AND 00000001B;
 14   1         MAINT$DOOR$1 = SHR(IN$PORT$0, 3) AND 00000001B;
 15   1         MAINT$DOOR$2 = SHR(IN$PORT$0, 2) AND 00000001B;
 16   1         MAINT$DOOR$3 = SHR(IN$PORT$0, 1) AND 00000001B;
 17   1         MAINT$DOOR$4 = IN$PORT$0 AND 00000001B;

 18   1         ALARM$1 = OPERATIONAL AND (MAINT$DOOR$1 OR MAINT$DOOR$2 OR MAINT$DOOR$3
                          OR MAINT$DOOR$4);
 19   1         ALARM$2 = OPERATIONAL AND NOT (OP$DOOR$1 XOR OP$DOOR$2);
 20   1         OUTPUT(0) = SHL(ALARM$2, 1) OR ALARM$1;

 21   1         HUNDREDS = IN$PORT$1 AND 00001111B;
 22   1         TENS = SHR(IN$PORT$2, 4);
 23   1         UNITS = IN$PORT$2 AND 00001111B;
 24   1         REF$TEMP = UNITS + 10*TENS + 100*HUNDREDS;
 25   1         ACTUAL$TEMP = (184*IN$PORT$4)/100;
 26   1         TEMP$DIFF = REF$TEMP - ACTUAL$TEMP;
 27   1         CURRENT = SHR(TEMP$DIFF*101, 8);
 28   1         OUTPUT(1) = CURRENT;

 29   1      END FURNACE$CONTROL;
```

of any statement, does not have a statement number. Statement 1 is the DO statement. We may recall, from the brief mention in Chapter 1, that every program must be enclosed between the reserved words DO and END, and that the opening DO must have a label followed by a colon.

THE DECLARE STATEMENTS

The program opens with declarations of its variables. In contrast with the DECLARE statements of the program in Chapter 1, each DECLARE statement here gives the characteristics of two or more variables. When this is done, the variable names are enclosed in parentheses. This is called *factored declaration*. The idea is that, in the case of the first DECLARE, for instance, instead of writing:

```
DECLARE IN$PORT$0 BYTE;
DECLARE IN$PORT$1 BYTE;
DECLARE IN$PORT$2 BYTE;
DECLARE IN$PORT$4 BYTE;
```

we can "factor out" the word BYTE and enclose within parentheses the variable names to which it applies. We shall see in later chapters that there are attributes other than BYTE and ADDRESS that may appear in DECLARE statements; these may also be factored.

Observe that in four cases the variables named in DECLARE statements have been written on one line, whereas the other DECLARE has been written on seven lines, one line for each identifier. This is to demonstrate that there are many possible ways to write program elements so as to promote clarity of meaning and ease of understanding. The PL/M compiler is indifferent to such matters of program style, and we are free to do anything that we think may assist in making a program easier for a human being to understand. In a DECLARE statement, such style conventions are largely a matter of taste; but in later chapters we shall insist on certain conventions for handling other matters.

GETTING THE INPUT

Before anything else can be done, it is necessary to obtain values from the four input ports. This is done with four assignment statements containing references to INPUT, which is built into the PL/M system. The four eight-bit values are assigned to four variables with names that clearly convey their meaning. (Actually, if the inputs are latched into the ports, these steps would not be necessary, since the ports could simply be read repeatedly. The method shown here is perhaps a little more general and has no important penalties).

TESTING THE DOORS FOR ALARM CONDITIONS

The first thing the program does after getting the input is to determine whether the positions of the doors violate either of the specified conditions. Before actually carrying out the logic of the condition testing, it is necessary to get the bits representing the positions of the six doors and the console switch into the same bit position of seven BYTE variables. Looking back at Fig. 2.1 or the program preamble, we see that these seven bits are by now arranged in the variables named IN$PORT$0 as follows:

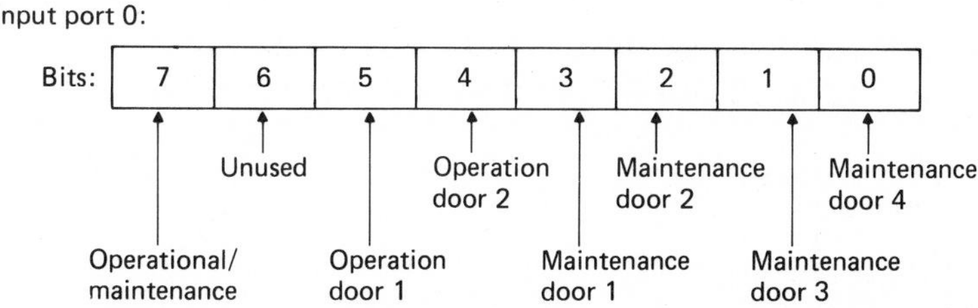

For the purposes of the logic operations that will follow, it would not make any difference which bit position we put these bits into; the rightmost position (bit zero) is as good as any. Bit 7 can be moved to bit zero by a shift of seven places to the right. All of the seven rightmost bits of IN$PORT$0 will be discarded by the shift and zeros will be entered on the left. There are no unwanted bits to mask off. Statement 11 calls for the necessary shift and stores the resulting byte in the variable named OPERATIONAL.

Bit 6 is unused. Bit 5 is shifted five places to the right by statement 12. After this shift there could be a one bit in position 2, shifted over from its original position in bit 7. This unwanted bit can be masked off by ANDing the result of the shift with a mask value consisting of a 1 in the position we want to keep, and zeros elsewhere. This mask could be written in any number system we please, since a one is a one regardless of how you write it. We prefer to show masks as binary constants since that makes it easy to visualize what is happening to individual bit positions. Statements 13–17 place the other five bits of IN$PORT$0 into appropriate variables. Observe that no shifting is required in the last of these. It would not do to call for a shift of zero positions here in order to maintain a consistent pattern, since the result of shift by zero positions is undefined.

Now we are ready to carry out the logic required to determine whether the door positions are other than those permitted during operation of the furnace. Remember that the first condition was that no maintenance door should be open while the furnace is operating. Statement 18 expresses this requirement. (Recall from the preamble that a one bit designates that the furnace is in operation or that a door is open.) We see here an example where parentheses are required within an expression containing only logical operators. Without parentheses the AND would operate only on the variables OPERATIONAL and MAINT$DOOR$1, since AND ranks higher than OR. The effect then would be to signal an alarm if maintenance doors 2, 3, or 4 were open even though the furnace was not operating.

The second alarm condition specifies that, during operation, exactly one of the operational doors must be open. That is, it is not permitted that both of them be open or both of them be closed. This condition could be expressed a number of ways, but the simplest is to use the exclusive OR operator, as shown here. The result of the operation in parentheses in statement 19 will have a one in bit position zero if either door is open but not both. This can also be expressed by saying that the result will be a zero in bit position zero if both doors are open or both doors are closed —which is the alarm condition. The NOT operator outside the parentheses complements this value, which means that we will have a 1 in bit position zero if the alarm condition is present. We are also guaranteed to have ones in the other seven bit positions after complementing the result of the exclusive OR, but they will be discarded in the AND operation that now takes place. This is required in order to meet the specification that we give the alarm only if the furnace is operational.

We now need to get these two alarm bits to output port zero in the required bit positions. This can be done simply by shifting ALARM$2 one position left and ORing it with ALARM$1.

COMPUTING THE REFERENCE TEMPERATURE

Input ports one and two give the three digits of a reference temperature, which is the desired operating temperature of the furnace. Each digit is binary-coded into four bits. For ease of understanding, we do the shifting and masking necessary to separate these binary-coded digits into three separate statements, and move each value to its own variable. The conversion from binary-coded decimal to pure binary is then carried out in statement 24. Everything in statements 21–24 could have been done in one statement, but the savings in running time and storage would not be worth the increased complexity and difficulty of understanding of the one combined statement.

To convert the thermocouple output to temperature we now have the problem of multiplying the value in IN$PORT$4 by 1.84, remembering that all quantities in PL/M programs are integers. The simplest way to do this is to multiply by 184 and then divide by 100, since 1.84 = 184/100.

It is essential to understand what is meant by a statement like "1.84 = 184/100," in the context of the fact that, in PL/M, we can work only with integers; 1.84 is certainly not an integer. We surely cannot try it this way:

```
ACTUAL$TEMP = (184 / 100) * IN$PORT$4;
```

The result of the division would be an integer one, since 184 divided by 100 is in fact 1 with a remainder of 84. What we do instead is write

```
ACTUAL$TEMP = (184 * IN$PORT$4) / 100;
```

which forces the multiplication to be done first. When we later divide the product by 100, we have achieved multiplication by 1.84 even though only integers have been used.

This formulation makes no provision for rounding the result, but this is easily enough accomplished, as we shall see in later case studies.

It is always extremely important to be sure that results of arithmetic operations do not exceed the space available for them. We are on safe ground in statement 25 since multiplication always gives an ADDRESS result. Since IN$PORT$4 is at most eight bits, multiplying its value by 184 cannot produce a product that will exceed the 16 bits of an ADDRESS variable.

COMPUTING THE TEMPERATURE DIFFERENCE

The computation of the temperature difference in statement 26 is straightforward enough except for the possibility that the actual temperature might *exceed* the reference temperature. Since there is no automatic handling of negative numbers in PL/M, this situation would produce a very large positive number, which would create serious problems in the following statements. If actually implemented in this way, it would probably burn out the heater. This undesirable state of affairs will be dealt with in the next chapter.

COMPUTING THE DESIRED CURRENT

The program specifications require that the temperature difference now be multiplied by 0.394. This constant is not expressible as the quotient of two integers smaller than 197/500. Although it would be possible to use the same techniques as before, multiplying by 197 and dividing by 500, we shall instead show an alternative technique. This is to find a quotient of two integers which, although not exactly equal to 0.394, is acceptably close, and where the denominator is a power of 2, permitting the "division" to be done by a right shift. This is based on the fact that shifting a binary number one place to the right has the effect of dividing it by 2, just as shifting a decimal number one place to the right divides it by 10. Similarly, shifting a binary number two places to the right divides it by $2^2 = 4$, shifting it three places to the right divides it by $2^3 = 8$, etc. A right shift of eight places divides by $2^8 = 256$. Shifting is preferable to division, when there is a choice, because shifting is considerably faster in most cases.

As it happens, $101/256 = 0.39453125$, which we shall assume is sufficiently close to 0.394 for the purposes of this application. Multiplication by 0.394 can thus be achieved by a multiplication by 101, followed by a right shift of eight places, as in statement 27. Statement 28 places this result on output port 1, and we are finished.

It is obviously highly unrealistic to set up a process-control program that executes once and stops. In the extension of this case study in the next chapter, we shall see how to make the program repeat indefinitely.

EXERCISES

***1.** Indicate which of the following are PL/M identifiers, and state why the others are not identifiers.

a) `Q`

b) `Q13`

c) `13Q`

d) `ENDOFTEXT`

e) `END-OF-TEXT`

f) `END$OF$TEXT`

g) `PROCESS$12`

h) `PROCESS 12`

i) `'VARIABLE'`

j) `SECTION501(C)3`

* Answers to starred exercises appear at the end of the text.

k) FIFTY$PERCENT

l) FIFTY$

m) FIFTY%

n) 50

o) CASE

p) DO CASE

q) DO$CASE

2. Indicate which of the following are PL/M identifiers, and state why the others are not identifiers.

a) GO

b) GOTO

c) GOTO$ROUTE$66

d) ROUTE$66

e) ROUTE66

f) ROUTE-66

g) ROUTE$'66'

h) /*IDENTIFIER*/

i) LEVEL77

j) 77LEVEL

k) ITERATION$NUMBER

l) TOLERANCE

m) DOLLAR$$SIGNS

n) INPUT 1

o) INPUT(1)

p) TEMP$MANIFOLD$J25

***3.** Do the following pairs of constants represent the same value in each case?

a)	7	7Q
b)	7D	7H
c)	1101$1000$0001B	110110000001
d)	23	23.0

e) 253 -3

f) 2FH 37Q

g) BAH 186D

h) 39Q 390

i) 19 13H

4. Do the following pairs of constants represent the same value in each case?

a) 12 12D

b) 12 140

c) 12 14Q

d) 140 14Q

e) 140 140

f) 1234 1,234

g) 1010$1100B 10101100B

h) 1BH 27

i) AE 174

***5.** Could 469 be the value of a BYTE variable?

***6.** Could 212 be the value of an ADDRESS variable, considering that the value would fit in a BYTE variable?

***7.** Suppose that, in a certain machine configuration, there is no storage with addresses greater than 32767. Could 34567 be the value of an ADDRESS variable in such a machine?

***8.** All of the following are illegal PL/M constants. Why?

```
46.7

-12

65547

46P

123HEX
```

***9.** Which of the following are legal PL/M expressions?

a) `B * C / D`

b) `B + C + C`

c) `LOOP$1 + 12`

d) `LOOP$2 - 7.5`

e) `(FLOW$1 + FLOW$2) / 2`

f) `PRESSURE$AT$MIXER$6 ** 2`

g) `(A + B) * (C - D)`

10. Which of the following are legal PL/M expressions?

a) `A - B * C`

b) `B12 * 12`

c) `RETURN + 29`

d) `(FLOW$1 + FLOW$2) * 0.5`

e) `(FLOW$1 + FLOW$2 + FLOW$3) DIV 3`

f) `REACTION$TEMP$16 + 273`

g) `(4*VESSEL$9$PRESSURE + 59) / 4`

***11.** Given the declaration shown, state the value(s) assigned in each of the following assignment statements.

```
DECLARE (A, B, C) BYTE;
DECLARE (X, Y, Z) ADDRESS;
```

a) `A = 15 + 4 * 8;`

b) `A = 15 * 15 + 35;`

c) `X = 15 * 15 + 35;`

d) `X = 256 * 100H;`

e) `X = 1;`

f) `A, B, C = 12;`

g) `A = SHL(1, 8);`

h) `X = SHL(1, 8);`

i) `A = (9 * 33) AND 0FFH;`

j) `X = (9 * 33) AND 0FFH;`

12. Given the declaration shown in Exercise 11, state the value(s) assigned in each of the following assignment statements.

a) `A = 29;`

b) `X = 29;`

c) `A = 150 + 150;`

d) `X = 150 + 150;`

e) `X = 4 * 16383 + 5;`

f) `A = SHR(1, 1);`

g) `X, Y, Z = 0;`

h) `A = SHL(1, 9);`

i) `X = SHL(1, 9);`

***13.** Are the following pairs of expressions equivalent?

a) `A + B` `A+B`

b) `A + B * C` `(A + B) * C`

c) `12 * X` `12X`

d) `X * 12` `X12`

e) `A / B * C` `(A / B) * C`

f) `(T$1 + T$2)/2` `T$1/2 + T$2/2`

14. Are the following pairs of expressions equivalent?

a) `TEMP$12+273` `TEMP$ 12 + 273`

b) `(A + B)/2` `A + B/2`

c) `Q * 19+6` `Q * 25`

d) `Q * (A + B)` `Q*A + Q*B`

e) `12h` `12*H`

f) `A + B * C / D` `A + (B * C) / D`

***15.** Write assignment statements to carry out the following operations.

a) Give the value zero to a variable named INITIAL$PRESSURE.

b) Add 12 to the value of the variable named A and give that value to the variable named B, replacing any previous contents of B.

c) Add 1 to the value of the variable named ITERATIONS and replace the present value of ITERATIONS with the sum.

d) Multiply the value of X by itself and assign that value to a variable named XSQUARED.

e) Add the values of the variables named TEMP$1, TEMP$2, TEMP$3. Divide their sum by 3 and assign the quotient to the variable named MEAN$TEMP.

f) Place the four leftmost bits of the variable named INPORT$1 into the rightmost four bit positions of the variable named DIGIT$1 with zeros in the four leftmost bit positions of DIGIT$1.

g) Divide the value of A by the sum of the values of B and C and place the quotient in Y.

h) Assign to NEXT$DIGIT the remainder obtained when the value of NUMBER is divided by the value of BASE.

i) Place in HALF$VALUE the result of shifting the quantity in VALUE one binary place to the right.

j) Place in ROUNDED$HALF$VALUE the results of adding one to the quantity in VALUE and then shifting the sum one binary position to the right.

16. Write assignment statements to carry out the following operations.

a) Assign the value 1 to the variable named GOOD$POINTS.

b) Make the value of the variable named A the same as the value of the variable named B, replacing the previous value of A.

c) Subtract 1 from the value of the variable named COUNTDOWN and replace the previous value of the variable named COUNTDOWN with that difference.

d) Multiply the value of A by the value of X, add the value of B, and give the resulting value to the variable named POLY.

e) Divide the sum of the values of A and B by the value of C and assign the quotient to the variable named X.

f) Cube the value of X and assign the result to the value of the variable named XCUBED.

g) Assign to REMAINDER the remainder obtained upon dividing the value of NUMBER by 10.

h) X is a BYTE variable containing one binary number in its leftmost four bits and one binary number in its rightmost four bits. Place in SUM the sum of these two binary numbers.

i) Place in QUARTER$VALUE the result of shifting the quantities in VALUE two binary places to the right.

j) Place in ROUNDED$QUARTER$VALUE the result of adding a binary 1 in bit position 1 of the quantity in VALUE and shifting the results two binary places to the right.

k) Using one statement, assign the value of the variable named POINTS$READ to the variables named COUNT$1, COUNT$2, and GOOD$POINTS.

l) In one statement, give the value zero to both TOTAL$1 and TOTAL$2.

***17.** Show the results in each of the following expressions.

a)
```
NOT 10111110B
```

b)
```
    10011010B
AND 11110000B
```

c)
```
    10011010B
AND 10101010B
```

d)
```
    11011001B
OR  10101010B
```

e)
```
    11011001B
XOR 10101010B
```

18. Show the results in each of the following expressions.

a)
```
NOT 11100111B
```
b)
```
    10110110B
AND 11000011B
```
c)
```
    10110110B
AND 10100110B
```
d)
```
    10110110B
OR  10100101B
```
e)
```
    10110110B
XOR 10100101B
```

***19.** Do these two operations produce the same result?

```
SHR(INPUT$1 AND 00000010B, 1);

SHR(INPUT$1, 1) AND 00000001B;
```

20. Do these two operations produce the same result?

```
SHL(MARKER, 4) AND 11110000B;

SHL(MARKER, 4);
```

21. Modify the program in Fig. 2.1 to incorporate the following changes in specifications.

a) The furnace operation has been changed so that, for normal operation, both operational doors must be closed; the program should alarm if *either* of them is open.

b) The furnace can operate normally with either all maintenance doors closed, or with at most one of them open. The program should alarm if *more than one* is open.

c) A new thermocouple is to be installed, leading to a new formula for getting the actual temperature from the thermocouple voltage:

Actual temperature = 1.72 * ADC output from thermocouple.

d) A new heater is to be installed, requiring a greater current computed from:

Current = 0.457 * (set temperature − actual temperature).

CHAPTER 3

CONDITIONALS AND DO GROUPS

INTRODUCTION

In this chapter we take up the fundamental topics of conditionals, which permit us to make decisions in a program, and various kinds of DO blocks, which permit a group of statements to be treated as a unit for purposes of control of program execution. Both will be heavily used in programs in the remainder of the book. We shall show several small examples in the body of the text, and then use the new techniques in expanding the work of the furnace-control application begun in the case study of the previous chapter.

THE IF STATEMENT

When an action must be done only if some condition is true, we turn to the IF statement. To illustrate, we might write:

```
IF CONTROL$VALUE > 4 THEN
   ALARM$3 = 1;
```

This means to compare the value of the variable named CONTROL$VALUE with 4; if it is greater, carry out the indicated assignment. If the value of CONTROL$VALUE is equal to or less than 4, the assignment is not carried out. In other words, the execution of the assignment statement is *conditional,* depending on the current value of CONTROL$VALUE.

It should be clear that, as the statement has been written, nothing at all will be done to ALARM$3 if the value of CONTROL$VALUE is not greater than 4. But what if we wanted to set ALARM$3 to zero in that case? Easy!—like this:

```
IF CONTROL$VALUE > 4 THEN
   ALARM$3 = 1;
ELSE
   ALARM$3 = 0;
```

Now we have specified what to do if the condition is false as well as what to do if it is true.

Let us pause now to broaden our understanding of the IF statement, looking at it more generally. The general form of the statement, as we have seen it so far, is this:

```
IF expression THEN
   basic statement 1;
ELSE
   basic statement 2;
```

What follows the IF has been stated as "expression" because we can write any PL/M expression there. If the expression is a condition, as it usually will be, the value of the expression is a zero if the condition is false and a byte of all 1 bits if it is true. In any event, the object program is set up simply to inspect the rightmost bit of the value resulting from evaluating the expression, executing the statement after the THEN if the value is 1 and executing the statement after the ELSE if it is zero. The ELSE portion may be omitted if there is *no* action to be taken when the rightmost bit of the expression is zero.

Observe that semicolons are required after the statements controlled by the THEN and ELSE portions of the IF statement, but must not be written after the words THEN and ELSE themselves.

The "basic statement" referred to here can be of several types, most of which we have not yet encountered. For now, the only kind of basic statement we know is the assignment statement.

Note the way the IF statement has been written on four lines, with the conditionally executed statements indented three spaces from the IF and ELSE, which are vertically aligned. Actually, none of this is required by PL/M, which permits us to write the entire statement on one line if we choose. We shall always follow this convention, however, and the reader is strongly urged to do likewise. In the attempt to make programs easy to understand, it is important to correctly convey the intention of the logic of the program. Writing the controlled statements on separate lines and indenting them is a major contribution to program understandability.

Following some indentation convention is important; the details of the convention chosen are not. Whether one indents three spaces, or two, or four, is not too important; other authors may recommend other conventions for the placement of the THEN or the ELSE. The main thing is to pick some meaningful convention and use it consistently.

The expression that is written in an IF statement can involve any of the following *relational operators:*

=	equal	>=	greater than or equal to
>	greater than	<=	less than or equal to
<	less than	<>	not equal to

The operands connected by a relational operator are permitted to be any arithmetic expressions. Thus, we can write statements like these:

```
IF A = 2 * B THEN . . .
IF A / (B + C) < X - 3 THEN . . .
IF (IN$PORT$16 AND 01111111B) = ODH THEN . . .
```

Observe the parentheses in the last example, which are necessary if we intend the AND to be carried out before the test for equality. Without the parentheses, the test for equality between 01111111B and ODH would be carried out first, leading to a result of **false,** which gives a byte of all zeros, and then this would be ANDed with the value of INPORT$16, again giving all zeros.

The complete ranking of operators, from highest to lowest, is as follows. Operators listed on the same line are of equal precedence:

```
unary "-"

* / MOD

+ -

= < > <= >= <>

NOT

AND

OR XOR
```

Summarizing, this means that *arithmetic* is done before *relation tests,* which are done before *logical operations.*

Next we note that we are not actually restricted to writing one condition, but in fact may write any logical expression, as in these examples:

```
IF A = 2 OR A = 3 THEN . . .
IF (IN$PORT$16 AND 00001000B) = 00001000B THEN . . .
IF SHR(A, 3) = 1BH AND SHR(B, 3) = 0CH THEN . . .
```

We can write statements containing no relations at all, such as this:

```
IF IN$PORT$16 THEN . . .
```

This is a simple way to look at just the least significant bit of a variable, to determine whether it is odd or even. We can also write:

```
IF A OR B OR C OR D THEN . . .
```

The expression is true if any one or more of the four variables has a 1 bit in its low-order position. Or, we could write

```
IF SHR(A, 1) OR A THEN . . .
```

which responds to a 1 bit in either bit 1 or bit zero of variable A. This has the same effect as the following:

```
IF (A AND 00000011B) > 0 THEN . . .
```

THE SIMPLE DO BLOCK FOR STATEMENT GROUPING

A problem arises with what we have seen of the IF so far when we wish to conditionally execute more than one statement. It will not do to write something like

```
IF A = B THEN
   ALARM$4 = 0;
   COUNT = COUNT + 1;
```

because the first semicolon would terminate the scope of the control of the IF, and the second assignment would always be executed. The answer is the simple DO statement, which we shall see has other uses as well. For this example, we could write:

```
IF A = B THEN
DO;
   ALARM$4 = 0;
   COUNT = COUNT + 1;
END;
```

Now, the two statements have been combined into a *unit;* both will be executed if the condition is true, and neither will be executed if the condition is false.

The DO–END grouping of statements can be used in both parts of the IF, as in this example:

```
IF A > B THEN
DO;
   LARGER = A;
   A$COUNT = A$COUNT + 1;
END;
ELSE
DO;
   LARGER = B;
   B$COUNT = B$COUNT + 1;
END;
```

DO–END grouping can be used around a single statement, if it is desired to maintain consistency in appearance. In the case-study program for this chapter, for instance, we have this statement:

```
IF REF$TEMP > ACTUAL$TEMP THEN
DO;
   TEMP$DIFF = REF$TEMP - ACTUAL$TEMP;
   CURRENT = SHR(TEMP$DIFF * 101, 8);
END;
ELSE
DO;
   CURRENT = 0;
END;
```

The effect of the statement is to determine whether the reference temperature is greater than the actual temperature, and to compute the current from the formula only if it is. If not, the current is set equal to zero. This solves the problem mentioned in the case study of Chapter 2—the possibility that an actual temperature greater than the reference temperature could lead to a very large computed temperature difference, since there are no negative numbers in PL/M.

THE DO–WHILE STATEMENT

Computer programming makes heavy use of the repetitive execution, or *looping,* of parts of programs. Perhaps some operation needs to be done a number of times on different data, or possibly a formula has to be evaluated repeatedly until a process of successive approximation converges, or maybe the program is looping indefinitely, waiting for inputs from a manufacturing process that it is controlling. In these and many other circumstances, we need a way to specify that a block of the program is to be repeated.

This need is answered in PL/M by the DO–WHILE statement, and also by the iterative DO statement that we shall study in the next chapter. (At an earlier time, when flowcharts were popular, such statements were called *loops,* and the name has stuck.) The general form of a DO–WHILE block, or loop, is

```
DO WHILE EXPRESSION;
   UNIT;
END;
```

For "expression," we may write any of the kinds of things we can write in an IF statement. The program inspects the rightmost bit of the value of the expression; if the bit is a 1, the statements in the "unit" are executed and the process repeats. Most commonly the expression is some kind of condition. For the "unit," or "body" of the DO, we may write one or more basic statements, or an IF statement, or a DO block.

Here is an example of a program segment employing a DO–WHILE block.

```
N = 1;
DO WHILE N <= 12;
   OUTPUT(1) = N * N;
   N = N + 1;
END;
```

With N started at 1, the condition N <= 12 is certainly met the first time, so $1 * 1 = 1$ is written to output port 1, and 1 is added to N. Now the test is made again, and since 2 is also less than 12, the two controlled statements are executed again, this time writing $2 * 2 = 4$ to the port. Again 1 is added to N. When the process reaches 11, $11 * 11 = 121$ will be written to the port and 1 added to N. Since 12 is less than or equal to 12, the body of the DO is executed again, this time writing $12 * 12 = 144$ and adding 1 to N. Now, finally, 13 is *not* less than or equal to 12, and the body is not executed. Instead, program control passes to whatever follows the END statement. The net effect, therefore, is to write the squares of the first 12 integers to output port 1.

USING THE DO–WHILE TO PRODUCE A RAMP FUNCTION

For another example of the use of the DO–WHILE, consider the following requirement, which will be part of the case study at the end of the chapter.

We are given a value of CURRENT, which must be reduced to 20 in steps of 1—assuming it is greater than 20 to begin with, of course. Each value is to be sent to output port 1. In the program, this reduction must be done at a rate of 1 amp per second, but let us first write a program segment that ignores this feature.

The program is actually quite simple:

```
DO WHILE CURRENT > 20;
   CURRENT = CURRENT - 1;
   OUTPUT(1) = CURRENT;
END;
```

If the value of CURRENT is less than or equal to 20 when the program segment is entered (i.e., if the value of CURRENT is not greater than 20), then the statements controlled by the DO–WHILE will not be executed at all, as desired. If the value of CURRENT is greater than 20 initially, the controlled statements will be executed as many times as necessary to reduce CURRENT to 20, at which point repetitions will cease.

All this would take place at the rate at which the microprocessor can execute the rather few machine instructions that would be generated by the compiler from this PL/M code. To get the reduction to be at the rate of 1 amp/sec, we must introduce a *time delay*. There are several possible ways to do this, the simplest of which is to use a PL/M procedure named TIME.

We write the reserved word CALL followed by the name of the procedure, which in this case is TIME, followed by an expression enclosed in parentheses. For example, we might write:

```
CALL TIME(1);
```

The result would be to give program control to the procedure named TIME, which is supplied with PL/M. This procedure has been written to retain control in units of 100 microseconds. In the statement just shown, the procedure would delay 100 microseconds before returning control to the statement after the CALL. If we write

```
CALL TIME(2);
```

the TIME procedure would delay 200 microseconds. If we write

```
CALL TIME(N);
```

and N has the value 200, the delay will be $200 * 100 = 20{,}000\ \mu s = 20\ ms = 0.02$ sec.

The number written in parentheses after the procedure named TIME is called the *argument* of the procedure. This procedure, which is supplied as part of the PL/M system, expects a BYTE argument; if we write an argument having a value larger than 255, bits other than the low-order eight will be ignored. (This is the same thing as saying that the value used by the procedure is the argument as written, modulo 256.) The longest time delay we can get with this procedure is therefore 0.0255 sec, which is not long enough for our needs.

The answer to this problem is to call the TIME procedure repeatedly. Suppose we use an argument of 200, getting a 0.02-sec delay; we would therefore need to carry out the function 50 times to get a 1-sec delay. This is readily done with another DO–WHILE. Writing this part of the program by itself, we would have:

```
COUNTER = 1;
DO WHILE COUNTER <= 50;
   CALL TIME(200);
   COUNTER = COUNTER + 1;
END;
```

All of this may now be inserted into the program segment we saw before, giving this combination:

```
DO WHILE CURRENT > 20;
    COUNTER = 1;
    DO WHILE COUNTER <= 50;
        CALL TIME(200);
        COUNTER = COUNTER + 1;
    END;
    CURRENT = CURRENT - 1;
    OUTPUT(1) = CURRENT;
END;
```

NESTING LEVEL NUMBERS

In the program just shown we see a DO block that contains another DO block. This is perfectly legal, and widely useful. In fact, this *nesting* of DO blocks is so common that the compiler provides us with some assistance in interpreting programs. This compiler-generated feature is the nesting-level number that appears just to the right of every statement number, which shows how many DOs enclose the statement. The DO that must begin every program is counted in this computation, and the END that matches a DO is counted as though included in the DO. This means that the DO at the beginning of a program has a nesting level of zero, and the END that ends the program has a nesting level of 1.

Here is the program just shown, written as a complete program so that we may show the DO and END at the beginning and end of the program.

```
 1          NESTING$LEVELS$EXAMPLE:
            DO;
 2   1         DECLARE (CURRENT, COUNTER) ADDRESS;

 3   1         DO WHILE CURRENT > 20;
 4   2            COUNTER = 1;
 5   2            DO WHILE COUNTER <= 50;
 6   3               CALL TIME(200);
 7   3               COUNTER = COUNTER + 1;
 8   3            END;
 9   2            CURRENT = CURRENT - 1;
10   2            OUTPUT(1) = CURRENT;
11   2         END;

12   1      END NESTING$LEVELS$EXAMPLE;
```

Statements 2 and 3, since they are enclosed in the DO of statement 1 and no other, are seen to have a nesting level of 1. Reading on through the program, we see that statements 9–11 are also enclosed in two DOs, and 6–8 are enclosed in three.

If there are the same number of DOs and ENDs in a program, as there should be, the final END will always be at nesting level 1; if the compiler finds otherwise, it signals an error. The nesting-level numbers are then sometimes helpful in locating the area where an END was omitted, which is one common cause of such an error.

A SQUARE-ROOT ROUTINE USING THE DO–WHILE

Many applications programs require the computation of the square root of a number. This turns out to be a fairly simple task using the DO–WHILE construct.

The usual way to compute square roots in a computer utilizes the Newton–Raphson method. Given a positive number N, we begin with any positive and nonzero approximation to the square root x. $N/2$ is an adequate and easily computed choice. Then we repeatedly apply the formula

$$x_{\text{new}} = (N/x + x)/2$$

each time replacing x by x_{new}, until we find that x and x_{new} are the same, at which point either of them is the square root of N. To see that this is true, note that when $x = x_{\text{new}}$ we can replace x_{new} by x, giving:

$$x = (N/x + x)/2$$

or

$$2x = N/x + x$$

which reduces to

$$x^2 = N$$

so x is the square root of N.

Unless N is a perfect square, and considering that in PL/M we are dealing entirely with integers, we must realize that the square root will not be exact, but an approximation. We shall consider this question a little more closely after writing the program.

It always is necessary to exercise caution in connection with integer division. We said we would begin with $N/2$ as a starting approximation. But what if $N = 1$? Then the integer division will give zero, and we are in deep trouble when we try to divide by zero in applying the formula. Therefore we shall use one-half of $(N + 1)$ as our starting approximation. In a somewhat similar fashion we have to add 1 to the quantity being divided by 2 in the approximation formula. This has the effect of rounding the quotient to the nearest integer, and prevents an endless oscillation between successive values differing by 1. (Try taking the square root of 8 without rounding, remembering to use integer division throughout; the successive approximations alternate between 2 and 3 indefinitely.)

With these preliminaries out of the way, and recalling that shifting right one place is equivalent to dividing by 2 (and much faster), the program itself is quite simple:

```
X = N;
X$NEW = SHR(N + 1, 1);
DO WHILE X <> X$NEW;
   X = X$NEW;
   X$NEW = SHR(N/X + X + 1, 1);
END;
```

The first statement, setting x equal to N, is needed to ensure that the DO–WHILE will not accidentally stop the iteration before the square root has been found. If we did not do this, it might happen that x would have the same value as the starting approximation, which would cause the DO–WHILE to skip over the application of the approximation formula and report the starting approximation as the square root. As the program is written, where we do give x the starting value of N, the skipping of the approximation calculation the first time can happen only if x is equal to 1, in which case the starting approximation of 1 is the correct square root.

It would be a worthwhile exercise for the reader to "play computer," "executing" this program with typical values.

Here are some values of N, and the successive values taken on by x, including the initializing statement that begins the program:

Approximation to x	Value of N: 1	2	3	4	5	200	20000
Starting	1	1	2	2	3	100	10000
Second		2	2	2	2	50	2502
Third		2			2	27	1254
Fourth						17	635
Fifth						14	333
Sixth						14	181
Seventh							146
Eighth							141
Ninth							141

A FIRST LOOK AT DEALING WITH FRACTIONS IN PL/M

Looking at the result for 20,000, we realize that, if we penciled in decimal points, we could regard 20,000 as 2.0000, and the resulting square root (141) as 1.41. Putting it another way, if we had to work with integer arithmetic but needed a more accurate approximation to the square root of 2 than 2—which is a rather poor approximation, after all!—we could shift the number left before going into the approximation formula. Mathematically, we have

$$\sqrt{10^{2n} \cdot N} = 10^n \cdot \sqrt{N}.$$

The basic idea is this. Even though we can, in fact, deal only with integers, the interpretation placed on those integers is up to us. If we want to ask for the square root of 20000 but think of the number as 2.0000, we are free to interpret the result (141) as 1.41, an approximation to the square root of 2. (If that is not enough precision, you must look into multiple-precision arithmetic, which is another story.)

But what if we are given a small integer, already in binary within the processor, and we need a better approximation to its square root than an integer? Should we multiply by the binary representation of a power of 10 and later divide by another power of 10? Not at all. Instead, we note that

$$\sqrt{2^{2n} \cdot N} = 2^n \sqrt{N}.$$

Suppose, for example, that we have a BYTE variable and want the best approximation of its square root that is possible without going to multiple precision. The answer is to shift it left eight positions, to the high-order portion of an ADDRESS variable. That gives eight bits after an imaginary binary point; the result will be an ADDRESS variable with four binary places after an imaginary binary point. Since the square root of a number has at most half as many digits as the number, we can be assured that the high-order half of the ADDRESS variable holding the square root will be a zero.

And what would one do with such a result? For one simple example, suppose that we wish to compute:

$$\text{Flowrate} = 348 \cdot \sqrt{\text{Pressure difference}}.$$

Here is how it could be done:

```
DECLARE PRESSURE$DIFF ADDRESS;
DECLARE (N, X, X$NEW, FLOW$RATE) ADDRESS;
N = SHL(PRESSURE$DIFF, 8);

/* NOW FOLLOWS SQUARE ROOT ROUTINE AS BEFORE */
X = N
X$NEW = SHR(N + 1, 1);
DO WHILE X <> X$NEW;
   X = X$NEW;
   X$NEW = SHR(N/X + x + 1, 1);
END;

FLOW$RATE = SHR(348 * X, 4);
```

In the last statement it is of course essential to multiply *before* shifting; otherwise we simply throw away the four extra bits we have arranged to compute.

This is intended merely as a sample, the barest introduction, to the subject of *scaling* of numbers in a computer. The reader concerned with such operations would need to study the subject in somewhat more detail.

NESTED IF STATEMENTS

Now that we have the DO block available to solve a problem that will arise, we may approach the topic of the *nested* IF*s*.

The general format of the IF statement as we have used it so far is:

```
IF expression THEN
   basic statement 1;
ELSE
   basic statement 2;
```

Actually, the statement is permitted to have a more general form, in that—with one restriction, shown later—IF statements are permitted where we have shown "basic statement." The subject can be approached through examples.

Suppose we write:

```
IF A = B THEN
   IF A = C THEN
      X = 1;
```

The second IF is reached only if the expression in the first IF gives a true result. The effect is the same as if we had written:

```
IF (A = B) AND (A = C) THEN
   X = 1;
```

This is one example of a *nested* IF. Here is another:

```
IF L = 10 THEN
   X = 1;
ELSE
   IF L = 14 THEN
      X = 2;
```

The meaning here is unambiguous. If L *is* equal to 10, X is set equal to 1 and nothing else happens. If L *is not* equal to 10 and L *is* equal to 14, X is set equal to 2. If L *is not* equal to 10 and L *is not* equal to 14, no action at all is taken.

Nested IFs of this form (where an IF appears in the ELSE part) can be *chained* to any needed length. If the chain is long, the previously used indentation scheme must be modified; here is one way to do it:

```
IF SALES$CODE = 1 THEN
   COMMISSION = 5;
ELSE IF SALES$CODE = 2 THEN
   COMMISSION = 10;
ELSE IF SALES$CODE = 7 THEN
   COMMISSION = SALES$AMOUNT / 20;
ELSE IF SALES$CODE = 9 THEN
   COMMISSION = 20 + SALES$AMOUNT / 50;
ELSE
   COMMISSION = 0;
```

Exactly one of the assignment statements here will be executed; if SALES$CODE is equal to 1, 2, 7, or 9, the assignment statement following that condition is executed and nothing else happens. If SALES$CODE is not equal to 1, 2, 7, or 9, which is presumably an error, the final assignment statement is executed.

Consider now this example:

```
IF A = B THEN
   IF C = D THEN
      X = 1;
   ELSE
      X = 2;
```

The ELSE is associated with the *second* IF, as the indentation suggests, just as if we had written:

```
IF A = B THEN
DO;
   IF C = D THEN
      X = 1;
   ELSE
      X = 2;
END;
```

The ELSE can be associated with the *first* IF by writing:

```
IF A = B THEN
DO;
   IF C = D THEN
      X = 1;
END;
ELSE
   X = 2;
```

The one restriction mentioned earlier is that the following construction is not permitted:

```
IF A = B THEN
    IF C = D THEN
        X = 1;
    ELSE
    X = 2;
ELSE
    X = 3;
```

The PL/M rule is that when an IF is nested within the THEN part, only one ELSE is permitted. If we really want to do the logic suggested by the indentation in this example, it is a simple matter to enclose the "inner" IF in a DO block.

Even when DO blocks are not *required,* however, it is a good idea to use them freely—just as we use parentheses freely—to convey meaning unambiguously to human readers of the program.

THE DO CASE BLOCK

It happens from time to time in programming that we need to execute one of a number of statements, depending on the value of a variable. In the case study for this chapter we shall read a value between zero and 4, inclusive, and use that value to determine which of five program segments to execute to change the heater current in our hypothetical furnace.

In skeleton form, the structure will be as follows:

```
DO CASE CONTROL$VALUE;
    UNIT FOR CASE 0;
    UNIT FOR CASE 1;
    UNIT FOR CASE 2;
    UNIT FOR CASE 3;
    UNIT FOR CASE 4;
END;
```

Each case must be a *unit,* either a single statement or a DO block.

If the value of CONTROL$VALUE is zero, the unit for case 0 is carried out and those for the other cases are skipped; execution continues with the statement after the END. If the value of CONTROL$VALUE is 1, the unit for case 1 is carried out, and again execution continues with the statement after the END, etc. If the value of CONTROL$VALUE is greater than 4, the result is undefined.

If there are any cases for which nothing is to be done, it is still necessary to provide the compiler with an indication that we have counted that case, so that the correct correspondence can be maintained between values of the expression in the DO CASE and the different cases. This does not mean that we must write dummy statements to fill up the space, however, since we are permitted in PL/M to write a *null* statement consisting of nothing but a semicolon.

For an example, consider the scoring of the game of (American) football. One point is given for a conversion, two points for a safety, three for a field goal, and six for a touchdown. We suppose that there is a variable named SCORE that contains the number of points awarded, and that we want to update the value of whichever of CONVERSIONS, SAFETIES, FIELDGOALS, or TOUCHDOWNS corresponds to this value. Since there are no actions to be taken for the cases of 0, 4, or 5, we must provide null statements as follows:

```
DO CASE SCORE;
   ;
   CONVERSIONS = CONVERSIONS + 1;
   SAFETIES = SAFETIES + 1;
   FIELD$GOALS = FIELD$GOALS + 1;
   ;
   ;
   TOUCHDOWNS = TOUCHDOWNS + 1;
END;
```

In both examples here, we have shown a single variable after the words DO CASE, but actually we are permitted to write any expression.

CASE STUDY: A SECOND VERSION OF THE PROGRAMMED CONTROL IN AN ELECTRICALLY HEATED FURNACE

To see the techniques studied in this chapter in the context of a fairly realistic application, let us turn again to the idea of an electrically heated furnace that we saw in the case study of the previous chapter.

The first thing we shall do is set the program up to repeat indefinitely, rather than just executing once. The major new feature of the application requirement is that we must now respond to a thumbwheel on the process operator's console that dictates how the heater current is to be handled. The legitimate control values that can be read from this thumbwheel and their meanings are as follows:

Control value	Action to be taken
0	Shut off current.
1	Set current at 200 amps.
2	Increase current from 2 to 100 amps in steps of 2 amps per second, then switch to continuous control.
3	Continuous control; handle as before.
4	Decrease from present setting to 20 amps, in steps of one amp per second.

In real life a mechanical stop on the thumbwheel would probably prevent any other values from being set; here, for practice, we shall alarm any illegal values.

A final new requirement is that the furnace temperature be tested against a limit. If the temperature is greater than this limit, we are to turn on two fans and an alarm. If the actual temperature is not greater than the limit but is greater than the reference temperature, then we are to turn off the current, turn on *one* fan and no alarm.

THE NEW INPUT DATA

The only information required by this program that was not also required by the previous version is the value of the thumbwheel that specifies the treatment of the heater current. This will be read on the previously unused high-order four bits of input port 1. We much prefer to utilize these bits in preference to assigning an additional port, in the interest of saving hardware costs.

The only new output consists of a bit for the new alarm and two bits for the two fans. These bits can be incorporated in the unused bit positions of output port 0.

THE LITERALLY DECLARATION

A declaration using the reserved word LITERALLY has the general form

DECLARE identifier LITERALLY 'substitution text';

This causes any occurrence of the identifier, anywhere in the program after this declaration, to be treated as though the substitution text appeared there instead. The identifier must conform to the rules for forming PL/M identifiers, but the LITERALLY feature applies more generally than this requirement might suggest.

For example, in the program for this case study, we have the declaration

```
DECLARE FOREVER LITERALLY 'WHILE 1';
```

Now, when later in the program we have the statement

```
DO FOREVER;
```

the result is that the system, *before compilation,* will substitute the WHILE 1 in place of the FOREVER, so that what the compiler sees is

```
DO WHILE 1;
```

In the program listing, however, we have the FOREVER, as originally written.

For another example, the program contains this declaration:

```
DECLARE LIMIT LITERALLY '460';
```

Later, we have

```
IF ACTUAL$TEMP > LIMIT THEN
```

The effect is as if we had written

```
IF ACTUAL$TEMP > 460 THEN
```

If the identifier LIMIT appeared many times in the program, 460 would be substituted for all of them. Then if the specifications changed, making it necessary to change the limit to, say, 435, we could change just the one LITERALLY declaration and recompile, with assurance that all instances of the constant have been modified.

We shall see many other instances of the usefulness of the LITERALLY feature in promoting program understandability and maintainability, in other case studies.

THE PROGRAM

The program shown in Fig. 3.1 begins with declarations that are quite similar to those in Fig. 2.2, although we now have some new variables. After the declarations, everything else in the program is part of a DO FOREVER loop. We understand that the DO FOREVER will become a DO WHILE 1. All the rest of the program will therefore be repeated indefinitely until the power is turned off or the process is somehow reset. In real life this would be too rudimentary, but it will serve our purposes here.

At the beginning of each execution of the program, we start, as in the Case Study in Chapter 2, by reading the values on the four ports. We get four bits more information than before because the high-order four bits of input port 1 now contain a value of the control thumbwheel. We mask off the other bits of the value read from this port and shift the bits representing the control value into the low-order positions.

We are now ready to decide on the basis of bit 6 of input port 0, whether we are required to alter the "profile" of the heater current. (The condition test in the IF statement looks only at bit zero, so we can safely ignore the operational/maintenance bit originally in bit position 7.) If we are so required, and if the control value is legitimate, then we carry out the DO CASE. Most of these either are very simple operations or have already been encountered earlier in the chapter. Observe that the statements for each of the five cases are enclosed in DO–END pairs even though the program would have worked the same if this had not been done for cases 0, 1, and 3, because they are single statements.

This is a good convention to follow since it is so easy to make mistakes that will associate statements with the wrong cases in such a way that the program is still *syntactically* correct. The compiler therefore gives no error indication, and we may have a very difficult time diagnosing the trouble. As an example of what can happen, suppose we omitted the DO–END in case 2. Then case 2 would consist

```
PL/M-80 COMPILER    FIG. 3.1                                                    PAGE   1

           /***************************************************************************
            *   SECOND VERSION OF A PROGRAM TO CONTROL AN ELECTRICALLY HEATED FURNACE   *
            ***************************************************************************/
           /*
           INPUTS AND OUTPUTS:
           ------ --- -------

           INPUT PORT 0: INDICATOR BITS: BIT 7: 1 = OPERATIONAL, 0 = MAINTENANCE
                                         BIT 6: IF 1, CHANGE HEATER CURRENT PROFILE
                                         BIT 5: OPERATIONAL DOOR 1 (0 = CLOSED, 1 = OPEN)
                                         BIT 4: OPERATIONAL DOOR 2
                                         BIT 3: MAINTENANCE DOOR 1
                                         BIT 2: MAINTENANCE DOOR 2
                                         BIT 1: MAINTENANCE DOOR 3
                                         BIT 0: MAINTENANCE DOOR 4

           INPUT PORTS 1 AND 2: THREE BCD DIGITS GIVING A REFERENCE TEMPERATURE:
                                         HUNDRED'S DIGIT: PORT 1, BITS 3-0
                                         TEN'S DIGIT:     PORT 2, BITS 7-4
                                         UNIT'S DIGIT:    PORT 2, BITS 3-0
                                ALSO, A BCD CONTROL THUMBWHEEL VALUE; SEE TEXT
                                         CONTROL VALUE    PORT 1, BITS 7-4

           INPUT PORT 4: BINARY ADC OUTPUT OF THERMOCOUPLE (8 BITS)

           OUTPUT PORT 0: BIT 0: ALARM (= 1) IF OPERATIONAL AND ANY MAINTENANCE
                                 DOOR IS OPEN
                          BIT 1: ALARM IF OPERATIONAL AND ZERO OR TWO OPERATIONAL
                                 DOORS OPEN
                          BIT 2: ALARM IF CONTROL THUMBWHEEL ILLEGAL VALUE
                          BIT 3: ALARM IF OVERTEMPERATURE
                          BIT 4: 1 = TURN ON FAN 1, 0 = TURN OFF FAN 1
                          BIT 5: 1 = TURN ON FAN 2, 0 = TURN OFF FAN 2

           OUTPUT PORT 1: BINARY OUTPUT, DESIRED HEATER CURRENT, COMPUTED FROM
                          CURRENT = .394 * (REFERENCE TEMPERATURE - ACTUAL TEMPERATURE)
           AND WHERE ACTUAL TEMPERATURE IS COMPUTED FROM
                          ACTUAL TERMPERATURE = 1.84 * ADC OUTPUT FROM THERMOCOUPLE
           */

  1        FURNACE$CONTROL:
           DO;
  2   1       DECLARE FOREVER LITERALLY 'WHILE 1';
  3   1       DECLARE LIMIT LITERALLY '460';
  4   1       DECLARE (IN$PORT$0, IN$PORT$1, IN$PORT$2, IN$PORT$4) BYTE;
  5   1       DECLARE OUT$PORT$0 BYTE;
  6   1       DECLARE (OPERATIONAL,
                    CHANGE$CURRENT$PROFILE,
                    OP$DOOR$1,
                    OP$DOOR$2,
                    MAINT$DOOR$1,
                    MAINT$DOOR$2,
                    MAINT$DOOR$3,
                    MAINT$DOOR$4) BYTE;
  7   1       DECLARE (UNITS, TENS, HUNDREDS) BYTE;
  8   1       DECLARE (REF$TEMP, ACTUAL$TEMP, TEMP$DIFF, CURRENT) ADDRESS;
  9   1       DECLARE CONTROL$VALUE ADDRESS;
 10   1       DECLARE (ALARM$1, ALARM$2, ALARM$3) BYTE;
 11   1       DECLARE TIME$COUNTER ADDRESS;

 12   1       DO FOREVER;

 13   2          IN$PORT$0 = INPUT(0);
 14   2          IN$PORT$1 = INPUT(1);
 15   2          IN$PORT$2 = INPUT(2);
 16   2          IN$PORT$4 = INPUT(4);

 17   2          CONTROL$VALUE = SHR(IN$PORT$1, 4);
```

```
18   2           IF (SHR(INPORT$0, 6)) AND (CONTROL$VALUE < 5) THEN
19   2           DO CASE CONTROL$VALUE;
                    /* CASE 0: SHUT OFF CURRENT */
20   3              DO;
21   4                 CURRENT = 0;
22   4              END;

                    /* CASE 1: SET MAXIMUM CURRENT */
23   3              DO;
24   4                 CURRENT = 200;
25   4              END;

                    /* CASE 2: INCREASE CURRENT FROM 2 TO 100 IN STEPS OF 2 AMP PER SEC */
26   3              DO;
27   4                 CURRENT = 0;
28   4                 DO WHILE CURRENT < 100;
29   5                    TIME$COUNTER = 1;
30   5                    DO WHILE TIME$COUNTER <= 50;
31   6                       CALL TIME(200);
32   6                       TIME$COUNTER = TIME$COUNTER + 1;
33   6                    END;
34   5                    CURRENT = CURRENT + 2;
35   5                    OUTPUT(1) = CURRENT;
36   5                 END;
37   4              END;

                    /* CASE 3: CONTINUOUS CONTROL - NOTHING TO BE DONE HERE */
38   3              DO;
39   4                 ;
40   4              END;

                    /* CASE 4: DECREASE FROM PRESENT TO 20 AMPS, 1 AMP PER SEC */
41   3              DO WHILE CURRENT > 20;
42   4                 TIME$COUNTER = 1;
43   4                 DO WHILE TIME$COUNTER <= 50;
44   5                    CALL TIME(200);
45   5                    TIME$COUNTER = TIME$COUNTER + 1;
46   5                 END;
47   4                 CURRENT = CURRENT - 1;
48   4                 OUTPUT(1) = CURRENT;
49   4              END;
50   3           END;    /* END OF DO CASE */


         /* GET TEMPERATURES FROM THUMBWHEELS AND THERMOCOUPLE VOLTAGE */
51   2           HUNDREDS = IN$PORT$1 AND 00001111B;
52   2           TENS = SHR(IN$PORT$2, 4);
53   2           UNITS = IN$PORT$2 AND 00001111B;
54   2           REF$TEMP = UNITS + 10*TENS + 100*HUNDREDS;
55   2           ACTUAL$TEMP = (184*IN$PORT$4)/100;    /* 1.84 * REFERENCE TEMP */

         /* COMPUTE CONTINUOUS-CONTROL CURRENT IF CONTROL VALUE DICTATES */
56   2           IF CONTROL$VALUE = 2 OR CONTROL$VALUE = 3 THEN
57   2           DO;
58   3              IF REF$TEMP > ACTUAL$TEMP THEN
59   3              DO;
60   4                 TEMP$DIFF = REF$TEMP - ACTUAL$TEMP;
61   4                 CURRENT = SHR(TEMP$DIFF*101, 8);  /* 0.394 * TEMP DIFF */
62   4              END;
                    ELSE
63   3              DO;
64   4                 CURRENT = 0;
65   4              END;
66   3           END;

         /* WRITE CURRENT, REGARDLESS HOW COMPUTED */
67   2           OUTPUT(1) = CURRENT;
```

```
PL/M-80 COMPILER    FIG. 3.1                                              PAGE   3


              /* CHECK FOR ALARM CONDITIONS, TURN FANS ON OR OFF */
68    2           OPERATIONAL   = SHR(IN$PORT$0, 7);
69    2           OP$DOOR$1     = SHR(IN$PORT$0, 5) AND 00000001B;
70    2           OP$DOOR$2     = SHR(IN$PORT$0, 4) AND 00000001B;
71    2           MAINT$DOOR$1 = SHR(IN$PORT$0, 3) AND 00000001B;
72    2           MAINT$DOOR$2 = SHR(IN$PORT$0, 2) AND 00000001B;
73    2           MAINT$DOOR$3 = SHR(IN$PORT$0, 1) AND 00000001B;
74    2           MAINT$DOOR$4 = IN$PORT$0 AND 00000001B;

75    2           ALARM$1 = OPERATIONAL AND (MAINT$DOOR$1 OR MAINT$DOOR$2 OR MAINT$DOOR$3
                              OR MAINT$DOOR$4);
76    2           ALARM$2 = OPERATIONAL AND NOT (OP$DOOR$1 XOR OP$DOOR$2);
77    2           IF CONTROL$VALUE > 4 THEN
78    2              ALARM$3 = 1;
                  ELSE
79    2              ALARM$3 = 0;
80    2           IF ACTUAL$TEMP > LIMIT THEN
81    2              OUT$PORT$0 = 00111000B; /* BOTH FANS AND ALARM 4 ALL ON */
                  ELSE
82    2           DO;
83    3              IF ACTUAL$TEMP > REF$TEMP THEN
84    3                 OUT$PORT$0 = 00010000B;   /* FAN 1 ON, FAN 2 AND ALARM 4 OFF */
                     ELSE
85    3                 OUT$PORT$0 = 00000000B; /* BOTH FANS AND ALARM 4 OFF */
86    3           END;

              /* COMBINE ALARM AND FAN-CONTROL BITS */
87    2           OUT$PORT$0 = OUT$PORT$0 OR ALARM$1 OR SHL(ALARM$2, 1) OR SHL(ALARM$3, 2);
88    2           OUTPUT(0) = OUT$PORT$0;

89    2        END; /* END OF DO FOREVER */

90    1     END FURNACE$CONTROL;
```

solely of the statement CURRENT = 2, case 3 would consist of the DO–WHILE immediately following, case 4 would be the null statement, and there would be a case 5 to which no reference would ever be made. Needless to say, the compiler does not take meaning from the comments; but in trying to check out the program, we would be guided by the comments and might have a rather difficult time figuring out what happened.

Observe the nesting-level numbers in the DO CASE. We begin in statement 19 at level 2, since at that point we were already nested within the DO FOREVER. After getting as high as level 6 in statements 31–33 and then again to level 5 in statements 44–46, we work our way back out to level 2 after statement 50. One way in which the nesting-level numbers may be used is to assist in detecting missing ENDs for DOs. Since the DO CASE was at level 2, statement 51 after the END of the DO CASE must also be at level 2. If it were not, some kind of mismatch between DOs and ENDs would be indicated. The compiler can always give an indication that something has gone wrong, but in extreme cases this will not be until the end of the program has been reached. The nesting-level numbers can then sometimes be useful in locating the error.

COMPUTING THE CONTINUOUS CONTROL CURRENT

Computation of the two temperatures in statements 51–55 is as before, although in this program we are placing these operations before the checking for alarm conditions.

We now need to decide whether it is necessary to compute the current. The idea here is that, if we are dealing with cases 0, 1, or 4, then the process operator wishes to leave the current at 0, 200, or 20 amps, respectively. It obviously would not make sense to set the current at 0, say, and immediately recompute it from the formula as some other value.

However, after increasing the current slowly in case 2, we do then want to switch to continuous control of the current, according to whatever values the reference and actual temperatures indicate. Accordingly, in statement 56 we inquire whether the control value is either 2 or 3, and if so carry out a calculation of the heater current.

This computation is as it was in case study 2, with one important difference: We take account of the possibility that the reference temperature might be *less* than the actual temperature, as, for example, when the process operator has just decreased the reference temperature. When this condition arises, the current should be shut off.

We now place the value of the current on output port 1, regardless of which of the various paths of program execution has computed that value. For cases 2 and 4, this will be sending to the port the same final value of current that is already there, but there is no harm in that.

CHECKING THE ALARM CONDITIONS

Statements 68–76 are identical to the same operations in the previous case study. We then have a new statement to set an alarm bit if the control thumbwheel contains an illegal value.

Now comes a nested IF statement to distinguish the three possibilities regarding the temperatures. First, if the actual temperature is greater than the specified limit, we set bits that will turn on the two exhaust fans and an alarm. If the actual temperature is not greater than the limit, it might still be greater than the reference temperature. On the ELSE path of the IF in statement 80, therefore, we place another IF statement (83) that makes this test. In this case we are to turn on one exhaust fan and reset the other two bits. If the actual temperature is not greater than the reference temperature, then we will execute statement 85, which resets all three of these bits.

COMBINING BITS FOR OUTPUT

The operations in statements 80–86 have now given desired values to bits 3, 4, and 5. In OUT$PORT$0 it is now necessary to get the values of the bits controlling the other three alarms into bits 0, 1, and 2 of OUT$PORT$0. This is readily done with a combination of left shifts and ORs in statement 87, after which we send the byte containing all of this information to output port 0. We realize, of course, that statements 87 and 88 could readily have been combined into one statement.

THE END OF THE PROGRAM

This completes the work of the program so we now write the END that terminates the DO FOREVER. Since this END matches a DO that is about two pages away, we have included a brief comment to identify what it matches, even though this can be unambiguously deduced from the nesting-level numbers. The END that terminates the program is written as a labelled END, meaning that it is written with the label that begins the program for statement 1. What this buys us is that the compiler checks the matching of labels associated with DOs and ENDs. If, through some error, a labelled END does not in fact match the corresponding DO (often because of omission of an END earlier in the program), then we get a diagnostic message from the compiler. This is a simple and helpful check.

This program was compiled with the compiler reporting no programming errors. We realize, however, that a program with no errors detectable by the compiler may still not do what we want it to. In order to check out the program on a Microcomputer Development System, it is necessary to modify the program slightly, using techniques discussed in later chapters. With the modified program we can try a variety of combinations on the input values and try to satisfy ourselves that the program operates as desired. The process of ferreting out errors in the program and trying to assure ourselves of its correctness is discussed somewhat more fully in Chapter 9.

EXERCISES

***1.** Write IF statements to carry out the following operations.

a) Add 1 to a variable named LEGAL$ADULT if AGE is 18 or greater.

b) Add 1 to BIG if SIZE$A is greater than 800 and add 1 to LITTLE if SIZE$A is less than or equal to 800.

c) If the value of VAR$1 is greater than the value of VAR$2, move the contents of VAR$1 to TEMPORARY; if the value of VAR$1 is less than that of VAR$2, move the contents of VAR$2 to TEMPORARY; if the two values are equal, move either of them to TEMPORARY.

d) If the value of the variable named HOURS$WORKED is *anything but* 40, make NON$STANDARD equal to 1.

e) If the variable named DIGIT contains a value greater than or equal to 30H and less than or equal to 39H, make GOOD equal to 1; otherwise make GOOD equal to zero.

2. Write IF statements to carry out the following operations.

a) Add 1 to the variable named MAJOR$BILLING if ACCOUNT$TOTAL is greater than 1000.

b) Determine whether the value of the variable named FINAL$BILL is greater than 999; if it is, make APPROVAL$REQUIRED equal to 1; otherwise make APPROVAL$REQUIRED equal to zero.

c) If the variable named CHAR$1 is equal to 41H and the variable named CHAR$2 is equal to 42H, move 12 to CODE$AB.

d) If the variable named LETTER contains 20H, or if it is in the range of 41H to 5AH inclusive, move 1 to GOOD; otherwise move zero to GOOD.

***3.** Three examination grades are named GRADE$1, GRADE$2, and GRADE$3. If the average of the three is 65 or greater, PASS is to be made equal to 1; if not, PASS is to be made equal to zero.

4. Values having been given to the variables by previous statements that you do not write, write a statement that will move either REORDER$QTY or zero to ORDER$AMOUNT, depending on whether or not the sum of ON$HAND and ON$ORDER is less than REORDER$POINT.

***5.** What will the following sets of statements do?

a)
```
BIG = A;
IF B > A THEN
    BIG = B;
```

b)
```
IF A > B THEN
    BIG = A;
ELSE
    BIG = B;
```

c)
```
IF A > B THEN
    BIG = A;
IF A <= B THEN
    BIG = B;
```

6. The following program will set ODDBIT to 1 if any of bits 1, 3, 5, or 7 of the byte variable named A is equal to 1, and will set ODDBIT equal to zero otherwise. Write a much shorter statement to do the same thing with only one relation test.

```
IF     ((A AND 00000010B) = 00000010B)
    OR ((A AND 00001000B) = 00001000B)
    OR ((A AND 00100000B) = 00100000B)
    OR ((A AND 10000000B) = 10000000B) THEN
    ODDBIT = 1;
ELSE
    ODDBIT = 0;
```

7. Identify any syntactic errors in the following:

a)
```
IF A > 12 THEN;
    BIG = A;
```

b)
```
IF PORT$6 = 00000011B THEN
    FLAG$1 = 1
ELSE
    FLAG$1 = 0;
```

c)
```
IF FLOWRATE > 80 THEN
    FLAG = 1;
    PROCESS$RATE = 16;
ELSE
    FLAG = 0;
```

d)
```
IF LAST$CHAR = 40H
    THEN BLANK
= 1;ELSE;
```

*8. Do these two program segments produce the same results for all values of the variables?

a)
```
IF A = B AND C = D AND E = F THEN
    G = 1;
ELSE
    G = 2;
```

b)
```
IF A = B THEN
    IF C = D THEN
        IF E = F THEN
            G = 1;
        ELSE
            G = 2;
```

9. Do these two program segments produce the same results for all values of the variables?

a)
```
IF A = B AND C = D AND E = F THEN
    G = 1;
ELSE
    G = 2;
```

b)
```
IF A = B THEN
    IF C = D THEN
        IF E = F THEN
            G = 1;
        ELSE
            G = 2;
    ELSE
        G = 2;
ELSE
    G = 2;
```

***10.** Given a value of ANNUAL$EARNINGS, write statements that will compute TAX from the following table:

ANNUAL$EARNINGS	TAX
Not over $2000	Zero
Over $2000 but not over $5000	2% of the amount over $2000
Over $5000	$60 plus 5% of the amount over $5000

11. Given FLOW, the value of FLOW$ZONE is to be found from the following:

If FLOW is	THEN FLOW$ZONE is
$=0$	0
>0 and $<=10$	1
>10 and $<=25$	2
>25 and $<=37$	3
>37 and $<=77$	4
>77 and $<=151$	5
>151	6

The numerical values defining the zones are such that there is no simple formula for converting from FLOW to FLOW$ZONE, so an IF statement or a combination of IF statements must be used. Find a way to get the value of FLOW$ZONE that minimizes the number of comparisons that must be made. If it matters to your choice of method, you may assume that small flows are more likely than large.

***12.** What will this program do?

```
N = 12;
DO WHILE N > 0;
   OUTPUT(1) = N * N;
   N = N - 1;
END;
```

13. What will this program do?

```
N = 1;
DO WHILE N < 100;
   X = N:
   X$NEW = SHR(N + 1, 1);
   DO WHILE X <> X$NEW;
      X = X$NEW;
      S$NEW = SHR(N/X + X + 1, 1);
   END;
   OUTPUT(1) = X$NEW;
   N = N + 2;
END;
```

***14.** Write a program to count from zero to 59, one count per second, and send each count to output port 16.

15. The cube root of a positive number N may be found by repeated application of the approximation formula

$$x_{new} = (2x^3 + N)/3x^2$$

Write a program to find a cube root using this method.

16. In a computer without a hardware multiply instruction, such as the Intel 8080, multiplication is ordinarily done by calling a procedure that examines all bits of the multiplier to determine whether the multiplicand is to be added in that position. Suppose that we have a multiplier, call it MULTIPLIER, which we are guaranteed has at most three ones, in bit positions 0–2. Write a program that will examine these three bit positions, adding a BYTE variable named MULTIPLICAND to the proper position of PRODUCT to get the product of MULTIPLIER and MULTIPLICAND. (As a side project you might try to determine the difference in speed between your program and the procedure that would be invoked if you simply wrote

```
PRODUCT = MULTIPLIER * MULTIPLICAND;
```

***17.** Given N and X, both BYTE variables, the Legendre Polynomials of order N = 0, 1, 2, and 3 are:

$$P_0(X) = 1$$
$$P_1(X) = X$$
$$P_2(X) = (3X^2 - 1) / 2$$
$$P_3(X) = (5X^3 - 3X) / 2$$

Write a program using a DO CASE statement to compute the appropriate polynomial and place its value in P. If N is greater than 3, place zero in P.

18. A certain company has four discount formulas, corresponding to four values of a discount code K. S is the sale price and D is the discounted price:

Code	Formula
1	D = S (No discount)
2	D = 0.98 S
3	D = S − 5% of amount by which S exceeds 100
4	If S <= 100, D = S If S > 100, D = S − 10

Assume BYTE variables, so that, for instance, multiplying by 98 and then dividing by 100 to get 0.98 will not cause loss of digits. Write a program using a DO CASE statement to carry out the appropriate calculation. If the code K is not in the range of 1–4, set BAD$CODE to 1.

***19.** Write a program to sample the value of input port 1 every 0.1 second for ten seconds, then place the average of the 100 sample values on output port 2.

20. Write a program to sample the value on input port 1 every 0.01 second for one second, and place the average of the 100 values on output port 2. If any of the input values is less than 12 or greater than 60, set LIMIT$FLAG equal to 1 and continue with the process.

21. Write a program to read the values on input ports 1 and 2 (port 1 being considered the high-order byte of an ADDRESS variable), compute the square root of this number, and send the square root (which will fit in a BYTE variable) to output port 4.

22. Write a program that will read values from input port 1 until detecting a value of zero, then compute the average of the nonzero values and place it on output port 2. If more than 255 values are read without detecting a zero, place zero on the output as the average. (*Note.* Adding 1 to a BYTE variable value of 255 produces zero.)

23. Write a program to carry out the following operations. Send to output port 1 a byte containing a 1 bit in the rightmost position. Then obtain a byte from input port 2 every 100 ms, so long as the rightmost bit of that byte is still a 1. Place a count of the number of times the input port was read in TIMER.

(If the output bit starts a one-shot multivibrator circuit, with the duration of the one-shot pulse controlled by a variable resistance in an external circuit, this technique suggests an inexpensive way to "read" the value of an analog variable.)

24. Write a program to determine the speed of a model train, as follows: Read input port 8 continuously, until detecting a 1 in bit position 7. At that point start counting milliseconds, using the TIME function with an appropriate argument, meanwhile continuing to input port 1. When bit 6 of the input value becomes 1, divide the value of DISTANCE by the count of milliseconds. Assuming that DISTANCE contains 1000 times the distance in millimeters between the two sensors represented by the two bits of the input port, this will give the speed of the train in mm/sec. Use ADDRESS variables.

CHAPTER 4

ARRAY AND STRUCTURE VARIABLES

INTRODUCTION

We have now learned a good deal about how to make effective use of PL/M in preparing programs for microcomputer applications; but there is a whole class of problems that we need new tools for, and that class consists of applications where many data values need to be referred to by one general name rather than giving each one a distinct name. In one program in this chapter, for example, we shall be interpolating in a table to find the temperature corresponding to a thermocouple voltage. Since the table has dozens of entries and, in principle, could have hundreds, it would be unworkable to give each value a distinct name. Doing so would make it impossible to write a simple loop to find the correct place in the table, as we shall be able to do using the new techniques.

ARRAYS

Arrays, also called *subscripted variables,* provide a powerful technique for dealing with this kind of situation. With an array we give one name to an entire collection of data. In the interpolation program we shall use the name X to represent the array of voltages.* Then, to indicate to PL/M which one of the voltages we want in a

* This name was chosen because it ties in with a geometrical interpretation of interpolation that will be discussed later. If it were not for this consideration, we might have used a name like VOLTAGE or THERMOCOUPLE$OUTPUT.

particular case, we follow the name with parentheses enclosing a subscript expression. For example, having named the array of voltages X, we can call for the first element of the array by writing X(0). Note that PL/M subscripts are numbered from *zero,* so that the second element in the array would be referenced by X(1). If the array had a total of 20 elements, the last one would be referenced by X(19).

SUBSCRIPT EXPRESSIONS

The real power of subscripted variables appears when we permit a subscript to be *any* expression, rather than just constants as in the examples so far. Then we can do such things as arranging for the subscript expression to take on a sequence of values as the elements in the array are processed.

In PL/M a subscript is permitted to be any expression, no matter how complex. In practice we will have little occasion to use highly complicated subscript expressions, but the facility is there if needed.

In applications where speed is an important consideration, we try to keep subscripts simple and to use BYTE variables, wherever possible, since doing so will usually result in a faster-running object program.

DECLARING AN ARRAY

It is necessary to inform the PL/M compiler that an identifier represents not just one value, as heretofore, but a collection of values. This is rather simply done. All we need do is, in the DECLARE statement, follow the identifier with parentheses giving the number of elements in the array. Thus, if our array of voltages, X, is to contain 20 values, we could write

```
DECLARE X(20) ADDRESS;
```

This tells the compiler that, in this program, X will be written with a subscript, and directs the compiler to allocate the required memory space for the elements of the array.

When several arrays are declared with factoring, the dimension information *must* be factored. Thus we may write:

```
DECLARE (X, Y, Z)(20) BYTE;
```

It would not be correct to write

```
DECLARE (X(20), Y(20), Z(20)) BYTE;
```

This would have no special value even if we could do it, but we might wish it were possible to write something like:

```
DECLARE (A(10), B(15), C(25)) BYTE;
```

This cannot be done, however; we must either use three declarations, or use

```
DECLARE A(10) BYTE, B(15) BYTE, C(25) BYTE;
```

VARIABLE INITIALIZATION WITH THE DATA AND INITIAL ATTRIBUTES

We pause briefly to introduce the concept of initializing a variable, in a declaration, using the DATA or INITIAL attribute. With either of these reserved words, we may assign to a variable a value that will be placed in the memory location for that variable before program execution begins. For example, we might write:

```
DECLARE TEMPERATURE ADDRESS INITIAL(0);
DECLARE PRESSURE ADDRESS DATA(760);
DECLARE TIME$BASE BYTE DATA(20);
DECLARE CRLF(2) BYTE DATA(0DH, 0AH);
DECLARE VOLTAGE(5) ADDRESS INITIAL(10, 39, 67, 98, 132);
```

Without DATA and INITIAL it would be necessary to begin the program with assignment statements establishing values for all such variables, since memory cannot be assumed to contain any specific values. The difference between the two forms is that variables initialized with DATA are assumed never to change and therefore may be assigned to Read-Only Memory (ROM), whereas variables initialized with INITIAL are assumed to be changeable and must therefore be assigned to Random Access Memory (RAM). (Control of storage assignment is considered briefly in Chapter 9.)

FINDING THE MEAN OF THE VALUES OF AN ARRAY

For an example of the use of these ideas in a small but realistic program, consider the task of writing a program to find the mean of the values of an array, which must be done by programs in many applications. To keep things simple in our first example, we shall show the array elements as program data and not concern ourselves with output.

Figure 4.1 is a program to carry out the necessary calculations using an array. We see that X has been declared to be an array of ten BYTE values and that the elements are given values using the DATA attribute in the DECLARE. SUM and MEAN are identifiers having fairly obvious purposes. SUM was declared to be of

```
PL/M-80 COMPILER    FIG. 4.1                                           PAGE   1

                /*************************************************************/
                /* A FIRST PROGRAM TO FIND THE MEAN OF THE 10 VALUES OF AN ARRAY */
                /*************************************************************/

 1              MEAN10:
                DO;
 2    1             DECLARE X(10) BYTE DATA(23,2,18,0,20,14,45,27,8,33);
 3    1             DECLARE SUM ADDRESS;
 4    1             DECLARE (MEAN, I) BYTE;

 5    1             SUM = 0;
 6    1             I = 0;
 7    1             DO WHILE I <= 9;
 8    2                 SUM = SUM + X(I);
 9    2                 I = I + 1;
10    2             END;
11    1             MEAN = SUM / 10;

12    1         END MEAN10;
```

type ADDRESS, to provide space for accumulating the BYTE values. MEAN was declared BYTE, since the mean of a set of values cannot be larger than the largest member of the set. The variable I will be used as a subscript. Since the subscript will never exceed 9, we assign it to a BYTE variable, which can hold a value as large as 255.

The basic idea is that we are going to start the variable named SUM at zero and then add all of the elements of the array to it. Statement 5 accordingly initializes SUM, as required. To access the ten elements of the array in succession, we wish to have the subscript I take on the values of 0 to 9 in succession. In statement 6 we therefore start I at zero.

Now comes a DO–WHILE that controls the repeated execution of the statements that accumulate the sum and advance the subscript. The first time statement 8 is executed, SUM and I will both be zero, so the result will be to add the value of X(0) to zero and place the result in SUM. Statement 9 increments I and the body of the loop is executed again. This time the value of X(1) is added to SUM—which contains X(0) from the previous execution—and the result is again placed in SUM. This process is repeated until statement 8 has been executed with I equal to 9, at which point the sum of all ten values is in SUM. This time when I is incremented, it goes to 10 and the DO–WHILE terminates repetition of the loop. Statement 11 then computes the mean, to the nearest smaller integer.

THE ITERATIVE DO

The operation of giving a variable a succession of values occurs so frequently that it is helpful to have a language feature to simplify it. PL/M provides the *iterative* DO. A very simple example of the statement appears in Fig. 4.2, a revision of the

```
PL/M-80 COMPILER    FIG. 4.2                                    PAGE   1

              /*****************************************************************/
              /* A SECOND PROGRAM TO FIND THE MEAN OF THE 10 VALUES OF AN ARRAY */
              /*****************************************************************/

 1            MEAN10:
              DO;
 2    1         DECLARE X(10) BYTE DATA(23,2,18,0,20,14,45,27,8,33);
 3    1         DECLARE SUM ADDRESS;
 4    1         DECLARE (MEAN, I) BYTE;

 5    1         SUM = 0;
 6    1         DO I = 0 TO 9;
 7    2           SUM = SUM + X(I);
 8    2         END;
 9    1         MEAN = SUM / 10;

10    1       END MEAN10;
```

program to find the mean of the ten elements of an array. The two programs give the same answers and carry out the calculations in exactly the same sequence.

The iterative DO, as it appears here, is seen to consist of an *index variable,* a *start expression,* and a *bound expression:*

```
DO index-variable = start-expression TO bound-expression;
```

The effect is to give index-variable all of the values from start-expression to bound-expression, in steps of 1. The two expressions in the example of this program are both constants, but in general they may be any expressions. We shall see many occasions to write start and bound expressions that involve at least simple arithmetic on variables. In later discussions, an index-variable will usually be referred to simply as an index.

If it is desired to increment the index variable by some other value than 1, it is possible to add a *step-expression.* For example, if we wanted a variable named CURRENT to take all the values from 2 to 100 in steps of 2, we could write

```
DO CURRENT = 2 TO 100 BY 2;
```

Again, we are not limited to a constant value, but may write any expression as a step expression. (Recall the furnace-control operation from the previous chapter. Statements 28–36 of Fig. 3.1 could be slightly simplified using the statement just shown.)

The iterative DO will be used very frequently to get values of subscripts in processing arrays, but we see in the furnace-control application one example of the many ways in which the iterative DO is useful even when arrays are not involved.

THE LENGTH AND THE LAST BUILT-IN FUNCTIONS

There can be problems with a program that contains statements like

```
DO I = 0 TO 9;
MEAN = SUM / 10;
```

where the 9 and 10 relate to the size of an array. The problem has to do with maintenance of the program: What happens when the program must be modified to process an array having a different number of elements? Finding and modifying all references to the size of such an array is a time-consuming and error-prone process.

Two methods of resolving this problem are available. One is to use the LITERALLY feature so that all explicit references to dimension information for an array appear in only one place. With this method our averaging program could be as shown in Fig. 4.3.

```
PL/M-80 COMPILER    FIG. 4.3                                          PAGE   1

          /*************************************************************************/
          /* A THIRD PROGRAM TO FIND THE MEAN OF THE 10 VALUES OF AN ARRAY */
          /*************************************************************************/

  1       MEAN10:
          DO;
  2   1      DECLARE ARRAY$SIZE LITERALLY '10';
  3   1      DECLARE X(ARRAY$SIZE) BYTE DATA(23,2,18,0,20,14,45,27,8,33);
  4   1      DECLARE SUM ADDRESS;
  5   1      DECLARE (MEAN, I) BYTE;

  6   1      SUM = 0;
  7   1      DO I = 0 TO ARRAY$SIZE - 1;
  8   2         SUM = SUM + X(I);
  9   2      END;
 10   1      MEAN = SUM / ARRAY$SIZE;

 11   1   END MEAN10;
```

The other alternative is to use the built-in PL/M functions named LENGTH and LAST. When we write

```
LENGTH(X)
```

the value supplied is the number of elements in X. This can be used in place of the 10 in computing the mean. When we write

```
LAST(X)
```

the value supplied is the element number of the last element in the array. Since elements are numbered from zero in PL/M, we have the formal relationship that LAST delivers a value that is one less than that delivered by LENGTH. We accordingly could get by with either of these functions alone; both are provided since both are frequently needed.

Using these PL/M procedures, we can rewrite our program as shown in Fig. 4.4. Now all the dimensioning information is also localized in one place, namely the array declaration.

A related procedure SIZE has occasional usefulness. It returns the number of bytes in the array given as its argument. For a BYTE array, SIZE and LENGTH give the same value, and for an ADDRESS array SIZE returns twice the value returned by LENGTH.

```
PL/M-80 COMPILER    FIG. 4.4                                PAGE   1

        /*******************************************************************/
        /* A FOURTH PROGRAM TO FIND THE MEAN OF THE 10 VALUES OF AN ARRAY */
        /*******************************************************************/

        MEAN10:
        DO;
           DECLARE X(10) BYTE DATA(23,2,18,0,20,14,45,27,8,33);
           DECLARE SUM ADDRESS;
           DECLARE (MEAN, I) BYTE;

           SUM = 0;
           DO I = 0 TO LAST(X);
              SUM = SUM + X(I);
           END;
           MEAN = SUM / LENGTH(X);

        END MEAN10;
```

A PROGRAM TO IMPLEMENT A SUBSTITUTION CIPHER

To broaden our understanding of the usefulness of arrays and to see some more techniques in working with them, let us consider a very simple encryption program. The scheme to be implemented is simply to replace each character of a message with some other character according to a fixed substitution rule. To keep things simple and let us focus on one thing at a time, we shall in fact deal with a "message" consisting of only one input character.

In the first version of the program we shall use a loop to search through a table looking for the input character. When a match is found, a variable named I will have been given a value equal to the element number of the character. I is then used as a subscript to access a second table the same length as the first, which gives the substitution.

```
PL/M-80 COMPILER    FIG. 4.5                                          PAGE   1


                  /*********************************************************/
                  /* A FIRST PROGRAM TO IMPLEMENT A SUBSTITUTION CIPHER */
                  /*********************************************************/

  1               CIPHER:
                  DO;
  2    1            DECLARE CHAR$TABLE(*) BYTE
                       DATA('ABCDEFGHIJKLMNOPQRSTUVWXYZ 0123456789,./?;+!"#$%&():*-=');
  3    1            DECLARE SUBSTITUTE$CHAR$TABLE(*) BYTE
                       DATA('1!QAZ2"WSX3#EDC4$RFV5%TGB6&YHN7UJM8(IK,9)OL.0P;+/?:*-= ');
  4    1            DECLARE (INPUT$CHAR, OUTPUT$CHAR, I) BYTE;

  5    1            INPUT$CHAR = INPUT(10);

  6    1            I = 0;
  7    1            DO WHILE INPUT$CHAR <> CHAR$TABLE(I) AND I <= LAST(CHAR$TABLE);
  8    2               I =  I + 1;
  9    2            END;

 10    1            OUTPUT(12) = SUBSTITUTE$CHAR$TABLE(I);

 11    1          END CIPHER;
```

A program to do all this is shown in Fig. 4.5. The first new feature we note is the use of *implicit dimensioning*. In this case we don't really care how long the two tables are so long as they are the same length, which is easily checked visually. Therefore instead of counting the number of elements in the array and entering that number as the dimension, we write an asterisk and let the compiler figure out the actual size by counting the number of elements in the initialization.

The actual search through the table is a rather simple matter, with a DO–WHILE condition doing most of the work. With I started at zero, the DO–WHILE asks whether the input character is equal to the zeroth element of CHAR$TABLE. If the two are not equal, meaning that we have not found a match, the subscript is incremented. This process is repeated until we either find a match or the second part of the DO–WHILE condition determines that we have run through the table without finding a match.

Statement 10 then uses the value of I to pick up the element in SUBSTITUTE$ CHAR$TABLE corresponding to the element in CHAR$TABLE for which a match was found. This is a rather inadequate way of handling the possibility of an invalid input character, since what we will get in that case is a subscript point to the next byte after the end of CHAR$TABLE, with no error indication. It is obviously possible to test for this possibility and handle it other ways; we shall see one other way in the next version of the program.

Note the presence of the character "blank" between Z and zero. If the text containing blanks is to be processed, this is a necessary provision, although where it is placed is not crucial.

A FASTER CIPHER ROUTINE

If one really wanted to implement this extremely simple encryption algorithm, one would be concerned about the speed of its operation. One obvious way to accelerate it would be to revise the tables so that the characters appearing most frequently in the clear text would appear early in the table. But even this is inferior to a scheme that involves no searching at all.

To see how this could work we must be clear about the internal representation of the input characters that we wish to translate. Figure 4.6 shows the hexadecimal representation of the 64 graphic symbols according to the American National Standard Code for Information Interchange. This code, called *ASCII* and pronounced

00	NUL		22	"	44	D		66	f	
01	SOH		23	#	45	E		67	g	
02	STX		24	$	46	F		68	h	
03	ETX		25	%	47	G		69	i	
04	EOT		26	&	48	H		6A	j	
05	ENQ		27	'	49	I		6B	k	
06	ACK		28	(	4A	J		6C	l	
07	BEL		29	)	4B	K		6D	m	
08	BS		2A	*	4C	L		6E	n	
09	HT		2B	+	4D	M		6F	o	
0A	LF		2C	,	4E	N		70	p	
0B	VT		2D	–	4F	O		71	q	
0C	FF		2E	.	50	P		72	r	
0D	CR		2F	/	51	Q		73	s	
0E	SO		30	0	52	R		74	t	
0F	SI		31	1	53	S		75	u	
10	DLE		32	2	54	T		76	v	
11	DC1	(X-ON)	33	3	55	U		77	w	
12	DC2	(TAPE)	34	4	56	V		78	x	
13	DC3	(X-OFF)	35	5	57	W		79	y	
14	DC4	~~(TAPE)~~	36	6	58	X		7A	z	
15	NAK		37	7	59	Y		7B	{	
16	SYN		38	8	5A	Z		7C	|	
17	ETB		39	9	5B	[		7D	}	
18	CAN		3A	:	5C	\				(ALT MODE)
19	EM		3B	;	5D	]		7E	~	
1A	SUB		3C	<	5E	∧	(↑)	7F	DEL	
1B	ESC		3D	=	5F	—	(←)			(RUB OUT)
1C	FS		3E	>	60	`				
1D	GS		3F	?	61	a				
1E	RS		40	@	62	b				
1F	US		41	A	63	c				
20	SP		42	B	64	d				
21	!		43	C	65	e				

Fig. 4.6. Hexadecimal representation of 64 characters, in ASCII code. The first 16 characters, 00H through 1FH, refer to communications functions.

"As-key," is used by PL/M compilers to represent characters. We see that the codes for the characters that can be entered from an upper-case-only keyboard range from 20H (space) to 5FH (the underscore), which is 32D to 95D. Thus if we subtract 20H from the internal representation of an input character, the result will be a number in the range of 0 to 3FH = 63D. This latter quantity can then be used directly to access a substitution table without any sort of searching loop. In fact, a program based on this method need have only one table.

```
PL/M-80 COMPILER    FIG. 4.7                                                    PAGE   1


          /*****************************************************************************/
          /* A SECOND PROGRAM TO IMPLEMENT A SUBSTITUTION CIPHER                       */
          /*****************************************************************************/

  1       CIPHER2:
          DO;
  2   1       DECLARE SUBSTITUTE$CHAR$TABLE(64) BYTE
                  DATA('!1QAZ"2WSX #3EDC$4RFV%5TGB&6YHN^''7UJM](8IK[,<)9O_L\.>0P@;+/?:*-=');
  3   1       DECLARE (INPUT$CHAR, OUTPUT$CHAR, I) BYTE;

  4   1       INPUT$CHAR = INPUT(10);

  5   1       IF INPUT$CHAR >= 20H AND INPUT$CHAR <= 5FH THEN
  6   1           OUTPUT(12) = SUBSTITUTE$CHAR$TABLE(INPUT$CHAR - 20H);
              ELSE
  7   1           OUTPUT(12) = 0FFH;
  8   1   END CIPHER2;
```

A program based on this method is shown in Fig. 4.7. Note the use of two successive single quotes to represent the single quote character. We realize that if a single quote were written to stand for itself, the compiler would of necessity mistakenly assume it to be the end of the DATA character string. By convention two successive single quotes within a quoted string are processed as a single quote.

The actual processing is done with an IF statement to handle the possibility of an invalid character more gracefully than our previous version did. The solution here is to substitute a character of all 1 bits when this happens. If it were not for the desirability of making this test, the entire processing could be done with the following statement:

```
OUTPUT(12) = SUBSTITUTE$CHARACTER$TABLE(INPUT(10) - 20H);
```

As a matter of fact, the entire program could be written in this fashion and would still handle invalid input, at the expense of a substitution table of 128 bytes giving the substitutions desired for all possible characters. This is typical of the space-versus-time tradeoffs encountered in programming.

A SIMPLE SORTING ROUTINE

It happens frequently, in certain types of data processing applications, that information must be put into sequence on the basis of some kind of criterion called a *key*. For example, employee time records might need to be sorted into ascending sequence on employee number, to simplify further processing. The employee number is the key in this case. In a retail banking application, it might be desirable to sort records corresponding to customer checks into sequence on check number as the key. Many other occasions arise.

For a first example of the kinds of techniques that can be used, we shall sort "records" each consisting of a single character. In later versions each record will contain a key of one or more characters and additional associated information. Here, however, the one-character key is the entire record. For concreteness we shall sort a group of records consisting of all the characters having graphic symbols on the keyboard of the CRT used to prepare programs for this book.

A great many sorting methods are known. Much research has been devoted to devising methods that are especially fast, or which take into account special characteristics of the information being sorted, or which minimize the amount of additional storage required, or which have other useful characteristics. This book is not the place to explore such matters, and we shall rather uncritically use the method which is conceptually simplest and easiest to explain. Rudimentary though the method is, we shall see, in the final version of the program at the end of the chapter, that under certain circumstances it is actually not a bad method.

The technique is one version of what is called *exchange sorting*. To explain it, we shall deal with the exercise at hand—sorting one-character records—and we shall consider a character to be "smaller" or "larger" than another based on their ASCII representations.

The method is this: We compare the first character with the second; if the first is larger, we exchange them in storage. We now compare the character in the first position—which may originally have been second, of course—with the character in the third position and exchange them if the first is larger. This process is repeated until the first character has been compared with all others in the array. When this has been done, we are guaranteed that the first position contains the smallest character in the whole set. We now compare the *second* character with the third, fourth, . . . , etc., until it has been compared with all the other characters in the array. Now we compare the *third* character with all characters that follow it. This process is continued until a final comparison determines whether the last and the next-to-last characters need to be exchanged.

At the end of this process the entire array is guaranteed to be in ascending sequence. There may have been a great deal of movement, or there may have been none if the array was already sorted to begin with. One of the reasons the method is rudimentary is that it takes no advantage of any initial ordering of the array.

The program to do all this is shown in Fig. 4.8. The characters to be sorted are entered with an INITIAL attribute in the DECLARE statement. We also declare two

```
PL/M-80 COMPILER    FIG. 4.8                                                    PAGE    1

              /*****************************************************************************/
              /* A FIRST SORTING ROUTINE - SORTS AN INPUT STRING OF CHARACTERS              */
              /*****************************************************************************/

  1           SORT$1:
              DO;
  2    1        DECLARE STRING(*) BYTE
                  INITIAL('1234567890:-QWERTYUIOPASDFGHJKL;ZXCVBNM,./ !"#$%&''()*=_@[\+ƀ]<>?');
  3    1        DECLARE (I, J, TEMP) BYTE;

  4    1        DO I = 0 TO LAST(STRING) - 1;
  5    2          DO J = I + 1 TO LAST(STRING);
  6    3            IF STRING(I) > STRING(J) THEN
  7    3            DO;
  8    4              TEMP = STRING(I);
  9    4              STRING(I) = STRING(J);
 10    4              STRING(J) = TEMP;
 11    4            END;
 12    3          END;
 13    2        END;
 14    1      END SORT$1;
```

variables named I and J that will be used as subscripts and a variable named TEMP that will be used in the exchanging.

As the sorting proceeds we are always dealing with two characters. The one controlled by the index I is successively compared with all characters later in the array. It therefore needs to start at zero, which accesses the first element in the array, and run through one less than the last element number in the array. The iterative DO in statement 4 accomplishes this. The second character in the comparison ranges from the one immediately after the first, up through the last element of the array. The index J, which indexes this character, may accordingly be started at I + 1. It runs through the element number of the last element of the array, which is given by LAST(STRING).

The comparison and—if necessary—exchange are carried out by statements 6 through 11. If the first character in the comparison is larger than the second and we want to exchange the two, it is done in a three-statement process as shown.

In checking out this program, a version was written that prints the array STRING after it has been sorted. Here is its output:

```
!"#$%&'()*+,-./0123456789:;<=>?@ABCDEFGHIJKLMNOPQRSTUVWXYZ[\]ƀ_
```

Naturally the program prints nothing corresponding to the character "blank," but from the position of the output on a printer or CRT, it could be seen that the blank did sort as the "smallest" character, as Fig. 4.6 tells us it should.

AN INTERPOLATION ROUTINE

A program to interpolate in a table will show the use of arrays and subscripting in the context of a realistic application.

The table in which we shall interpolate gives data from the National Bureau of

Standards on the output (in millivolts) for temperatures in degrees Celsius of type J thermocouples. In an application program, we would be entering this table with a value of the thermocouple output and seeking the corresponding temperature. For our purposes, therefore, the voltage is the independent variable.

The idea behind this application is that, even though the curve of the relationship between temperature and voltage is nonlinear, it can be adequately approximated by a sequence of short straight lines. In regions where the curvature is small, the line segments can be longer. We assume, for this application, that a temperature within 1° is close enough; and from this we establish that the thermocouple output must be accurate to hundredths of a millivolt. Thus the thermocouple output for a temperature of 700° is 39.13 mV; in the program, this voltage will be represented by 3913 as an integer.

The program that we shall write is to read such a voltage from an input port, find two table values that bracket it, and then use linear interpolation to find the corresponding temperature. The search process consists of a loop to find the smallest table value that is larger than or equal to the input voltage. We shall call this value of the voltage x_i. The corresponding value of temperature is y_i. The geometric picture is then as shown in Fig. 4.9. The algebra of the situation then says that:

$$\frac{y_{\text{out}} - y_{i-1}}{x_{\text{in}} - x_{i-1}} = \frac{y_i - y_{i-1}}{x_i - x_{i-1}},$$

from which we obtain

$$y_{\text{out}} = y_{i-1} + \frac{(x_{\text{in}} - x_{i-1})(y_i - y_{i-1})}{(x_i - x_{i-1})}.$$

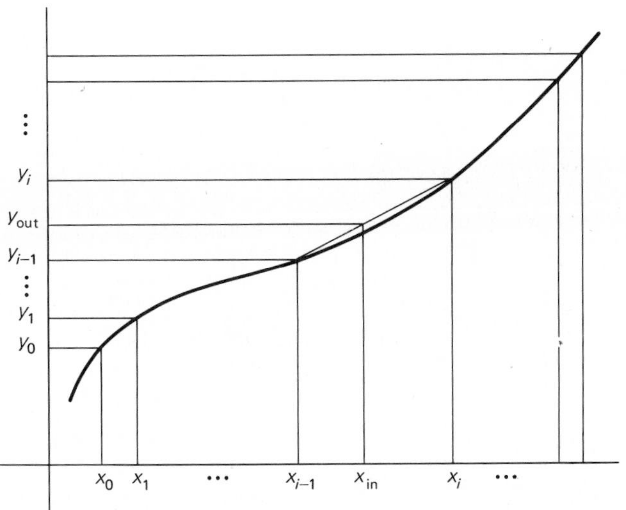

Fig. 4.9. Geometrical representation of the interpolation process.

This is the calculation that the program must carry out once it has established which value of temperature corresponds to x_i.

The program is shown in Fig. 4.10. Let us begin studying it by making sure that the meaning of the two tables is clearly understood. The declarations say that X(0) and Y(0) are both zero. This means simply that a temperature of zero degrees corresponds to a thermocouple output of zero. The next entries in the two tables establish that X(1) is 51 (= .51 mV) which corresponds to Y(1) = 10°. The last entries in the two tables establish that 45.50 mV corresponds to a temperature of 800°. Since we do not really care how many entries there are in the tables so long as they have been carefully checked to be sure that they are the same length, we have used the asterisk notation in the declaration. The values here were chosen to guarantee that a temperature accurate to within 1° can be found. With further work, the number of entries in the table could probably be reduced and still meet this requirement.

The searching loop is closely related to the one we saw in the first version of the encryption routine. (For our purposes here we choose not to concern ourselves with the possibility that the thermocouple voltage might be outside the range of the table. Providing such a test would not be difficult.)

```
PL/M-80 COMPILER    FIG. 4.10                                         PAGE   1


         /***********************************************************************/
         /*  A PROGRAM TO INTERPOLATE IN A TABLE OF VOLTAGES, X, TO FIND A    */
         /*  CORRESPONDING TEMPERATURE, Y.                                    */
         /***********************************************************************/

         INTERPOLATE:
         DO;
            DECLARE X(*) ADDRESS DATA(0,51,102,154,206,258,365,472,581,746,911,
            1078,1411,1743,2074,2405,2739,2879,3021,3164,3310,3457,3607,3759,
            3913,4038,4165,4292,4421,4550);
            DECLARE Y(*) ADDRESS DATA(0,10,20,30,40,50,70,90,110,140,170,200,
            260,320,380,440,500,525,550,575,600,625,650,675,700,720,740,760,
               780,800);
            DECLARE (I, X$IN, NUMERATOR, Y$OUT) ADDRESS;

         /* STATEMENTS HERE WOULD GIVE A VALUE TO X$IN */

            I = 0;
            DO WHILE X$IN > X(I);
               I = I + 1;
            END;

            /* SHIFT FOR ROUNDING */
            NUMERATOR = SHL((X$IN - X(I-1)) * (Y(I) - Y(I-1)), 1);
            Y$OUT = Y(I-1) + SHR(NUMERATOR/(X(I) - X(I-1)) + 1, 1);

         /* STATEMENTS HERE WOULD USE THE VALUE OF Y$OUT */

         END INTERPOLATE;
```

The computation of the interpolated value of the temperature is set up to round the quotient, to give a result that is accurate to within one-half unit in the last place. Rounding requires that we provide one extra digit in the quotient. As in any number system, we then add to this position a quantity equal to one-half the value of the position to its left, which is the last one that will be kept. In binary this is just a one. If the last position contains a one, there will be a carry into the last position to be kept. (This is a simple method of rounding; more complex methods are beyond the scope of this book.)

Consider an example. Suppose we wish to find the quotient (11 * 4)/10, which in binary would be:

$$\frac{0000\ 1011\ *\ 0000\ 0100}{0000\ 1010}$$

Multiplying, we get:

$$\frac{0000\ 0000\ 0010\ 1100}{0000\ 1010}$$

Shifting the numerator left one position gives:

$$\frac{0000\ 0000\ 0101\ 1000}{0000\ 1010}$$

The division now yields:

0000 1000

Adding one in the last position does not cause a carry, so after shifting right one place, the final result is 0000 0100. And 44/10 is indeed 4, to the nearest unit.

Now suppose everything is as before except that the divisor is 9, which in binary is 0000 1001. Now, the division yields

0000 1001.

Adding one in the last position does cause a carry into the position to the left, so that, after the final right shift, we have 0000 0101. This means that 44/9 is 5, to the nearest unit, rather than the 4 we would get without rounding.

It is essential, in doing all this, to be sure that no result exceeds the capacity of the variable in which it will be held. The multiplication is no problem, since the product of two BYTE variables will always fit in an ADDRESS variable, as NUMERATOR was declared to be. The shifting, however, could cause the loss of a leading bit; it is our responsibility to be sure that the data values are such that this cannot happen. This in fact sets a limit, as this program is written, on the maximum length of the straight-line segments used for interpolation. This kind of consideration will frequently arise in microcomputer programming. An alternative would be to arrange the computation to do the division before multiplication. Shifting and rounding could still be used. Either way, the entire computation could of course be done with just one statement, at the expense of making that one statement somewhat less easy to understand.

This interpolation routine is incorporated in the case study in the next chapter, where we once again take up the furnace-control application studied in the previous two chapters.

STRUCTURE VARIABLES

We have, so far, seen simple variables in which an identifier refers to a single BYTE or ADDRESS item, and arrays in which a single identifier refers to an entire set of items, which must be either all BYTE quantities or all ADDRESS quantities. We shall now investigate *structures,* in which one identifier refers to a collection of *structure members,* which need not be of the same type. Each member of a structure has a *member identifier*.

Here is a simple example of the declaration of a structure:

```
DECLARE RECORD STRUCTURE (KEY BYTE, CONTENTS ADDRESS);
```

This declares that KEY is a BYTE variable and that CONTENTS is an ADDRESS variable. These are the two members of the structure RECORD. We see that member identifiers and their attributes must be enclosed in parentheses.

This declares the structure. To refer to the members we would write RECORD.KEY or RECORD.CONTENTS.

Structures can be much larger and more complex than this. Limits are established by the compiler and the size of available memory, but in practice these would not be found restrictive.

ARRAYS OF STRUCTURES

The next step in the development is that, instead of declaring just one structure associated with a structure identifier, we may, in fact, have many structures associated with the same identifier. For instance we can write

```
DECLARE RECORD(10) STRUCTURE (KEY BYTE, CONTENTS ADDRESS);
```

This declares RECORD to consist of ten structures each of which contains a KEY and a CONTENTS. Now we specify which one of the structures we mean by writing a subscript following the structure name. Thus we might write things like this:

```
RECORD(0).KEY
RECORD(7).KEY
RECORD(K + 1).CONTENTS
```

A SECOND SORTING ROUTINE WITH A SIMPLE STRUCTURE

We can use the structure just declared to implement a slightly more realistic sorting routine. The method is still exchange sorting as we studied it earlier in the chapter, but now we have in each record not only a key on which the records are to be sorted, but also additional information (CONTENTS) which must be carried along with the key. We could think of the key as being a stock number and the contents as the quantity of that item currently on hand in inventory.

The program is shown in Fig. 4.11. The declaration of the structure is as just shown, except that we have also given initial values to the structure members, using an INITIAL list. When giving values to a structure, we simply list them in a linear sequence, first giving all the member values for structure zero, then all the member values for structure one, etc.

The program is very similar to the one we saw in Fig. 4.8, except that when an exchange is necessary we must now exchange both the KEY and the CONTENTS. Since KEY is a BYTE variable and CONTENTS is ADDRESS, it is best to have two temporary storage locations. It would be permissible to use a temporary location of type ADDRESS for the KEY exchange, but this would force PL/M into some useless and time-consuming conversions between BYTE and ADDRESS representations.

It will perhaps be apparent that if the record were of a size corresponding to the requirements of realistic applications—perhaps 50 or 100 bytes—the amount

```
PL/M-80 COMPILER    FIG. 4.11                                    PAGE   1

/*********************************************************************/
/* A SECOND SORTING ROUTINE - SORTS A STRUCTURE OF SIMPLE RECORDS */
/*********************************************************************/

SORT$2:
DO;
    DECLARE RECORD(10) STRUCTURE (KEY BYTE, CONTENTS ADDRESS)
        INITIAL('D',429,'N',20881,'F',560,'B',1201,'X',500,'7',12300,'Q',
        1292,'C',9810,'A',300,'G',0);
    DECLARE (I, J, TEMP$BYTE) BYTE;
    DECLARE TEMP$ADDRESS ADDRESS;

    DO I = 0 TO LAST(RECORD) - 1;
        DO J = I + 1 TO LAST(RECORD);
            IF RECORD(I).KEY > RECORD(J).KEY THEN
            DO;
                TEMP$BYTE = RECORD(I).KEY;
                RECORD(I).KEY = RECORD(J).KEY;
                RECORD(J).KEY = TEMP$BYTE;
                TEMP$ADDRESS = RECORD(I).CONTENTS;
                RECORD(I).CONTENTS = RECORD(J).CONTENTS;
                RECORD(J).CONTENTS = TEMP$ADDRESS;
            END;
        END;
    END;
END SORT$2;
```

of data movement involved in actually exchanging the records could become prohibitive. After we have studied some more of the capabilities provided by structures, we shall take up this sorting problem again and see how this question may be answered.

ARRAYS WITHIN STRUCTURES

An array may be used as a member of a structure. The following example is taken from *PL/M-80 Programming Manual,* Intel document 98–268, copyright 1976:

```
DECLARE PAYCHECK STRUCTURE (
    LAST$NAME (15) BYTE,
    FIRST$NAME (15) BYTE,
    MIDDLE$INITIAL BYTE,
    DOLLARS ADDRESS,
    CENTS ADDRESS);
```

This structure is seen to consist of the following members: two 15-element BYTE arrays, PAYCHECK.LAST$NAME and PAYCHECK.FIRST$NAME; the BYTE variable PAYCHECK.MIDDLE$INITIAL; and two ADDRESS variables PAYCHECK.DOLLAR and PAYCHECK.CENTS.

We use subscripting to refer to particular elements of the member arrays, writing such things as

```
PAYCHECK.LAST$NAME(0)
PAYCHECK.FIRST$NAME(J)
```

So far we have done nothing with structures that could not have been done—although perhaps less conveniently—in other ways. Now we come to the features that make structures really interesting: We are permitted to have an array of structures in which there are arrays inside the structures. Here, for example, is a declaration based on the final version of the sort program that we shall be considering later.

```
DECLARE RECORD(NUMBER$OF$RECORDS) STRUCTURE
    (
    SN(5) BYTE,          /* STOCK NUMBER */
    DESCRIPTION(20) BYTE,
    ORDER$QTY ADDRESS,
    QTY$ON$HAND ADDRESS,
    QTY$ON$ORDER ADDRESS,
    REORDER$POINT ADDRESS,
    REORDER$QTY ADDRESS,
    LOC(8) BYTE          /* WAREHOUSE LOCATION */
    );
```

We see that RECORD is now many structures, each of which contains three BYTE arrays and five ADDRESS variables. Now we are able to write statements like this:

```
IF RECORD(I).SN(K) > RECORD(J).SN(K) THEN . . .
```

We shall pursue this example later.

STRUCTURES CONSIDERED AS TWO-DIMENSIONAL ARRAYS

When we have an array of structures where the structure members are arrays, we may, if we wish, think of the aggregate as a two-dimensional variable. To fully specify a particular element within the structure, we must give two subscripts, one identifying the structure and one identifying the member within that structure. The interpretation placed on the collection is up to us so long as the PL/M syntax rules are obeyed. We can, therefore, write such a declaration as

```
DECLARE ROW(20) STRUCTURE (COLUMN(20) ADDRESS);
DECLARE SUM ADDRESS;
DECLARE X(20) ADDRESS;
```

and think of the structure as a 20-by-20 matrix. Now we may write statements such as

```
SUM = SUM + X(J) * ROW(I).COLUMN(J);
```

which could be part of a procedure for solving a system of simultaneous equations. In many programming languages, variables are permitted to have more than one subscript, in which case we would write variable references such as MATRIX(I,J). PL/M permits only one-dimensional arrays but, using arrays within structures, we get exactly the same effect as with a two-dimensional array.

Arrays of three and higher dimensions, however, must be approached in other ways, since PL/M does not permit structures within structures. One of the examples in Chapter 5 will show a simple approach to this question.

A PROGRAM USING STRUCTURE VARIABLES TO DETERMINE WHETHER AN INPUT STRING IS A RESERVED WORD

The following example uses a structure essentially as a two-dimensional variable along the lines just described. The application is to accept a group of characters and determine whether it represents a PL/M reserved word. If the input string is a reserved word, the program prints its number (0 to 38) and otherwise prints the response NOT A RESERVED WORD.

We shall set up a table of the 39 reserved words in PL/M. Since all elements of an array within a structure must be of the same length, we shall supply trailing blanks for the reserved words that are shorter than the maximum of nine characters. For programming simplicity we shall require that the input string also be nine characters long, with trailing blanks if necessary; this unrealistic restriction could easily be removed. In the program shown in Fig. 4.12, the 39 reserved words are shown on 39 separate lines, in an attempt to make the meaning and arrangement of data as clear as possible, but this would not be required. It is also not required that the opening and closing parentheses around the data be on separate lines, although the practice has much to recommend it.

In order to show the program in operation, we shall jump ahead of our story a bit and use procedures named READ, WRITE, and NUMOUT to let us run the program on an Intellec Microcomputer Development System and see it in operation. This requires the declarations in statements 7–9, the CALL READ in 30 and 31, and the various operations in statements 46 and following. We shall make no attempt to explain these operations at this stage, but simply content ourselves with the fact that the general meaning is clear from the statements as written. The details will be explained later, in Chapters 6 and 9. The statements in the program that relate to these unexplained details have been marked with a vertical line to the right of the statement numbers. The reader is urged to try to ignore these lines at this stage, or at least not to be discouraged if the details are unclear.

The basic approach of the program is to compare the input string with each reserved word in the table in the structure until either finding a match or reaching the end of the table without finding a match. We shall need a variable, named WORD$NO in the program, that keeps track of the word numbers of the reserved word currently being checked, and a variable named LETTER$NO to keep track of which letter we are currently inspecting.

At the level of the word number we need a flag indicating that no match has been found so far, to control a DO–WHILE (statement 34) that runs through the words in the list. This flag is called NO$MATCH$FOUNDSOFAR. So long as it is true, it says that we are still searching and keeps this DO–WHILE loop repeating.

The second flag, called MATCH$FLAG, also begins as true and controls the DO–WHILE in statement 37. We can think of this loop as saying "the input string and the reserved word currently being examined will be assumed to be the same until proven otherwise." Within this loop we compare the current pair of letters, one from the input string and one from the reserved word identified by WORD$NO, to see if they are equal. If they are not, MATCH$FLAG is set to false; we have established that the input string is not the same as this reserved word, and we wish to stop further comparison of letters. If the current pair of letters are the same, then we increment LETTER$NO to prepare for looking at the next pair. As seen by the condition in statement 37, this comparison will stop either on finding a no match or on completing the comparison of all nine letters.

When we get out of this DO–WHILE loop, we need to know which condition it was that terminated it. If MATCH$FLAG is still true, then we have found a match and the DO–WHILE in statement 34 should be terminated. Otherwise we wish to examine the next word.

```
PL/M-80 COMPILER    FIG. 4.12                                          PAGE   1

            /***************************************************************************/
            /* A PROGRAM USING STRUCTURE VARIABLES TO DETERMINE IF AN INPUT STRING   */
            /* IS A RESERVED WORD                                                     */
            /***************************************************************************/

 1          RESERVED$WORD$CHECK:
            DO;
 2   1         DECLARE RESERVED$WORDS(39) STRUCTURE
                  (WORD(9) BYTE)
                  DATA (
                        'ADDRESS  ',
                        'AND      ',
                        'AT       ',
                        'BASED    ',
                        'BY       ',
                        'BYTE     ',
                        'CALL     ',
                        'CASE     ',
                        'DATA     ',
                        'DECLARE  ',
                        'DISABLE  ',
                        'DO       ',
                        'ELSE     ',
                        'ENABLE   ',
                        'END      ',
                        'EOF      ',
                        'EXTERNAL ',
                        'GO       ',
                        'GOTO     ',
                        'HALT     ',
                        'IF       ',
                        'INITIAL  ',
                        'INTERRUPT',
                        'LABEL    ',
                        'LITERALLY',
                        'MINUS    ',
                        'MOD      ',
                        'NOT      ',
                        'OR       ',
                        'PLUS     ',
                        'PROCEDURE',
                        'PUBLIC   ',
                        'REENTRANT',
                        'RETURN   ',
                        'STRUCTURE',
                        'THEN     ',
                        'TO       ',
                        'WHILE    ',
                        'XOR      '
                       );
 3   1         DECLARE (WORD$NO, LETTER$NO) BYTE;
 4   1         DECLARE (NO$MATCH$FOUND$SO$FAR, MATCH$FLAG) BYTE;
 5   1         DECLARE STRING(128) BYTE;
 6   1         DECLARE TRUE LITERALLY '0FFH', FALSE LITERALLY '0';
 7   1         DECLARE (COUNT, STATUS) ADDRESS;
 8   1         DECLARE CRLF(2) BYTE DATA(0DH, 0AH);
 9   1         DECLARE BUFFER(128) BYTE;

            $INCLUDE (:F1:INOUT.SRC)
         =  $NOLIST
```

```
PL/M-80 COMPILER    FIG. 4.12                                              PAGE   2

30   1        CALL READ(1, .STRING, 128, .COUNT, .STATUS); /* TO CLEAR BUFFER */

31   1        CALL READ(1, .STRING, 128, .COUNT, .STATUS);
32   1        NO$MATCH$FOUND$SO$FAR = TRUE;

33   1        WORD$NO = 0;
34   1        DO WHILE NO$MATCH$FOUND$SO$FAR AND WORD$NO <= LAST(RESERVED$WORDS);
35   2           LETTER$NO = 0;
36   2           MATCH$FLAG = TRUE;
37   2           DO WHILE MATCH$FLAG AND LETTER$NO <= LAST(RESERVED$WORDS.WORD);
38   3              IF STRING(LETTER$NO) <> RESERVED$WORDS(WORD$NO).WORD(LETTER$NO) THEN
39   3                 MATCH$FLAG = FALSE;
                    ELSE
40   3                 LETTER$NO = LETTER$NO + 1;
41   3           END;
42   2           IF MATCH$FLAG THEN
43   2              NO$MATCH$FOUND$SO$FAR = FALSE;
                 ELSE
44   2              WORD$NO = WORD$NO + 1;
45   2        END;
46   1        IF NO$MATCH$FOUND$SO$FAR THEN
47   1           CALL WRITE(0, .('NOT A RESERVED WORD'), 19, .STATUS);
              ELSE
48   1        DO;
49   2           CALL NUMOUT(WORD$NO, 10, 0, .BUFFER, 2);
50   2           CALL WRITE(0, .BUFFER, 2, .STATUS);
51   2        END;
52   1        CALL WRITE(0, .CRLF, 2, .STATUS);
53   1        CALL EXIT;
54   1     END RESERVED$WORD$CHECK;
```

When the DO–WHILE of statement 34 terminates, either we have found a match or we haven't. This can be established by looking at NO$MATCH$FOUNDSOFAR; if this is still true, then the input string is not a reserved word, and we print a comment to that effect. If NO$MATCH$FOUNDSOFAR is now false, then we have found a match, so we convert WORD$NO to its representation as an ASCII character—which is the function of NUMOUT—and write it. Either way, we then (statement 52) write a carriage return and line feed, and exit the program. (The CALL EXIT returns control to the ISIS-II operating system; see Chapter 9.)

THE FINAL VERSION OF THE SORTING ROUTINE

We now have the techniques available to deal with the sorting problem in a fairly realistic way, given certain assumptions about the records to be sorted. These assumptions are:

1. All of the records are in random-access storage when we begin the program. This excludes situations where there might, for instance, be many thousands of records on a diskette or other external storage media.

2. The number of records is sufficiently large that speed of execution of the program is an important consideration.
3. The records are sufficiently large that actually exchanging them in memory every time the key comparison indicated the need for an exchange would carry a high penalty in execution speed.

With these assumptions, exchange sorting is actually a fairly attractive method if we can somehow get around the massive data movement addressed by assumption 3—and it turns out that we can. The heart of the approach is the provision of an auxiliary array called RANK, which, when the program has completed execution, will show the order in which the records should be accessed to get them in ascending sequence on a key. For example, suppose that there are ten records and that at the end of the execution of the program the elements of RANK are found to be

5, 8, 3, 7, 0, 2, 9, 1, 6, 4.

This means that, if we picked up record 5, we would be getting the one having the smallest key in the original ordering; if we picked up record 8 next we would be getting the one with the next larger key, etc.; and record 4 is the one having the largest key in the original ordering.

The real heart of the scheme is that we will exchange the elements of RANK and never move the actual records. RANK will be initialized so that

```
RANK(I) = I
```

This says that we begin with the assumption that the records are in sequence and then make whatever exchanges of the elements of RANK the actual keys dictate. With this background, the program in Fig. 4.13 is actually fairly straightforward. The crucial change is in statement 34 where, in specifying the two records involved, we write not I and J but RANK(I) and RANK(J). This means that, in picking up the two keys, the object program goes to the array RANK to find what the current numbers associated with I and J are and uses them to access two records. Let us see in more detail how this works.

Consider the sample data shown in the declaration in statement 2 of Fig. 4.13. As the sorting process begins in statement 32, RANK will have been initialized to 0, 1, 2, 3, 4, 5, 6, 7, 8, 9. With I set to zero and J set to 1, the first time statement 34 is executed I and RANK(I) will both be zero, and J and RANK(J) will both be 1. After the iterative DO in statement 33 has been completely executed, however, and we go to the next iteration of statement 32, things will be different. The contents of RANK will now be 5, 1, 2, 0, 4, 3, 6, 7, 8, 9. (Work out the comparisons in this first pass, recalling that any digit is "smaller" than any letter.) Now we begin the second pass with I = 1 and (initially) J = 2. Statement 34 is thus equivalent to

```
IF RECORD(RANK(1)).KEY > RECORD(RANK(2)).KEY THEN
```

```
PL/M-80 COMPILER    FIG. 4.13                                        PAGE   1

          /*************************************************************************
           *                                                                       *
           *    A THIRD SORTING ROUTINE - USES ADDRESS SORTING TO SORT A STRUCTURE *
           *                                                                       *
           *************************************************************************/

          SORT$3:
          DO;
             DECLARE RECORD(10) STRUCTURE (KEY BYTE, CONTENTS ADDRESS)
                DATA('D',429,'N',20881,'F',560,'B',1201,'X',500,'7',12300,'Q',
                1292,'C',9810,'A',300,'G',0);
             DECLARE RANK(10) BYTE;
             DECLARE (I, J, TEMP$BYTE) BYTE;
             DECLARE LAST$RECORD$NUMBER LITERALLY '9';

             DECLARE BUFFER(5) BYTE;
             DECLARE (COUNT, STATUS) ADDRESS;
             DECLARE CRLF(2) BYTE DATA (0DH, 0AH);

          $INCLUDE (:F1:INOUT.SRC)
      =   $NOLIST

             /* INITIALIZE RANK ARRAY */
             DO I = 0 TO LAST$RECORD$NUMBER;
                RANK(I) = I;
             END;

             DO I = 0  TO LAST$RECORD$NUMBER - 1;
                DO J = I + 1 TO LAST$RECORD$NUMBER;
                   IF RECORD(RANK(I)).KEY > RECORD(RANK(J)).KEY THEN
                   DO;
                      TEMP$BYTE = RANK(I);
                      RANK(I) = RANK(J);
                      RANK(J) = TEMP$BYTE;
                   END;
                END;
             END;
             DO I = 0 TO 9;
                CALL WRITE(0, .RECORD(RANK(I)).KEY, 1, .STATUS);
                CALL NUMOUT(RECORD(RANK(I)).CONTENTS, 10, '0', .BUFFER, 5);
                CALL WRITE(0, .BUFFER, 5, .STATUS);
                CALL WRITE(0, .CRLF, 2, .STATUS);
             END;
             CALL EXIT;
          END SORT$3;
```

Looking at the current contents of RANK, we see this is further equivalent to

```
IF RECORD(1).KEY > RECORD(2).KEY THEN
```

Looking at the keys of records 1 and 2, we see that this will cause an exchange of elements 1 and 2 of RANK, after which the contents of RANK will be 5, 2, 1, 0, 4,

3, 6, 7, 8, 9. When statement 34 is executed next we will have the effect of

```
IF RECORD(RANK(1)).KEY > RECORD(RANK(3)).KEY THEN
```

which reduces to

```
IF RECORD(2).KEY > RECORD(0).KEY THEN
```

As it happens this will call for another exchange. This process goes on through the I and J loops until in the end the elements of RANK have been rearranged so as to specify the order in which the records should be picked up to have them in ascending sequence on the keys. The effort of working through the entire sample, showing the contents of RANK after each execution of statements 34–39, will be rewarded with a thorough understanding of how the program operates.

Statements 42–47 clearly exhibits what we mean by claiming to have "sorted" these records even though they never moved, even though we still do not wish to study the details of how the procedure calls work. We see that the first record written is the one specified by element 0 of RANK. For that record we write the key, which is a BYTE variable, convert CONTENTS to a form suitable for output, and write it. We next pick up the record specified by element 1 of RANK, etc. Here is the output produced when this program was directed to print its results on a line printer.

```
712300
A00300
B01201
C09810
D00429
F00560
G00000
N20881
Q01292
X00500
```

THE FINAL SORTING PROGRAM

We now look at a final version of the sorting routine, in which the records are considerably longer than the rather skeletal items that we have dealt with so far. As seen in the program in Fig. 4.14, each record contains 43 bytes including a 5-byte stock number, a 20-byte description, and an 8-byte warehouse location. The ADDRESS quantities are five items related to an inventory-control application.

We assume that the records have been placed in storage by a previous program and that the purpose of the application is to prepare a listing of these records that is in sequence on warehouse location and stock number. The idea is to produce what is called a *picking list,* which presents the information in the easiest form for use by an order clerk who is "picking" the items to fill an order. We realize that these records are being used both for inventory-control purposes and for order-fulfillment purposes and that not every item in the record is needed for both of these functions. We also realize that for other purposes it might be necessary to sort these same records into sequence on stock number alone. This is typical of many data-processing applications.

The most important regard in which this program differs from the previous version is that the key has two parts, both of which are more than one byte. The first part of the key is the location, which can be called the *major key* since it is more

```
PL/M-80 COMPILER    FIG. 4.14                                                    PAGE   1

           /*****************************************************************************
            *                                                                           *
            *  A FINAL SORTING PROGRAM - SORTS STRUCTURE RECORDS BY ADDRESS SORTING     *
            *  THE KEY OF EACH RECORD CONSISTS OF TWO PARTS, EACH HAVING MULTIPLE BYTES *
            *                                                                           *
            *****************************************************************************/

  1        SORT$4:
           DO;
  2   1       DECLARE NUMBER$OF$RECORDS LITERALLY '10';
  3   1       DECLARE RECORD(NUMBER$OF$RECORDS) STRUCTURE
                (
                SN(5) BYTE,            /* STOCK NUMBER */
                DESCRIPTION(20) BYTE,
                ORDER$QTY ADDRESS,
                QTY$ON$HAND ADDRESS,
                QTY$ON$ORDER ADDRESS,
                REORDER$POINT ADDRESS,
                REORDER$QTY ADDRESS,
                LOC(8) BYTE            /* WAREHOUSE LOCATION */
                )
                INITIAL
               (
               '04950BOLT, 3 INCH X 1/2  ',100,111,40,120,40,'A002    ',
               '00989BUSHING, 2 INCH OD  ',50,210,100,300,100,'A007    ',
               '04802BOLT, 4 INCH X 1/2  ',10,73,0,60,40,'A002    ',
               '00209NUT, 1/2 INCH       ',120,200,100,350,100,'A016    ',
               '00099WASHER, 2 INCH      ',25,199,1000,2000,500,'A006    ',
               '54320GADJET, BLUE        ',1234,2233,0,1000,1000,'WHS9A029',
               '00820COTTER PIN, 2 IN    ',250,1000,100,1200,200,'A007    ',
               '00819DRILL, 8 SPINDLE    ',1,10,0,8,5,'A120B006',
               '54329GADJET, RED         ',2233,3322,0,1000,1000,'WHS9A030',
               '00821COTTER PIN, 3 IN    ',6,1062,0,1000,200,'A007    '
               );

  4   1       DECLARE RANK(NUMBER$OF$RECORDS) BYTE;
  5   1       DECLARE (I, J, K, TEMP$BYTE) BYTE;
  6   1       DECLARE TRUE LITERALLY '0FFH', FALSE LITERALLY '0';
  7   1       DECLARE (EXCHANGE$NEEDED, KEYS$STILL$EQUAL) BYTE;
  8   1       DECLARE BUFFER(70) BYTE;
  9   1       DECLARE STATUS ADDRESS;
 10   1       DECLARE CRLF(2) BYTE DATA(0DH, 0AH);
 11   1       DECLARE BLANKS(4) BYTE DATA('    ');

           $INCLUDE (:F1:INOUT.SRC)
      =    $NOLIST
```

```
PL/M-80 COMPILER    FIG. 4.14                                    PAGE   2

                 /* INITIALIZE RANK ARRAY */
     1           DO I = 0 TO NUMBER$OF$RECORDS - 1;
     2              RANK(I) = I;
     2           END;

                 /* THE SORTING ROUTINE */
     1           DO I = 0 TO NUMBER$OF$RECORDS - 2;
     2              DO J = I + 1 TO NUMBER$OF$RECORDS - 1;
     3                 EXCHANGE$NEEDED = FALSE;
     3                 KEYS$STILL$EQUAL = TRUE;

                       /* MAJOR KEY: WAREHOUSE LOCATION */
     3                 K = 0;
     3                 DO WHILE KEYS$STILL$EQUAL AND K < LAST(RECORD.LOC);
     4                    IF RECORD(RANK(I)).LOC(K) > RECORD(RANK(J)).LOC(K) THEN
     4                    DO;
     5                       EXCHANGE$NEEDED = TRUE;
     5                       KEYS$STILL$EQUAL = FALSE;
     5                    END;
                          ELSE
     4                       IF RECORD(RANK(I)).LOC(K) < RECORD(RANK(J)).LOC(K) THEN
     4                       DO;
     5                          KEYS$STILL$EQUAL = FALSE;
     5                       END;
                          K = K + 1;
     4                 END;

                       /* MINOR KEY: STOCK NUMBER */
     3                 K = 0;
     3                 DO WHILE KEYS$STILL$EQUAL AND K < LAST(RECORD.SN);
     4                    IF RECORD(RANK(I)).SN(K) > RECORD(RANK(J)).SN(K) THEN
     4                    DO;
     5                       EXCHANGE$NEEDED = TRUE;
     5                       KEYS$STILL$EQUAL = FALSE;
     5                    END;
                          ELSE
     4                       IF RECORD(RANK(I)).SN(K) < RECORD(RANK(J)).SN(K) THEN
     4                       DO;
     5                          KEYS$STILL$EQUAL = FALSE;
     5                       END;
                          K = K + 1;
     4                 END;
     3                 IF EXCHANGE$NEEDED THEN
     3                 DO;
     4                    TEMP$BYTE = RANK(I);
     4                    RANK(I) = RANK(J);
     4                    RANK(J) = TEMP$BYTE;
     4                 END;
     3              END;
     2           END;
```

```
PL/M-80 COMPILER    FIG. 4.14                                        PAGE   3

                    /* WRITE THE SORTED RECORDS -- WHICH HAVE NEVER MOVED, OF COURSE */
 73   1             DO I = 0 TO NUMBER$OF$RECORDS - 1;
 74   2                 CALL WRITE(0, .RECORD(RANK(I)).LOC, 8, .STATUS);
 75   2                 CALL WRITE(0, .BLANKS, 3, .STATUS);
 76   2                 CALL WRITE(0, .RECORD(RANK(I)).SN, 5, .STATUS);
 77   2                 CALL WRITE(0, .BLANKS, 4, .STATUS);
 78   2                 CALL WRITE(0, .RECORD(RANK(I)).DESCRIPTION, 20, .STATUS);
 79   2                 CALL WRITE(0, .BLANKS, 2, .STATUS);
 80   2                 CALL NUMOUT(RECORD(RANK(I)).ORDER$QTY, 10, ' ', .BUFFER, 7);
 81   2                 CALL WRITE(0, .BUFFER, 7, .STATUS);
 82   2                 CALL NUMOUT(RECORD(RANK(I)).QTY$ON$HAND, 10, ' ', .BUFFER, 7);
 83   2                 CALL WRITE(0, .BUFFER, 7, .STATUS);
 84   2                 CALL NUMOUT(RECORD(RANK(I)).QTY$ON$ORDER, 10, ' ', .BUFFER, 7);
 85   2                 CALL WRITE(0, .BUFFER, 7, .STATUS);
 86   2                 CALL NUMOUT(RECORD(RANK(I)).REORDER$POINT, 10, ' ', .BUFFER, 7);
 87   2                 CALL WRITE(0, .BUFFER, 7, .STATUS);
 88   2                 CALL NUMOUT(RECORD(RANK(I)).REORDER$QTY, 10, ' ', .BUFFER, 7);
 89   2                 CALL WRITE(0, .BUFFER, 7, .STATUS);
 90   2                 CALL WRITE(0, .CRLF, 2, .STATUS);
 91   2             END;

 92   1             CALL EXIT;

 93   1         END SORT$4;
```

important in determining sequence than is the second part, the stock number, which is called the *minor key*. The idea is that, if two items are in different aisles in the warehouse, we don't care how their stock numbers compare. However, if they are in the same aisle, the records should be in sequence on stock number. This means that we can start comparing pairs of characters with byte zero on the warehouse location; when we have inspected all the pairs of characters in the two locations, we proceed through the stock number. Whenever we find a pair of characters that are not the same, we can terminate the comparisons since nothing to the right of these two characters could have any influence on the relative size of the keys. Putting it another way, this means both that we can stop the comparison of locations upon finding two unequal characters and that if the locations have been found to be unequal we don't need to examine the stock numbers at all.

All of this is embodied in the logic of statements 35–72. EXCHANGE$NEEDED is a flag that signals the detection of a character in the first key that is larger than the corresponding character in the second key. KEYS$STILL$EQUAL is a flag that says that we have so far not found any differences in the two keys. These two flags do necessarily have different functions; although EXCHANGE$NEEDED does imply that the keys are no longer equal, we want to stop the comparison process on detecting unequal characters even though no exchange is needed.

The handling of the two parts of the key is accomplished here simply by two similar routines one after the other, being careful to do the test of the major key first. The condition in the DO–WHILE of statement 53 guarantees that if the major keys are unequal there will be no processing of the minor keys at all.

What this all boils down to is that the processing time for this sorting method depends mostly on the number of records. It doesn't depend on the size of the records at all and only slightly on the length of the keys, since key comparison is stopped as soon as an unequal position is detected.

The output statements at the end of the program arrange the different numbers in an order that reflects the function of the different items rather than presenting them in the same order in which they appear in the record. Here is the output when this program was run using the ten illustrative records provided in the structure declaration.

```
A002        04802    BOLT, 4 INCH X 1/2         10      73     0     60    40
A002        04950    BOLT, 3 INCH X 1/2        100     111    40    120    40
A006        00099    WASHER, 2 INCH             25     199  1000   2000   500
A007        00820    COTTER PIN, 2 IN          250    1000   100   1200   200
A007        00821    COTTER PIN, 3 IN            6    1062     0   1000   200
A007        00989    BUSHING, 2 INCH OD         50     210   100    300   100
A016        00209    NUT, 1/2 INCH             120     200   100    350   100
A120B006    00819    DRILL, 8 SPINDLE            1      10     0      8     5
WHS9A029    54320    GADJET, BLUE             1234    2233     0   1000  1000
WHS9A030    54329    GADJET, RED              2233    3322     0   1000  1000
```

We should not leave the reader with the impression that this is an ideal sorting method in general, however, as it still takes no advantage whatever of any existing order in the records and it involves on the order of $N^2/2$ key comparisons. The extensive research into sorting methods has led to techniques that eliminate both of these deficiencies. One such is considered in passing on page 139.

EXERCISES

*1. An array named B contains 20 elements. Write separate program segments to accomplish the following:
   a) Divide the sum of the first and second elements by the third element and place the result in ABC.
   b) Replace the last four elements by zeros without using a loop.
   c) If the tenth element is greater than the value of TEST, replace the tenth element by the mean of the ninth and eleventh elements.
   d) Add 1 to every element in the array, using a loop.

2. An array named A contains 10 elements. Write separate program segments to accomplish the following:
   a) Place the product of the first and second elements in PROD.
   b) Replace the third element by the average of the first, third, and fifth elements.
   c) If the last element is greater than 127, replace it by its complement, using the NOT function.
   d) Double every element in the array, using an interative DO.

*3. Identify any syntactic errors in the following statements:

a) `DO I = 1, 21, 2;`

b) `DO COUNT = N TO 1 BY -1;`

c) `DO N = 1 TO 10 WHILE EXCHANGE = FALSE;`

4. Identify any syntactic errors in the following statements:

a) `DO CASE N BY 2;`

b) `DO ITER TO 19;`

c) `DO UNTIL N > 20;`

*5. What will this program fragment do?

```
DO I = 1 TO 15 BY 2;
    OUTPUT(1) = I;
    OUTPUT(2) = I * I;
END;
```

6. What will this program fragment do?

```
DO I = 0 TO 29;
    OUTPUT(1) = 1;
    CALL TIME(100);
END;
```

*7. Given the declarations shown, do program fragments (a) and (b) give the same results?

```
    DECLARE I BYTE;
    DECLARE X(20) BYTE;
    DECLARE SUM ADDRESS;
/*  INPUT OPERATIONS HERE WOULD LOAD THE X ARRAY */
```

a)
```
SUM, I = 0;
DO WHILE I <= LAST(X);
    SUM = SUM + X(I);
END;
```

b)
```
SUM = 0;
DO I = 0 TO LAST(X);
    SUM = SUM + X(I);
END;
```

8. Given the declarations shown, do program fragments (a) and (b) give the same results?

```
DECLARE N BYTE;
DECLARE X(101) BYTE;
DECLARE SUM ADDRESS;
```

a)
```
SUM = 0;
DO N = 1 TO 100;
    SUM = SUM + X(N);
END;
```

b)
```
SUM = 0;
N = 100;
DO WHILE N > 0;
    SUM = SUM + X(N);
    N = N - 1;
END;
```

***9.** Given a set of values in an array, the *first differences* of the set are formed by subtracting each element except the last from the element immediately following it. Suppose, for example, that we have an array named X containing 50 elements. Write a program to compute the 49 elements of another array named DX defined by DX(i) = X(i + 1) − X(i), i = 0, 1, . . . , 48.

10. We are given an array named Y which contains 32 elements that are to be regarded as the 32 ordinates of a curve of experimental data with equally spaced abscissas. Assuming that a value has already been given to H, write a program to compute the integral of the curve represented approximately by the Y values, using the trapezoidal rule:

$$I = \frac{H}{2}(Y(0) + 2Y(1) + \ldots + 2Y(30) + Y(31)).$$

***11.** Write a program using iterative DOs that will send the integers from 0–59 in succession to output port 16, one each second.

12. Modify the program of Exercise 11 so that it reads a number, call it N, from input port 6 and then sends to output port 16 the integers from 0 to N − 1, one each second.

13. Modify the program of Exercise 12 so that it reads from input port 4 a number, call it M, as well as the number N from input port 6. It then sends integers from 0 to N − 1 to output port 16 with a delay between integers of M milliseconds (rather than one second).

***14.** Write a program that reads the value on input port 8 every 0.1 second for 10 seconds, placing the 100 values in an array named SAMPLES.

15. Modify the program in Exercise 14 so that, as the input values are being read, the same loop accumulates the sum of all the values and inspects for the largest and smallest values in the array. In other words, when the loop execution has been completed, SUM, LARGE, and SMALL should contain the appropriate values without any further computation.

16. Suppose that X and Y are both arrays having 20 BYTE elements. Write a program to produce the scalar product of two vectors represented by these arrays, which is given by:

$$\text{S.P.} = \sum_{i=0}^{19} X_i Y_i.$$

17. An array named R contains 40 BYTE values. Write a program segment to place in ZEROS the count of the number of elements of R that are zero.

18. Write a program to place in COUNT the number of binary 1's in an ADDRESS variable named LINES. (Recall that when an expression is written in an IF statement, the object program inspects only the rightmost bit of the value represented by the expression.)

***19.** Identify any syntactic errors in the following declarations.

a)
```
DECLARE INVENTORY STRUCTURE
    (QOH ADDRESS,
     QOO ADDRESS,
     RP  ADDRESS,
     RQ ADDRESS,
     LOCATION ADDRESS);
```

b)
```
DECLARE A STRUCTURE (B BYTE, C ADDRESS) (19);
```

c)
```
DECLARE R(19) STRUCTURE (S(20) BYTE, T(21) ADDRESS);
```

20. Identify any syntactic errors in the following declarations.

a)
```
DECLARE CLUB MEMBERS STRUCTURE(20)
    (ACTIVE BYTE, ASSOCIATE BYTE, RETIRED BYTE);
```

b)
```
DECLARE STANDING STRUCTURE (INITIAL BYTE, HIGH BYTE, LOW BYTE, FINAL BYTE);
```

c)
```
DECLARE STOPS STRUCTURE (DIAPASON, PRINCIPAL, FLUTE, GEMSHORN, GAMBA,
    MIXTURE, OBOE, TRUMPET);
```

21. Modify the program of Fig. 4.12 so that trailing blanks to fill out the input word to nine bytes are not required.

22. You are given an input string named STRING, which consists of words separated by blanks, and a structure defined by the declaration:

```
DECLARE WORDS(40) STRUCTURE (MEMBER(10) BYTE);
```

Write a program to blank the entire structure, then move each word of STRING to a structure member, beginning with the first and proceeding in succession. If any word is longer than ten letters, set LENGTH$ERROR$FLAG to one.

23. Modify the program of Exercise 22 so that the following declarations are used:

```
DECLARE WORDS(40) STRUCTURE (MEMBER(10) BYTE, CONTINUATION BYTE);
```

Now, so long as a word is no longer than ten letters, place a zero in the corresponding position of CONTINUATION. If any word is longer than ten letters, place the first ten in the appropriate position of MEMBER, place a one in the corresponding position of CONTINUATION, and continue with the eleventh and following letters in the next element of MEMBER. Continue in this way until the entire word has been stored; the element of CONTINUATION corresponding to the last element of MEMBER used should contain zero.

24. Modify the program of Fig. 4.13 so that KEY consists of two ADDRESS variables, KEY$1 and KEY$2, with KEY$1 being the more significant.

25. (For the mathematically oriented.) You are given the following declaration:

```
DECLARE ROW(20) STRUCTURE (COLUMN(20) ADDRESS);
DECLARE DIAGONAL(20) ADDRESS;
```

The structure can be thought of as a 20-by-20 matrix, and the array as a 20-element vector. Write a program to move the main diagonal elements of the matrix to the vector.

26. Using the structure declaration in Exercise 25, write a program to transpose the matrix. You may wish to utilize the fact that the following three-statement sequence interchanges the contents of variables A and B:

```
A = A XOR B;

B = A XOR B;

A = A XOR B;
```

27. A variable named DAYOFYEAR contains the day of the year; an array of 12 elements named DAYSINMONTH contains the number of days in each of the 12 months of the year. Write a loop that places in MONTH the number of the month (numbered from 1) corresponding to DAYOFYEAR, and in DAY the day of that month.

28. One small part of a chess-playing program is the determination of legal moves. Set up a structure to represent a board, and devise a numerical identification of the pieces, black and white. Then write a program that produces a listing of all the legal moves open to a rook on row M, column N, assuming no capture.

29. Set up a structure containing 400 records, each consisting of a BYTE variable named PITCH and an ADDRESS variable named DURATION. This is the representation of a musical melody, to be played by a synthesizer attached to the microcomputer. Write a program that "plays" the melody, starting with the first member and stopping when a note of duration zero is reached. For each note, send the value of PITCH to output port 4; this will control an oscillator through an ADC converter. Delay, while this note is being played, for a length of time equal (in milliseconds) to ten times the value of DURATION.

30. Page 96 shows the Braille code for the letters of the alphabet, where solid black circles denote raised dots and periods denote level areas (unused positions). Suppose you have a modified printer that will somehow make an indentation when printing a dot. Devise a way to convert a string of letters in an array named TEXT, to Braille characters. If you plan to print each Braille letter on three lines, bear in mind that you will need a preliminary pass to convert the characters of a line to some kind of coding in three separate arrays, since the first line prints on only the top two bits of all the cells for the line, etc. Also allow for the fact that the paper must be turned over for reading, so that the lines must be reversed.

(This is, of course, the lowest level of the use of Braille. In actual practice, there is heavy use of a system of abbreviations.)

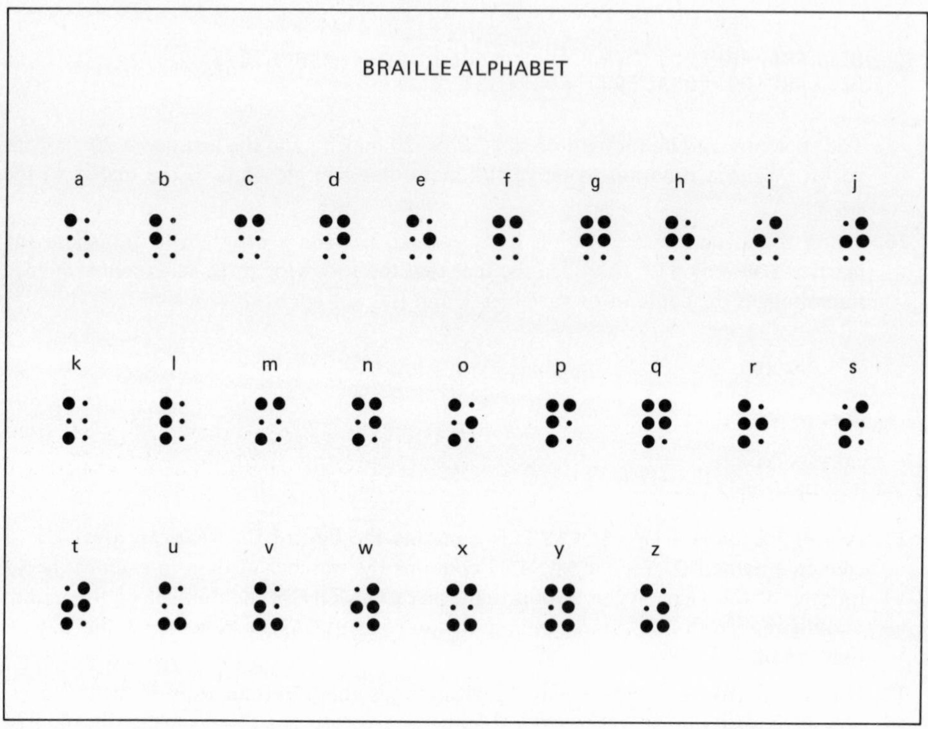

CHAPTER 5

PROCEDURES

INTRODUCTION

A PL/M procedure is a group of statements that is called into action from elsewhere in a program. Sometimes this *invocation* of the procedure is done with a CALL statement and sometimes simply by writing the name of the procedure. Either way, program control is then taken over by the procedure. When it has finished its work, control returns to the point in the calling program just beyond the invocation.

Procedures offer a number of significant advantages in programming, which we shall explore as we go along. Among these advantages are:

- If the same operations must be carried out at many points in the program, it saves program storage space to place those operations in one procedure rather than repeating them each place they are needed.
- If a procedure that carries out needed operations has already been written and checked out by someone else, it saves programming and checkout time to use the existing procedure rather than writing a new one. Organizations have been formed to facilitate exchange of programs among users of most computers. For the Intel 8080 family, the organization is called INSITE (Intel Software Index and Technology Exchange). At the time of writing, the INSITE users' library contained over 300 programs.

- Intelligent use of procedures can improve the understandability of programs by breaking them into simpler pieces. This improvement of program understandability is one of the most important reasons for using procedures. We shall be dealing with this issue throughout the rest of the book.

Let us begin by exploring the PL/M language features for using procedures.

PL/M PROCEDURE BASICS

The operations to be carried out by a PL/M procedure constitute its *body*. These are ordinary statements. Before the body of the procedure we write the procedure name followed by a colon and the word PROCEDURE. In many cases other information will be provided after the word PROCEDURE, but in some cases it is not necessary to provide anything else except the semicolon that terminates the statement. At the end of the procedure body we must provide an END statement. As with END statements that close complete programs, we may follow the word END with the name of the procedure for clarity of understanding and to take advantage of the syntax checking that the compiler can perform.

A procedure of this simplest form is invoked by writing a CALL statement that names it. When program execution reaches the CALL statement, program control is automatically transferred to the procedure; its operations are carried out, and program control returns to the statement after the CALL.

It is essential to distinguish carefully between the definition of a procedure and its execution. The procedure definition—that is, its name, the word PROCEDURE, the procedure body, and the END—must appear before any reference to the procedure in an executable statement. A procedure is never invoked except through the CALL mechanism or by writing its name in a function reference.

It is worth pausing over this fundamental idea. In schematic form our program organization is that shown in Fig. 5.1. We begin as always with declarations. After these we have all procedures. These procedures contain PL/M statements, of course, but these are not automatically executed when program execution begins. Eventually, somewhere in the program, there will be a first statement, other than a declaration, that is not within the body of a procedure. Execution will start with this statement, which in many cases will be a CALL although it is not required to be. Whenever program control reaches a CALL statement, the statements in the procedure body are executed and control returns to the statement after the CALL.

It will be convenient to speak of a program as a *module,* which is defined simply as a labeled DO block that is not nested in any other block. All the programs we have seen in the book have been modules. When we speak of the *module level* we mean *inside a module,* but not inside any procedures or DO blocks contained in the module.

Using this terminology, we can now say that, *in the simple form of procedure we have seen so far,* all variables appearing in the procedure body must have been

```
PROGRAM$NAME:
DO;

   Declarations

PROCEDURE$NAME:
PROCEDURE;
   Procedure body

END PROCEDURE$NAME;

Other procedures, if any

   First executable statement outside a procedure
      (Could be a CALL)
   CALL PROCEDURE$NAME;
   Other statements
   CALL PROCEDURE$NAME;
   Other statements

END PROGRAM$NAME;
```

Fig. 5.1. Schematic representation of the organization of a program containing a procedure.

declared at the module level. That is, they are declared outside the procedure and, like all declarations, they must appear earlier in the program than any reference to information contained in them.

A FIRST PROCEDURE EXAMPLE—FINDING THE MEAN OF FOUR NUMBERS

For an example of how these ideas work out in practice, suppose that, in a certain program, we have several occasions to find the mean of four BYTE values. In fact, we shall show the entire program doing nothing else, but the reader will understand that in a real-life situation there would be other operations carried out as well.

The program is shown in Fig. 5.2. We see that the procedure definition comes immediately after the declarations at the beginning of the program. The procedure body consists of one statement, in which we have used the DOUBLE operation to extend the first operand with eight high-order bits, making it an ADDRESS quantity, to avoid the possibility of losing significance in the addition.

The first executable statement outside the procedure is statement 6. After giving values to the four variables, in statement 10 we invoke the procedure. This will transfer control to the procedure and cause execution (for the first time) of statement 4. This gives a value to MEAN, which is written to output port 1 by statement 11. We now read four more values and again invoke the procedure to send their mean to output port 2. Now we set up the four values a third time to consist of: a constant,

```
PL/M-80 COMPILER    FIG. 5.2                                          PAGE   1

              /*************************************************************/
              /* A FIRST ILLUSTRATION OF A PROCEDURE                        */
              /*************************************************************/

 1            PROCEDURE$EXAMPLE$1:
              DO;
 2    1          DECLARE (RATE$1, RATE$2, RATE$3, RATE$4, MEAN) BYTE;

 3    1       MEAN$PROCEDURE$1:
              PROCEDURE;
 4    2          MEAN = (DOUBLE(RATE$1) + RATE$2 + RATE$3 + RATE$4) / 4;
 5    2       END MEAN$PROCEDURE$1;

              /* THE ROUTINE THAT CALLS THIS PROCEDURE INTO ACTION */

 6    1          RATE$1 = INPUT(1);
 7    1          RATE$2 = INPUT(2);
 8    1          RATE$3 = INPUT(4);
 9    1          RATE$4 = INPUT(8);
10    1          CALL MEAN$PROCEDURE$1;
11    1          OUTPUT(1) = MEAN;
12    1          RATE$1 = INPUT(33);
13    1          RATE$2 = INPUT(34);
14    1          RATE$3 = INPUT(36);
15    1          RATE$4 = INPUT(40);
16    1          CALL MEAN$PROCEDURE$1;
17    1          OUTPUT(2) = MEAN;
18    1          RATE$1 = 150;
19    1          RATE$2 = INPUT(65) AND 7FH;
20    1          RATE$3 = INPUT(66);
21    1          RATE$4 = INPUT(68) + INPUT(72);
22    1          CALL MEAN$PROCEDURE$1;
23    1          OUTPUT(4) = MEAN;

                 /* OTHER PROCESSING */

24    1       END PROCEDURE$EXAMPLE$1;
```

a port value with its high-order bit removed, another port value, and the sum of two more port values. The mean of these is sent to port 4 by invoking the procedure for the third time.

This program illustrates the most basic idea of the mechanism. We turn to the next step in the development.

PROCEDURE PARAMETERS

One of the most important facilities offered by procedures is that we are not restricted to always working on the same data. Using the mechanism of *formal parameters,* we can specify (in the procedure body) what operations are to be carried out; then when the procedure is invoked we can specify whatever actual values we wish to process in the invocation. In another invocation, entirely different values may be specified. Thus, in addition to the advantage of a procedure in saving memory space, we add the flexibility of being able to process whatever data we wish.

Formal parameters

In designing a procedure with parameters, we follow the word PROCEDURE with a list of parameter names, enclosed in parentheses and separated by commas. Within the body of the procedure there must be declarations containing the names of these parameters. The other statements within the procedure body may use these parameters freely as representing values sent to the procedure.

Actual parameters

When we invoke a procedure that has parameters, we follow the name of the procedure with parentheses enclosing PL/M expressions that specify values that the procedure is to process. There must be the same number of expressions, separated by commas, as there are parameters in the procedure parameter list. When the procedure is invoked the expressions representing the actual parameters are evaluated and those values are transmitted to the procedure. These values are then processed as specified by the operations on the formal parameters in the procedure body.

A SECOND PROCEDURE EXAMPLE—FINDING A MEAN WITH PARAMETERS

The program in Fig. 5.3 shows these ideas in operation. We see that a list of four parameters has been written in statement 3, that statement 4 declares these parameters to be of the type BYTE, and that the computation of the mean is now defined in terms of these formal parameters.

In statements 7–10 values are given to four variables just as in the program of Fig. 5.2. These become the actual parameters in the call of statement 11. These values are accordingly transmitted to the procedure, which assigns a value to the variable named MEAN—which is not a parameter.

It is actually unnecessary, however, to go through the operations of assigning values to four variables in this way. In statement 13 we see that four INPUT function references have been written as actual parameters. When this statement is executed, just as with any other procedure CALL, these four "expressions" will be "evaluated." "Evaluating" an "expression" consisting of an INPUT function reference means simply to read the specified port. The values so obtained are transmitted to the procedure.

To emphasize that an actual parameter may be any PL/M expression, observe that in statement 16 one of the actual parameters is a constant, one involves an AND operation, and another involves an addition. In every case, the expression is evaluated and the resulting value transmitted to the procedure.

```
PL/M-80 COMPILER    FIG. 5.3                                                        PAGE   1

                /*****************************************************************/
                /* A SECOND ILLUSTRATION OF A PROCEDURE: USES PARAMETERS */
                /*****************************************************************/

  1             PROCEDURE$EXAMPLE$2:
                DO;
  2    1           DECLARE (RATE$1, RATE$2, RATE$3, RATE$4, MEAN) BYTE;

  3    1        MEAN$PROCEDURE$2:
                PROCEDURE (PARAM$1, PARAM$2, PARAM$3, PARAM$4);
  4    2           DECLARE (PARAM$1, PARAM$2, PARAM$3, PARAM$4) BYTE;
  5    2           MEAN = (DOUBLE(PARAM$1) + PARAM$2 + PARAM$3 + PARAM$4) / 4;
  6    2        END MEAN$PROCEDURE$2;

                /* THE ROUTINE THAT CALLS THIS PROCEDURE INTO ACTION */

  7    1           RATE$1 = INPUT(1);
  8    1           RATE$2 = INPUT(2);
  9    1           RATE$3 = INPUT(4);
 10    1           RATE$4 = INPUT(8);
 11    1           CALL MEAN$PROCEDURE$2(RATE$1, RATE$2, RATE$3, RATE$4);
 12    1           OUTPUT(1) = MEAN;
 13    1           CALL MEAN$PROCEDURE$2(INPUT(33), INPUT(34), INPUT(36), INPUT(40));
 14    1           OUTPUT(2) = MEAN;
 15    1           RATE$1 = INPUT(65);
 16    1           CALL MEAN$PROCEDURE$2(150, INPUT(65) AND 7FH, INPUT(66), INPUT(68) + INPUT(72));
 17    1           OUTPUT(4) = MEAN;

                   /* OTHER PROCESSING */

 18    1        END PROCEDURE$EXAMPLE$2;
```

CALL-BY-VALUE, THE PARAMETER-PASSING MECHANISM IN PL/M

In the preceding we have emphasized repeatedly that what is passed to a procedure is the *value* obtained by evaluating the expression written as an actual parameter. It is necessary to distinguish this mechanism, which is designated as *call-by-value,* from other mechanisms that are sometimes used. With many other languages it is sometimes possible to pass the *name* of an actual parameter to a procedure, which makes it possible to do two things that are not possible with the techniques we shall study in this chapter.

1. If we confine ourselves to only those techniques available so far, we cannot pass a procedure the name of an array or a structure. We can only pass the *value* of one element, which will then be processed like any other value. We cannot, however, pass the name of an array and then have the procedure use the elements of the array.

2. A parameter may not be used to return a value to the calling program. For example, it would not work to declare MEAN as a parameter and try to send the result of the procedure back to the main program this way.

Both of these operations, which will seem natural to readers familiar with some other languages, can be done in PL/M using techniques that we shall study in the next chapter. The second of these operations—so long as we wish to return only one value—may also be done by a technique to which we now turn.

TYPED PROCEDURES

It is possible to declare a procedure to have a *type* of BYTE or ADDRESS. This is done by following the parameter list (if there is one) in the PROCEDURE statement with the word BYTE or ADDRESS. This has two results:

1. To invoke the procedure, we do not write the word CALL. Rather, the procedure is invoked simply by writing its name (with appropriate parameters, if any) wherever the name of a variable is permitted.
2. A value is automatically returned and is used where the name of the procedure is written. The procedure must include one or more RETURN statements in order to return such a value.

The invocation of a typed procedure (no CALL) means that the expressions written as actual parameters (if any) are evaluated; these values are passed to the procedure and assigned to the corresponding formal parameters; the procedure body is executed; a RETURN statement in the procedure body causes a value to be returned, and execution of the procedure terminates. The value returned by the procedure becomes an operand in the expression in which the procedure name appeared, and execution of the calling program proceeds with the evaluation of the expression.

A TYPED PROCEDURE TO FIND A MEAN

To see this new feature in operation, consider a third and final version of the procedure to find a mean, as shown in the program in Fig. 5.4. We see here the rather unusual case of a main program having no DECLARE statements at all. This will rarely, if ever, happen in actual practice and is done here only to make a point about parameters and typed procedures.

Looking at the procedure definition we see in statement 4 a RETURN. This means to evaluate the expression shown and send the resulting value back to the calling program. The RETURN also means to terminate execution of the procedure and go back to the point in the calling program immediately following the invocation. It is permissible for an untyped procedure to have RETURN statements also, if we wish to terminate procedure execution other than at the end of the procedure. A RETURN statement in an untyped procedure contains no expression. We shall not often do this. A procedure may have more than one RETURN, only one of which will be executed on any one invocation of the procedure.

```
PL/M-80 COMPILER    FIG. 5.4                                                   PAGE   1

            /*************************************************************************/
            /* A THIRD ILLUSTRATION OF A PROCEDURE: USES PARAMETERS AND IS TYPED */
            /*************************************************************************/

 1          PROCEDURE$EXAMPLE$3:
            DO;

 2   1      MEAN$VALUE:
            PROCEDURE (PARAM$1, PARAM$2, PARAM$3, PARAM$4) BYTE;
 3   2         DECLARE (PARAM$1, PARAM$2, PARAM$3, PARAM$4) BYTE;
 4   2         RETURN (DOUBLE(PARAM$1) + PARAM$2 + PARAM$3 + PARAM$4) / 4;
 5   2      END MEAN$VALUE;

            /* THE ROUTINE THAT CALLS THIS PROCEDURE INTO ACTION */

 6   1         OUTPUT(1) = MEAN$VALUE(INPUT(1), INPUT(2), INPUT(4), INPUT(8));
 7   1         OUTPUT(2) = MEAN$VALUE(INPUT(33), INPUT(34), INPUT(36), INPUT(40));
 8   1         OUTPUT(4) = MEAN$VALUE(150, INPUT(65) AND 7FH, INPUT(66), INPUT(68) + INPUT(72));

               /* OTHER PROCESSING */

 9   1      END PROCEDURE$EXAMPLE$3;
```

The calling program this time consists of just three statements. Everything in the previous two versions, other than the CALL statements, has now been collapsed to parameter evaluation.

A SQUARE-ROOT PROCEDURE WITH LOCAL VARIABLES

Let us now consider another feature of procedures in the context of a useful application.

We recall from Chapter 3, page 43, that the Newton–Raphson method for finding a square root involves a process of successive approximations. Computing these approximations and determining whether the process has converged required two variables to hold the current and previous approximations to the square root. We know that the process has converged when the values are equal, at which point either of them is the best approximation of the square root we can obtain in the number of bits available.

The question before us is where to declare the variables to hold the two approximations. They certainly could be declared at the beginning of the program containing the square-root procedure—i.e., at the module level—but this would be potentially confusing to the reader of the program and would complicate the incorporation of programs from a user library.

The obvious answer is to declare these variables within the body of the procedure itself. Such variables are said to be *local* to the procedure in which the declarations appear, which means that they are unknown outside of that procedure. A local variable is in contrast to a *global* variable, which is one that is declared outside a procedure but is nevertheless known within it. As a matter of fact, it is permissible for the same identifier to represent a global variable and a local variable in the same program. When this is done the two are entirely different variables. Within the procedure that identifier refers to the local variable only. That is, because of the declaration within the procedure, the global variable of the same name has become temporarily unknown.

This is a considerable abbreviation of the full story of the scope of variables. We shall consider the matter more thoroughly in Chapter 7.

The fact that a local variable is unknown outside of the procedure in which it is declared is actually a significant benefit of using procedures. It means, for example, that a programmer may borrow procedures from other programmers with no concern that the borrowed procedures might contain identifiers that are the same as identifiers in his program—which without the local–global variable mechanism, could cause compilation errors or, worse, incorrect operation of programs that would compile without error messages. More generally, local variables limit the amount of detail that must be kept in mind at any one time in trying to understand how a program works. In programs of realistic size—that is to say, much larger than most of the programs in this book—this can be a major advantage.

All of this would seem to be an argument against ever referring to global variables within a procedure. Some authors in fact urge exactly such a policy: A procedure body should use nothing but formal parameters and variables that are local to that procedure. There are indeed clear advantages to such a policy, but there are also some disadvantages, and we shall find it necessary to make compromises among conflicting goals.

The program in Fig. 5.5 begins by declaring a variable named NUMBER, which is used in the loop of statements 36–41 to run through a set of values, for each of which we find the square root. Statements 3–5 define variables used in the output procedure in that loop.

The square-root procedure is typed, meaning that writing its name (SQRT) will cause a value to be supplied where its name is written. The DECLARE statement in the procedure lists both the formal parameter, N, and two local variables, X, and X$NEW. This combining of the two rather different sorts of variables is permitted. The executable statements in the procedure are exactly the same as on page 44 except that when the process has converged we return X$NEW.

The loop that constitutes the main program runs through the values from 100 to 2000 in steps of 100. Each time through this loop, NUMOUT is used to convert NUMBER to ASCII representation for output. NUMOUT is also used to convert the square root of that number to ASCII; observe the use of the invocation of the

```
PL/M-80 COMPILER    FIG. 5.5                                          PAGE   1

                /*****************************************************************/
                /* A SQUARE ROOT PROCEDURE, AND A PROGRAM TO EXERCISE IT */
                /*****************************************************************/

  1             SQUARE$ROOT$PROGRAM:
                DO;
  2    1           DECLARE NUMBER ADDRESS;
  3    1           DECLARE BUFFER(128) BYTE;
  4    1           DECLARE STATUS ADDRESS;
  5    1           DECLARE CRLF(2) BYTE DATA(0DH, 0AH);

                $INCLUDE (:F1:INOUT.SRC)
           =    $NOLIST

 26    1        SQRT:
                PROCEDURE (N) ADDRESS;
 27    2           DECLARE (N, X, X$NEW) ADDRESS;
 28    2           X = N;
 29    2           X$NEW = SHR(N + 1, 1);
 30    2           DO WHILE X <> X$NEW;
 31    3              X = X$NEW;
 32    3              X$NEW = SHR(N/X + X + 1, 1);
 33    3           END;
 34    2           RETURN X$NEW;
 35    2        END SQRT;

                /* A PROGRAM TO EXERCISE THE SQUARE ROOT ROUTINE */

 36    1           DO NUMBER = 100 TO 2000 BY 100;
 37    2              CALL NUMOUT(NUMBER, 10, ' ', .BUFFER, 6);
 38    2              CALL NUMOUT(SQRT(NUMBER), 10, ' ', .BUFFER(6), 6);
 39    2              CALL WRITE(0, .BUFFER, 12, .STATUS);
 40    2              CALL WRITE(0, .CRLF, 2, .STATUS);
 41    2           END;

 42    1           CALL EXIT;

 43    1        END SQUARE$ROOT$PROGRAM;
```

procedure SQRT within the parameter list of another procedure. This is perfectly legal and frequently useful.

This loop could have used either X or N in place of NUMBER, in which case the meaning and operation of the program would have been absolutely unchanged. If N had been used, this would have meant that the same identifier was used as a formal and an actual parameter, but the distinction between the two is still very real. If X had been used, it would have been a global variable but unknown within the procedure because it was declared as local to that procedure. These kinds of multiple use of the same identifier will often occur in the normal course of events in writing large programs, especially when a number of programmers are involved. We avoid such things in writing illustrative programs because of the rather obvious potential for confusion.

Here is the output when this program was run.

```
 100    10
 200    14
 300    17
 400    20
 500    22
 600    25
 700    26
 800    28
 900    30
1000    32
1100    33
1200    35
1300    36
1400    37
1500    39
1600    40
1700    41
1800    42
1900    44
2000    45
```

AN INTERPOLATION ROUTINE AS A PROCEDURE

Rewriting the interpolation routine shown earlier in Fig. 4.10 will provide another example of the way in which it is useful to "hide" data within a procedure. It may be recalled that the table in which we are interpolating gives temperature as a function of thermocouple voltage. We assume that we need to be able to do this interpolation within a larger program that has no other need for the table data. The best way to handle this situation is to declare the table within the procedure so that it will not clutter up the declarations at the module level.

The procedure is shown in Fig. 5.6. We see that, in addition to the declarations for the table values, we also have a declaration that lists the formal parameters and two local variables.

When it is desired to use this procedure all that it is necessary to write is something like

```
ACTUAL$TEMP   = INTERPOLATE(TC$OUTPUT);
```

This statement is taken from the final version of the furnace-control program, which we shall consider at the end of the chapter.

```
PL/M-80 COMPILER    FIG. 5.6                                                    PAGE   1

             /*************************************************************************/
             /* A PROGRAM CONTAINING ONLY AN INTERPOLATION PROCEDURE                    */
             /*************************************************************************/

 1           FIVE$INTERP:
             DO;

 2   1       INTERPOLATE:
             PROCEDURE(X$IN) ADDRESS;
 3   2          DECLARE X(*) ADDRESS DATA(0,51,102,154,206,258,365,472,581,746,911,
                1078,1411,1743,2074,2405,2739,2879,3021,3164,3310,3457,3607,3759,
                3913,4038,4165,4292,4421,4550);
 4   2          DECLARE Y(*) ADDRESS DATA(0,10,20,30,40,50,70,90,110,140,170,200,
                260,320,380,440,500,525,550,575,600,625,650,675,700,720,740,760,
                   780,800);
 5   2          DECLARE (I, X$IN, NUMERATOR) ADDRESS;

 6   2          I = 0;
 7   2          DO WHILE X$IN > X(I);
 8   3             I = I + 1;
 9   3          END;

                /* SHIFT FOR ROUNDING */
10   2          NUMERATOR = SHL((X$IN - X(I-1)) * (Y(I) - Y(I-1)), 1);
11   2          RETURN Y(I-1) + SHR(NUMERATOR/(X(I) - X(I-1)) + 1, 1);

12   2       END INTERPOLATE;

13   1       END FIVE$INTERP;
```

THE ENCRYPTION PROGRAM AS A PROCEDURE

Rewriting the substitution cipher of Fig. 4.7 will provide an example of a subscripted actual parameter.

The procedure in the program of Fig. 5.7 involves only minor changes from the earlier program. We declare CHAR as the one formal parameter and make the encryption into a typed procedure. Here we have a natural use of two RETURN statements in one procedure.

The main program to exercise this procedure begins by reading an entire line of text of indefinite length into the array named INPUT$BUFFER. After completion of the READ procedure invoked in statement 32, COUNT will show how many characters there actually are in the line. We now encode the characters in this array, one at a time, using the typed procedure call of statement 34 in an iterative DO loop. The actual parameter of the procedure ENCRYPT is thus a subscripted identifier specifying one of the characters of the message. The encoded message is written in its entirety by statement 36.

```
PL/M-80 COMPILER    FIG. 5.7                                    PAGE   1

              /*************************************************/
              /* A PROGRAM USING A PROCEDURE TO ENCODE A MESSAGE */
              /*************************************************/

 1            CIPHER$3:
              DO;
 2   1           DECLARE (INPUT$BUFFER, OUTPUT$BUFFER)(128) BYTE;
 3   1           DECLARE CRLF(2) BYTE DATA(0DH, 0AH);
 4   1           DECLARE (I, COUNT, STATUS) ADDRESS;

              $INCLUDE(:F1:INOUT.SRC)
         =    $NOLIST

25   1        ENCRYPT:
              PROCEDURE (CHAR) BYTE;
26   2           DECLARE CHAR BYTE;
27   2           DECLARE SUBSTITUTE$CHAR$TABLE(64) BYTE
                   DATA('!1QAZ"2WSX #3EDC$4RFV%5TGB&6YHNƀ''7UJM](8IK[,<)9O_L\.>0P@;+/?:*-=');

28   2           IF CHAR >= 20H AND CHAR <= 5FH THEN
29   2              RETURN SUBSTITUTE$CHAR$TABLE(CHAR - 20H);
                 ELSE
30   2              RETURN 0FFH;
31   2        END ENCRYPT;

              /* A MAIN LINE ROUTINE TO EXERCISE THE PROCEDURE */

32   1           CALL READ(1, .INPUT$BUFFER, 128, .COUNT, .STATUS);
33   1           DO I = 0 TO COUNT - 1;
34   2              OUTPUT$BUFFER(I) = ENCRYPT(INPUT$BUFFER(I));
35   2           END;
36   1           CALL WRITE(0, .OUTPUT$BUFFER, COUNT, .STATUS);
37   1           CALL WRITE(0, .CRLF, 2, .STATUS);

38   1           CALL EXIT;

39   1        END CIPHER$3;
```

PROCEDURES FOR SUBSCRIPTING TRIANGULAR MATRICES

We pause to consider briefly two additional applications of procedures that will further illustrate the range of things that can be done with them. Readers not familiar with matrices may wish to omit this section.

Suppose that in a certain application it is necessary to process moderately large matrices (two-dimensional arrays) in which all elements above or below the main diagonal are zeros. It is, of course, possible to store such matrices in a computer in rectangular form, i.e., as an array of structures, and simply not use about half the elements; but this is very wasteful of space and limits the size of matrices that can be processed. It makes much more sense to store the elements in a one-dimensional array and implement a formula that converts the row and column numbers of the triangular matrices to corresponding element numbers in the array. This is readily done by using a simple procedure. Consider first a lower-triangular matrix, written in the conventional form with subscripts beginning with 1.

$$\begin{matrix} a_{11} \\ a_{21}\ a_{22} \\ a_{31}\ a_{32}\ a_{33} \\ .\ \ . \\ .\ \ .\ \ a_{ij} \\ .\ \ . \\ a_{n1}\ a_{n2}\ a_{n3}\ \ldots\ a_{nn} \end{matrix}$$

Let us work through the derivation of the formula that converts from an element number in this matrix to the element number in an array in which the elements are stored. Suppose that we are looking for the one-dimensional element number of the lower-triangular matrix element A_{ij}. Using a formula from algebra, we know that the number of elements in all rows r before the ith row is

$$\sum_{r=1}^{i-1} r = \frac{i(i-1)}{2}.$$

To this we add j for the number of elements in the ith row up to and including A_{ij}. Finally we subtract 1 to account for the fact that PL/M arrays have an origin of zero, not 1. Therefore, element A_{ij} is in location

$$\frac{i(i-1)}{2} + j - 1$$

of the array.

In a program utilizing this scheme, we will declare variables I and J and think of them as subscripts of the two-dimensional triangular matrix. However, the only place they will ever appear is as parameters of calls to a typed procedure that carries out the computation just shown.

We suppose that the application requires not only lower-triangular but also upper-triangular matrices of the following form:

$$\begin{matrix} a_{11} & a_{12} & a_{13} & \ldots & a_{1n} \\ & a_{22} & a_{23} & \ldots & a_{2n} \\ & & a_{33} & \ldots & a_{3n} \\ & & & .\ a_{ij}\ . & \\ & & & & . \\ & & & & . \\ & & & & a_{nn} \end{matrix}$$

```
PL/M-80 COMPILER    FIG. 5.8                                    PAGE   1

              /*******************************************************************/
              /* PROCEDURES FOR FINDING SUBSCRIPTS FOR TRIANGULAR MATRICES */
              /*******************************************************************/

 1            SUBSCRIPT$PROGRAM:
              DO;
 2    1          DECLARE (LOWER$MATRIX, UPPER$MATRIX) (820) ADDRESS;
 3    1          DECLARE (B, X) (40) ADDRESS;
 4    1          DECLARE (I, J) ADDRESS;
 5    1          DECLARE N ADDRESS DATA(40);
 6    1          DECLARE SUM ADDRESS;

 7    1       LOWER$SUBS:
              PROCEDURE (I, J) ADDRESS;
 8    2          DECLARE (I, J) ADDRESS;
 9    2          RETURN (I * (I - 1)) / 2 + J - 1;
10    2       END LOWER$SUBS;

11    1       UPPER$SUBS:
              PROCEDURE (I, J, N) ADDRESS;
12    2          DECLARE (I, J, N) ADDRESS;
13    2          RETURN (I - 1) * N - ((I - 1) * I) / 2 + J - 1;
14    2       END UPPER$SUBS;

              /* A FRAGMENT OF A MAIN PROGRAM TO SOLVE AN UPPER TRIANGULAR SYSTEM */

15    1          I = N;
16    1          DO WHILE I >= 1;
17    2             SUM = 0;
18    2             DO J = I + 1 TO N;
19    3                SUM = SUM + UPPER$MATRIX(UPPER$SUBS(I, J, N)) * X(J);
20    3             END;
21    2             X(I) = (B(I) - SUM) / UPPER$MATRIX(UPPER$SUBS(I, I, N));
22    2             I = I - 1;
23    2          END;

24    1       END SUBSCRIPT$PROGRAM;
```

The computation here is a bit more complex since it has to take into account the size of the matrix. We shall not go through the details of the derivation but it can be thought of as computing the number of elements in a full rectangle of rows before the *i*th row and then subtracting off a triangular subarray of elements that are not there.

The program in Fig. 5.8 incorporates typed procedures named LOWER$SUBS and UPPER$SUBS to do these computations and shows a small bit of code suggesting how they could be used in a main program. What the main program does is solve an upper-triangular system of simultaneous equations. We assume that other parts of the program would have given values to the arrays named UPPER$MATRIX and

B, which represent the coefficients and constant terms of the following system of simultaneous equations:

$$
\begin{aligned}
a_{11}x_1 + a_{12}x_2 + a_{13}x_3 + \ldots + a_{1n}x_n &= b_1 && (1)\\
a_{22}x_2 + a_{23}x_3 + \ldots + a_{2n}x_n &= b_2 && (2)\\
a_{33}x_3 + \ldots + a_{3n}x_n &= b_3 && (3)\\
\vdots \quad &\quad \vdots && \vdots\\
a_{nn}x_n &= b_n && (n)
\end{aligned}
$$

The obvious way to solve such a system is to find x_n first, then substitute that into equation $(n-1)$ to get x_{n-1}, etc. This can be incorporated into a loop as shown, which involves two considerations that should be noted. First we want the loop on I to run from N back through 1. This is done with a DO–WHILE loop since it is not possible to write

```
DO I = N TO 1 BY -1;
```

because there are no negative numbers in PL/M.

The second consideration, also involving an iterative DO, is what happens when the appropriate values are such as to make statement 18 execute as

```
DO I = 41 TO 40;
```

The answer is that the unit controlled by the DO is not executed at all, which is exactly what we want. This makes it possible to describe the computation of all values of X with the same loop.

Note the assumption, contained in the declarations, that we are dealing with the matrices having 40 rows; a triangular matrix of this size contains 820 elements. (Observe too the factored array declaration in statement 2: The dimensioning information and the attribute ADDRESS are both factored. This is the required PL/M form.)

Observe the use of actual values incorporating the number of rows into the declarations. It would have been possible to write something like

```
DECLARE NO$ROWS LITERALLY '40';
DECLARE (B, X)(NO$ROWS) ADDRESS;
.
.
.
DO J = I + 1 TO NO$ROWS;
```

but it would not have been possible then to say

```
DECLARE (LOWER$MATRIX, UPPER$MATRIX)(NO$ROWS * (NO$ROWS - 1) / 2) ADDRESS;
```

because the PL/M compiler does not allow an expression as the dimension specifier for an array. The dimension specifier must be a numeric constant, possibly supplied through a LITERALLY declaration.

A PROGRAM USING A RANDOM-NUMBER PROCEDURE

Many applications require the generation of random numbers. This illustration exhibits an algorithm for generating random numbers having certain characteristics, and then makes one of many possible tests of randomness.

We assume that 16-bit random numbers are needed and that it is desirable to generate as many different numbers as possible before the sequence repeats. In other words, we want the longest possible cycle of random numbers. With 16-bit numbers, the longest possible cycle is 2^{16}. Mathematical theory provides simple algorithms that are guaranteed to produce cycles of such length. (See Knuth, *The Art of Computer programming;* Vol. 2: "Seminumerical Algorithms"; Addison-Wesley, Reading, Mass., 1969.) The scheme is to start with any random number whatever. Then any time a new random number is needed we multiply the most recent one by a multiplier and add a constant. Theory dictates certain characteristics of the multiplier and the constant to obtain desired characteristics of the cycle. Values that will guarantee a cycle of length 2^{16} can be found, leading to the formula

$$X_{n+1} = (2053X_n + 13849) \bmod 2^{16}.$$

The modulo 2^{16} computation is automatic since all computations on ADDRESS values in PL/M are modulo 2^{16}. We may note for the record that

$$(ab + c) \bmod 2^{16} = ((ab \bmod 2^{16}) + c) \bmod 2^{16}.$$

The program in Fig. 5.9 utilizing a procedure to generate random numbers involves several interesting features.

First, note that RANDOM$NUMBER is declared in the main program and is therefore global to the procedure, which is named RANDOM$PROC.

The loop to exercise this procedure begins by reading a starting value for the random-number sequence, to permit testing the effect of that parameter on the process. The simple test that will be applied to the generator is to see how a sample of numbers is distributed into 16 ranges. Counters representing these ranges are accordingly initialized to zero. Now (statement 84) we have a loop to generate 1600 random numbers and classify them as to the ranges into which they fall, looking only at the leftmost four bits. The simplest way to handle this assignment of a random number to one of the 16 ranges is to use the leftmost four bits as a subscript. This could be done by shifting the random number 12 binary places to the right, but it is faster to pick up the higher-order byte, using the built-in PL/M procedure HIGH, and shift that four places to the right.

Observe that by writing the name RANDOM$PROC we accomplish two things. First, the procedure changes the value of the global variable named RANDOM-$NUMBER since this identifier appears on the left side of an assignment statement

```
PL/M-80 COMPILER    FIG. 5.9                                          PAGE   1

          /*************************************************************************/
          /* A PROGRAM TO GENERATE RANDOM NUMBERS AND TEST THEIR DISTRIBUTION */
          /*************************************************************************/

          RANDOM$NUMBER$PROGRAM:
          DO;
             DECLARE RANDOM$NUMBER ADDRESS;
             DECLARE BUCKET(16) BYTE;
             DECLARE (I, BUCKET$INDEX) ADDRESS;

             DECLARE BUFFER(128) BYTE;
             DECLARE (COUNT, STATUS, BUFFPTR) ADDRESS;
             DECLARE CRLF(2) BYTE DATA(0DH, 0AH);

          $INCLUDE(:F1:INOUT.SRC)
          $NOLIST NOCODE

          RANDOM$PROC:
          PROCEDURE ADDRESS;
             RANDOM$NUMBER = 2053 * RANDOM$NUMBER + 13849;
             RETURN RANDOM$NUMBER;
          END RANDOM$PROC;

          /* A LOOP TO GENERATE VALUES AND TEST THEM */

             CALL READ(1, .BUFFER, 128, .COUNT, .STATUS);   /* GET STARTING VALUE */
             BUFFPTR = .BUFFER;
             RANDOM$NUMBER = NUMIN(.BUFFPTR);  /* CONVERT FROM ASCII TO BINARY */

             DO BUCKET$INDEX = 0 TO 15;
                BUCKET(BUCKET$INDEX) = 0;        /* INITIALIZE COUNTERS TO ZERO */
             END;

             DO I = 0 TO 1599;
                BUCKET$INDEX = SHR(HIGH(RANDOM$PROC), 4);
                BUCKET(BUCKET$INDEX) = BUCKET(BUCKET$INDEX) + 1;
             END;

             DO BUCKET$INDEX = 0 TO 15;
                CALL NUMOUT(BUCKET$INDEX, 10, '0', .BUFFER, 2);
                CALL NUMOUT(BUCKET(BUCKET$INDEX), 10, ' ', .BUFFER(2), 6);
                CALL WRITE(0, .BUFFER, 8, .STATUS);
                CALL WRITE(0, .CRLF, 2, .STATUS);
             END;

             CALL EXIT;

          END RANDOM$NUMBER$PROGRAM;
```

in the procedure. Second, that value is returned to the point of the function reference because of the RETURN statement. These are two entirely distinct operations requiring separate statements in the procedure. If we wrote

```
RETURN 2053 * RANDOM$NUMBER + 13849;
```

a value would be generated and used in statement 85—but it would always be the same value because nothing would ever happen to RANDOM$NUMBER. If there were any advantage to it we could, however, use an imbedded assignment statement to write

```
RETURN (RANDOM$NUMBER := 2053 * RANDOM$NUMBER + 13849);
```

A simple loop now writes the counts in the 16 ranges.

Here is the output of this program when run with initial random numbers of 899 and zero.

```
00     94          00    112
01     95          01    104
02    100          02     85
03     90          03     86
04    109          04     94
05     98          05    105
06    110          06    120
07    108          07     86
08     94          08    101
09     93          09    106
10    121          10     87
11     98          11    131
12     98          12    103
13    113          13     91
14     96          14    102
15     83          15     87
```

Statistical tests can be used to determine whether such results are "sufficiently random" for the purposes to which the random numbers are to be put. If not, other algorithms can be employed, bringing into consideration factors other than the maximum cycle length.

(This program depends for its operation on a feature of the PL/M-80 compiler that is not guaranteed by the PL/M standard: Multiplication results larger than 16 bits are assumed to be correctly truncated to 16 bits. Some future compiler might produce a program that would not operate correctly, since the PL/M standard says that such products are "undefined." We have taken advantage of the special feature of PL/M-80 advisedly, since the method of generating random numbers could not be programmed without it, but realizing that we are taking the risk of producing a program not "portable" to other compilers unless they also go beyond the standard in the same way.)

CASE STUDY: THE FURNACE-CONTROL PROGRAM WITH PROCEDURES

For our major example of the use of procedures in an application program of more or less realistic size, we shall show one final version of the furnace-control program considered in Chapters 2 and 3. The revision will be largely a matter of reorganizing the program, utilizing procedures to make its structure and meaning clearer. We shall, however, expand its scope by incorporating the interpolation procedure studied earlier to make the temperature computation more accurate.

The program in Fig. 5.10 has been broken into pages for clarity by using the EJECT control. This has no effect except to move the listing to the start of a new page. Since we intend to organize the program around a set of procedures, it is helpful to have all or most of them begin at the top of their own page.

A PL/M syntax rule specifies that a procedure may not be invoked until a point in the program after its definition. This means that, if we want a main program consisting largely of procedure calls, then that main program must be the last thing in the module. We accordingly develop the habit of turning to the last page of a program to see what its overall shape is and then study the individual procedures in the order in which they are invoked by the main program. Understandability will often be furthered if the procedures appear in the program—to the extent possible—in the order in which they are invoked.

Looking at the main program in Fig. 5.10, we see that it begins by invoking a procedure named READALLPORTSANDCONVERT$DATA. An inspection of this routine, which is the first one after the module-level declarations, reveals that it uses three local variables for computations that can be invisible to the rest of the program. Otherwise it deals entirely with global variables. The only real purpose of this procedure is to promote an understandable program organization. This also makes it possible for the main program loop to provide a high-level overall view of what the program structure and execution is. That is, with meaningful procedure names having been used, a person approaching this program for the first time could get a bird's eye view of what it does and how it operates simply by looking at statements 93–101. A subsequent study of the details of the individual procedures would then be facilitated by having in mind where the individual parts fit into the overall structure.

The only processing in this procedure that is not a direct equivalent of similar operations in the program of Chapter 3 is the handling of the thermocouple voltage. This is now a 16-bit value, assembled from two ports. (We realize that analog-to-digital converters don't have that much precision, and the largest number to be processed has only 13 bits anyway, but accounting for these details would not add to the educational value of the program.) The assembly of the two bytes into one ADDRESS variable is done with a shift followed by an OR operation. To make the shift possible, the variable named IN$PORT$4 had to be declared to be of type ADDRESS.

The interpolation procedure is as we have already studied it. The computation of the continuous current, shown together with the interpolation routine, is the same as before. The procedure named MONITOR$PROCESS collects and names a group of operations that are the same as those in Chapter 3. The procedure named ALTER$HEATER$CURRENT$PROFILE carries out the same functions as the

```
PL/M-80 COMPILER    FIG. 5.10                                        PAGE    1

          /*************************************************************************/
          /* FINAL VERSION OF A PROGRAM TO CONTROL AN ELECTRICALLY HEATED FURNACE      */
          /* THIS VERSION IS ORGANIZED AROUND PROCEDURES CALLED BY A MAIN PROGRAM LOOP, */
          /* AND USES INTERPOLATION TO GET A MORE ACCURATE TEMPERATURE.               */
          /*************************************************************************/
          /*
          INPUTS AND OUTPUTS
          ------ --- -------

          INPUT PORT 0: INDICATOR BITS: BIT 7: 1 = OPERATIONAL, 0 = MAINTENANCE
                                        BIT 6: NOT USED
                                        BIT 5: OPERATIONAL DOOR 1 (0 = CLOSED, 1 = OPEN)
                                        BIT 4: OPERATIONAL DOOR 2
                                        BIT 3: MAINTENANCE DOOR 1
                                        BIT 2: MAINTENANCE DOOR 2
                                        BIT 1: MAINTENANCE DOOR 3
                                        BIT 0: MAINTENANCE DOOR 4

          INPUT PORTS 1 AND 2: THREE BCD DIGITS GIVING A REFERENCE TEMPERATURE:
                                        HUNDRED'S DIGIT: PORT 1, BITS 3-0
                                        TEN'S DIGIT:     PORT 2, BITS 7-4
                                        UNIT'S DIGIT:    PORT 2, BITS 3-0
                               ALSO, A BCD CONTROL THUMBWHELL VALUE; SEE TEXT
                                        CONTROL VALUE:   PORT 1, BITS 7-4

          INPUT PORT 4: BINARY ADC OUTPUT OF THERMOCOUPLE, HIGH-ORDER 8 BITS

          INPUT PORT 8: BINARY ADC OUTPUT OF THERMOCOUPLE, LOW-ORDER 8 BITS

          OUTPUT PORT 0: BIT 0: ALARM (= 1) IF OPERATIONAL AND ANY MAINTENANCE
                                DOOR IS OPEN
                         BIT 1: ALARM (= 1) IF OPERATIONAL, AND ZERO OR TWO OPERATIONAL
                                DOORS OPEN
                         BIT 2: ALARM IF CONTROL THUMBWHEEL ILLEGAL VALUE
                         BIT 3: ALARM IF OVERTEMPERATURE
                         BIT 4: 1 = TURN ON FAN 1, 0 = TURN OFF FAN 1
                         BIT 5: 1 = TURN ON FAN 2, 0 = TURN OFF FAN 2

          OUTPUT PORT 1: BINARY OUTPUT, DESIRED HEATER CURRENT, COMPUTED FROM
                         CURRENT = .394 * (REF TEMPERATURE - ACTUAL TEMPERATURE)
          WHERE ACTUAL TEMPERATURE IS FOUND BY INTERPOLATION IN A TABLE
          */

  1       FURNACE$CONTROL:
          DO;
  2   1      DECLARE FOREVER LITERALLY 'WHILE 1';
  3   1      DECLARE (IN$PORT$0, IN$PORT$1, IN$PORT$2, IN$PORT$8) BYTE;
  4   1      DECLARE IN$PORT$4 ADDRESS;
  5   1      DECLARE OUT$PORT$0 BYTE;
  6   1      DECLARE (OPERATIONAL, OP$DOOR$1, OP$DOOR$2, MAINT$DOOR$1, MAINT$DOOR$2,
                MAINT$DOOR$3, MAINT$DOOR$4) BYTE;
  7   1      DECLARE (REF$TEMP, ACTUAL$TEMP, CURRENT, TC$OUTPUT) ADDRESS;
  8   1      DECLARE CONTROL$VALUE ADDRESS;
  9   1      DECLARE TIME$COUNTER ADDRESS;
```

```
PL/M-80 COMPILER    FIG. 5.10                                    PAGE   2

              $EJECT
 10   1       READ$ALL$PORTS$AND$CONVERT$DATA:
              PROCEDURE;
 11   2          DECLARE (HUNDREDS, TENS, UNITS) BYTE;

 12   2          IN$PORT$0 = INPUT(0);
 13   2          OPERATIONAL  = SHR(IN$PORT$0, 7);
 14   2          OP$DOOR$1    = SHR(IN$PORT$0, 5) AND 00000001B;
 15   2          OP$DOOR$2    = SHR(IN$PORT$0, 4) AND 00000001B;
 16   2          MAINT$DOOR$1 = SHR(IN$PORT$0, 3) AND 00000001B;
 17   2          MAINT$DOOR$2 = SHR(IN$PORT$0, 2) AND 00000001B;
 18   2          MAINT$DOOR$3 = SHR(IN$PORT$0, 1) AND 00000001B;
 19   2          MAINT$DOOR$4 = IN$PORT$0 AND 00000001B;

 20   2          IN$PORT$1 = INPUT(1);
 21   2          IN$PORT$2 = INPUT(2);
 22   2          HUNDREDS = IN$PORT$1 AND 00001111B;
 23   2          TENS = SHR(IN$PORT$2, 4);
 24   2          UNITS = IN$PORT$2 AND 00001111B;
 25   2          REF$TEMP = UNITS + 10*TENS + 100*HUNDREDS;

 26   2          IN$PORT$4 = INPUT(4);
 27   2          IN$PORT$8 = INPUT(8);
 28   2          TC$OUTPUT = SHL(IN$PORT$4, 8) OR IN$PORT$8;

 29   2          CONTROL$VALUE = SHR(IN$PORT$1 AND 11110000B, 4);

 31   1       INTERPOLATE:
              PROCEDURE(X$IN) ADDRESS;
 32   2          DECLARE X(*) ADDRESS DATA(0,51,102,154,206,258,365,472,581,746,911,
                 1078,1411,1743,2074,2405,2739,2879,3021,3164,3310,3457,3607,3759,
                 3913,4038,4165,4292,4421,4550);
 33   2          DECLARE Y(*) ADDRESS DATA(0,10,20,30,40,50,70,90,110,140,170,200,
                 260,320,380,440,500,525,550,575,600,625,650,675,700,720,740,760,
                    780,800);
 34   2          DECLARE (I, X$IN, NUMERATOR) ADDRESS;

 35   2          I = 0;
 36   2          DO WHILE X$IN > X(I);
 37   3             I = I + 1;
 38   3          END;

                 /* SHIFT FOR ROUNDING */
 39   2          NUMERATOR = SHL((X$IN - X(I-1)) * (Y(I) - Y(I-1)), 1);
 40   2          RETURN Y(I-1) + SHR(NUMERATOR/(X(I) - X(I-1)) + 1, 1);

 41   2       END INTERPOLATE;


 42   1       COMPUTE$CONTINUOUS$CURRENT:
              PROCEDURE;
 43   2          IF REF$TEMP > ACTUAL$TEMP THEN
 44   2             CURRENT = SHR((REF$TEMP - ACTUAL$TEMP)*101, 8);
                 ELSE
 45   2             CURRENT = 0;
 46   2       END COMPUTE$CONTINUOUS$CURRENT;
```

```
PL/M-80 COMPILER    FIG. 5.10                                    PAGE   3

                 $EJECT
                 /* CHECK FOR ALARM CONDITIONS, TURN FANS ON OR OFF */
 47   1          MONITOR$PROCESS:
                 PROCEDURE;
 48   2             DECLARE (ALARM$1, ALARM$2, ALARM$3) BYTE;
 49   2             DECLARE LIMIT ADDRESS DATA(750);

 50   2             ALARM$1 = OPERATIONAL AND (MAINT$DOOR$1 OR MAINT$DOOR$2 OR MAINT$DOOR$3
                             OR MAINT$DOOR$4);
 51   2             ALARM$2 = OPERATIONAL AND NOT (OP$DOOR$1 XOR OP$DOOR$2);
 52   2             IF CONTROL$VALUE > 4 THEN
 53   2                ALARM$3 = 1;
                    ELSE
 54   2                ALARM$3 = 0;
 55   2             IF ACTUAL$TEMP > LIMIT THEN
 56   2                OUT$PORT$0 = 00111000B; /* BOTH FANS AND ALARM 4 ALL ON */
                    ELSE
 57   2                IF ACTUAL$TEMP > REF$TEMP THEN
 58   2                   OUT$PORT$0 = 00010000B;  /* FAN 1 ON, FAN 2 AND ALARM 4 OFF */
                       ELSE
 59   2                   OUT$PORT$0 = 00000000B; /* BOTH FANS AND ALARM 4 OFF */

                    /* COMBINE ALARM AND FAN-CONTROL BITS */
 60   2             OUT$PORT$0 = OUT$PORT$0
                             OR ALARM$1
                             OR SHL(ALARM$2, 1)
                             OR SHL(ALARM$3, 2);
 61   2             OUTPUT(0) = OUT$PORT$0;

 62   2          END MONITOR$PROCESS;
```

corresponding part of the program in Chapter 3. It is called into action only if bit 6 of the value from input port 0 is 1, indicating that the process operator wishes to change the heater current profile.

The invocation of these five procedures, together with sending the current value to an output port, are the components of an infinite loop, which will repeat as long as the power is on.

EXERCISES

*1. Write statements to add to the program of Fig. 5.2 so that it will find the mean of the following four quantities, and send the mean to output port 8:
The constant 12
The value from input port 24
The leftmost four bits of the value from port 25, shifted four binary places to the right
The rightmost four bits of the value from port 25

```
PL/M-80 COMPILER    FIG. 5.10                                              PAGE   4

              $EJECT
                 /* PROCEDURE TO ALTER HEATER CURRENT PROFILE
                 ENTERED ONLY AS A RESULT OF EXTERNAL INTERRUPT */

63    1          ALTER$HEATER$CURRENT$PROFILE:
                 PROCEDURE INTERRUPT 3;
64    2             DECLARE TIME$COUNTER ADDRESS;

65    2             CONTROL$VALUE = INPUT(1) AND 11110000B;

66    2             IF CONTROL$VALUE < 5 THEN
67    2             DO CASE CONTROL$VALUE;

                       /* CASE 0: SHUT OFF CURRENT */
68    3                DO;
69    4                   CURRENT = 0;
70    4                END;

                       /* CASE 1: SET MAXIMUM CURRENT */
71    3                DO;
72    4                   CURRENT = 200;
73    4                END;

                       /* CASE 2: INCREASE CURRENT FROM 2 TO 100 IN STEPS OF 2 AMP PER SEC */
74    3                DO CURRENT = 2 TO 100 BY 2;
75    4                   DO TIME$COUNTER = 1 TO 50;
76    5                      CALL TIME(200);
77    5                   END;
78    4                   OUTPUT(1) = CURRENT;
79    4                END;

                       /* CASE 3: CONTINUOUS CONTROL - NOTHING TO BE DONE HERE */
80    3                DO;
81    4                   ;
82    4                END;

                       /* CASE 4: DECREASE FROM PRESENT TO 20 AMPS, 1 AMP PER SEC */
83    3                DO WHILE CURRENT > 20;
84    4                   DO TIME$COUNTER = 1 TO 50;
85    5                      CALL TIME(200);
86    5                   END;
87    4                   CURRENT = CURRENT - 1;
88    4                   OUTPUT(1) = CURRENT;
89    4                END;

90    3             END;   /* END OF DO CASE */

91    2          OUTPUT(0FDH) = 20H;

92    2       END ALTER$HEATER$CURRENT$PROFILE;
```

```
PL/M-80 COMPILER    FIG. 5.10                                   PAGE   5

             $EJECT
             /* ***************************************************************
                ***************************************************************
                *                                                             *
                *                    MAIN PROGRAM LOOP                        *
                *                                                             *
                *************************************************************** */

      1         DO FOREVER;
      2            CALL READ$ALL$PORTS$AND$CONVERT$DATA;
      2            ACTUAL$TEMP = INTERPOLATE(TC$OUTPUT);
      2            IF CONTROL$VALUE = 2 OR CONTROL$VALUE = 3 THEN
      2               CALL COMPUTE$CONTINUOUS$CURRENT;
      2            OUTPUT(1) = CURRENT;
      2            CALL MONITOR$PROCESS;
      2         END;

      1      END FURNACE$CONTROL;
```

2. Write statements to add to the program of Fig. 5.2 so that it will find the mean of the four values represented by the leftmost and rightmost four bits from input ports 12 and 13, and send the mean to output port 12.

*3. Write a typed procedure named MAX3 that returns the largest of its three ADDRESS arguments.

4. Write a typed procedure named MIN3 that returns the smallest of its three BYTE arguments.

*5. Write a typed procedure named SUMSQ3 that returns the sum of the squares of its three BYTE arguments as an ADDRESS value.

6. Write a typed procedure that has four ADDRESS arguments. If no more than one of the arguments is zero, it should return a BYTE 1, and zero otherwise.

*7. Modify the program of Fig. 5.6 so that it gives a value of zero to the global BYTE variable named OUTOFRANGE if the value of the argument is less than X(0) or greater than X(LAST(X)), and 1 otherwise. (No PL/M quantity could be less than X(0) in the program as it stands, of course; the modification assumes the possibility of a more general interpolation routine in which the first X value is not zero.)

8. What would happen in the program of Fig. 5.7 if the ENCRYPT procedure, statements 25–31, were moved to the end of CIPHER$3, just before the END in statement 39?

9. Add to the program of Fig. 5.8 the statements necessary to solve a lower-triangular system of equations, with the coefficients being in LOWER$MATRIX.

***10.** What modifications would have to be made in the program of Fig. 5.9 if RANDOM$-NUMBER were declared within the procedure RANDOM$PROC?

11. Write statements to add to the program of Fig. 5.9 to determine whether the first random number is repeated within the maximum possible cycle length of 65,536.

***12.** Is the order of the procedures in Fig. 5.10 essential?

13. Write a program, along the lines of the square-root program in Fig. 5.5, to compute the cube root of N from the formula

$$x_{\text{new}} = (2x + N/x^2)/3.$$

14. Using the random-number generator shown in Fig. 5.9, write a program to generate multiplication drills. If you write it to run on the Intellec Microcomputer Development System, the program can ask for the maximum size numbers to be used, then generate multiplication exercises with factors in the range of zero (or one, or two) to the maximum requested. The program should read the student's response, then inform him whether his answer is correct. A slightly more elaborate program could retry on mistakes, up to perhaps three times, then give the correct value. The program could also give statistics for the training session; the end of the session might be signalled by a special code from the student, or the session might be established in advance as being some fixed number of exercises.

CHAPTER 6

BASED VARIABLES AND THEIR RELATION TO PROCEDURES

BASED VARIABLES

It is often convenient, for reasons that we shall see in the examples that make up the bulk of this chapter, to provide for an indirect form of reference to variables. Using a *based variable,* one variable name can refer to many different data items depending on the value of the base. The base is, in effect, an address in computer storage. The techniques we consider in this chapter amount to dealing with both data elements *and their addresses.* These techniques are very powerful and will be worth the study necessary to understand their power and to gain a very clear understanding of the difference between a value and its address.

A based variable is one that is pointed to by another variable called its *base.* The base and the based variable must be declared separately, in that order. For instance, we might write

```
DECLARE ITEM$POINTER ADDRESS;
DECLARE ITEM BASED ITEM$POINTER BYTE;
```

ITEM$POINTER is the base and ITEM is the based variable. In order to use ITEM meaningfully, a value must first have been given to ITEM$POINTER. We might write, for instance

```
ITEM$POINTER = 1200H;
```

thus giving the value of 1200H to ITEM$POINTER. If later in the program we write

```
SUM = SUM + ITEM;
```

the effect is to add to SUM the value of the byte currently contained in storage location 1200H.

So far this looks simply like a way of assigning identifiers to specific memory locations. If that is all that needs to be done, it can be done more simply with the AT attribute that we shall discuss in Chapter 8. But based variables do much more, since the value of the base is not fixed but may be altered by the program itself. If, at another point in our hypothetical program, we execute

```
ITEM$POINTER = 2345H;
```

then any subsequent references to ITEM deal with the contents of location 2345H. Or we could write this loop:

```
TOTAL = 0;
DO ITEM$POINTER = 2100H TO 2199H;
   TOTAL = TOTAL + ITEM;
END;
```

The effect would be to place in TOTAL the sum of the 256 (decimal) bytes in 2100H through 2199H.

These initial examples are designed to get us thinking in terms of the distinction between memory locations and their contents. Most of our subsequent illustrations, however, will not involve actual numeric addresses in this form.

RULES GOVERNING BASED VARIABLES

Let us collect some reference information about based variables before proceeding with further examples.

1. A variable is made *based* by inserting in its declaration the word BASED and the identifier of the base, which must already have been declared.
2. The base must be of type ADDRESS.
3. The base may not be subscripted; i.e., it may not be an array element.
4. The base may not itself be a based variable.
5. The word BASED must immediately follow the name of the variable in its declaration.
6. Before a based variable may be used meaningfully, a value must have been assigned to its base.
7. The declaration of a based variable does not cause any storage to be allocated to it.

The implications of some of these rules may be seen in the following set of declarations taken from the PL/M-80 Programming Manual.

```
DECLARE (AGE$PTR, INCOME$PTR, RATING$PTR, CATEGORY$PTR) ADDRESS;
DECLARE AGE BASED AGE$PTR BYTE;
DECLARE (INCOME BASED INCOME$PTR, RATING BASED RATING$PTR) ADDRESS;
DECLARE (CATEGORY BASED CATEGORY$PTR) (100) ADDRESS;
```

The first declaration specifies that the four variables named are of type ADDRESS. As it happens these are all used as bases in the following declarations, but, if one wished, they could be used for any other purpose. The second line is the simplest form of the declaration of a based variable, involving neither factoring nor arrays. The third declaration shows how the declarations for based variable may be factored. The last declaration shows that we give the dimensioning information of the based variable not after the identifier as we are accustomed to doing, but after the identification of the base. The parentheses shown around CATEGORY BASED CATEGORY$POINTER are optional, but recommended, since they may help reduce possible confusion caused by misreading the dimensioning information as applying to CATEGORY$PTR.

LOCATION REFERENCES

The *location reference* of an identifier is formed by writing the identifier with a dot (period or decimal point) immediately to the left of the identifier. The value of such an expression is its location, that is, the actual memory address of the variable when the program is run. For example if we write

```
.STRING
```

the value is the memory address at which STRING is stored. If we write

```
.ARRAY(23)
```

the value is the location at which element 23 (the 24th array element, numbering from zero) of ARRAY is stored, taking into account its type, since ADDRESS elements take two bytes each. If it is desired to refer to the first element of an array, it is permissible to omit the subscript. Either of the following gives the address of the first element of ARRAY:

```
.ARRAY
.ARRAY(0)
```

For structures we may use unqualified or partially qualified location references.

Consider, for example, the structure declaration from the program of Fig. 4.14, which, minus the INITIAL clause, was:

```
DECLARE RECORD(NUMBER$OF$RECORDS) STRUCTURE
   (
   SN(5) BYTE,          /* STOCK NUMBER */
   DESCRIPTION(20) BYTE,
   ORDER$QTY ADDRESS,
   QTY$ON$HAND ADDRESS,
   QTY$ON$ORDER ADDRESS,
   REORDER$POINT ADDRESS,
   REORDER$QTY ADDRESS,
   LOC(8) BYTE          /* WAREHOUSE LOCATION */
   );
```

(Recall that NUMBEROFRECORDS was set to 10.) With this declaration the value of .RECORD is the address of the first byte of the entire structure, namely the first byte of the array SN in RECORD(0). The location reference .RECORD(5).LOC specifies the first byte of the array LOC in RECORD(5). The location of the last byte in the entire structure would be given by .RECORD(9).LOC(7).

LOCATION REFERENCE OF A CONSTANT LIST

The location-reference mechanism can be used in one special way to refer to a set of constants and to cause the constants to be stored. The form is

```
.(constant list)
```

The constants in the list are separated by commas. Using this feature we can write such things as

```
.(0DH, 0AH)
```

which stores the two hexadecimal values shown in two contiguous byte locations and returns the address of the first. (These values happen to correspond to carriage return and line feed in ASCII code.) Or we can write

```
.('THIS IS A CHARACTER STRING')
```

which stores the string and returns the address of the first byte. (A string within quotes is considered to be one constant.)

With these preliminaries out of the way, we turn to an extended set of examples to see the wide usefulness of based variables and location references in practical applications.

A FIRST PROCEDURE TO GET THE MEAN OF THE VALUES OF AN ARRAY

Our first example involves a procedure to find the mean of the values of an array having ten elements. When we dealt with this problem before, in Chapter 4, we had to declare the array outside the procedures because we had no way to pass either the name of the array or its address as a parameter. We recall that in PL/M the parameter passing mechanism is call-by-value, which means that every parameter in a procedure call is reduced to one number, which is stored within an area allocated to the procedure.

To process an array in a procedure we pass the address of the array as a parameter and use that value as the base of a based variable. Figure 6.1 shows a simple typed procedure that computes the mean of ten values of an array. We see that its parameter has been named ARRAY$POINTER. This parameter is immediately declared as being of type ADDRESS and is used in declaring ARRAY as being a based array having ten elements. This last declaration does not cause the allocation of any storage. Any subsequent use of the identifier ARRAY means: whatever storage location is pointed to by ARRAY$POINTER. In different invocations of this procedure, many different arrays at varying locations can be involved.

```
PL/M-80 COMPILER    FIG. 6.1                                    PAGE   1

              /*********************************************************************/
              /* A PROCEDURE TO GET THE MEAN OF THE VALUES OF AN ARRAY             */
              /* THE PROCEDURE IS PLACED IN A MODULE TO PERMIT COMPILATION         */
              /*********************************************************************/

  1           SIX$MEAN1:
              DO;

              /* A FIRST PROCEDURE TO GET THE MEAN OF THE VALUES OF AN ARRAY */
  2    1      MEAN$OF$ARRAY$VALUES$1:
              PROCEDURE (ARRAY$POINTER) ADDRESS;
  3    2        DECLARE ARRAY$POINTER ADDRESS;
  4    2        DECLARE (ARRAY BASED ARRAY$POINTER) (10) ADDRESS;
  5    2        DECLARE (I, TEMP) ADDRESS;

  6    2        TEMP = 0;
  7    2        DO I = 0 TO LAST(ARRAY);
  8    3          TEMP = TEMP + ARRAY(I);
  9    3        END;
 10    2        RETURN TEMP / LENGTH(ARRAY);

 11    2      END MEAN$OF$ARRAY$VALUES$1;


 12    1      END SIX$MEAN1;
```

A simple loop computes the sum of the array values and divides by 10, the length of the array. The quotient is returned.

To see this procedure in operation, we imbed it in a program that supplies some values and calls it, as shown in Fig. 6.2. The first invocation is in statement 39, where we see that the parameter passed to the procedure is a location reference to FIRST$ARRAY. The address at which the compiler and the operating system store this array is therefore passed to the procedure. This address is used as a base, causing the procedure to access the ten values shown in statement 2.

Statement 40 causes the binary value in MEAN$1 to be converted to ASCII and stored in an array named BUFFER. We note that among other things passed to the procedure NUMOUT are the *value* of the number to be converted and the *address* of the buffer into which the converted values are to be placed. We shall study NUMOUT in detail shortly.

The number now in ASCII in BUFFER is next written (sent to the output device) using the call to the procedure WRITE in statement 41. The four parameters of this procedure are, in sequence:

1. A zero, having functions that we shall cover later;
2. The *address* of the first byte to be written;
3. The *number* of bytes to be written;
4. The *address* of a variable where the procedure returns certain information about its operation.

For now we concern ourselves only with the second and third parameters. The result of this call will be to write the four characters contained in BUFFER(0) through BUFFER(3) onto whatever has been established as the Intellec console device.

The WRITE in statement 42 sends a carriage return and line feed to this device.

For a second illustration of how this procedure would be called, we have the loop in statements 43–48 which produces *moving averages* of sets of ten values from SECOND$ARRAY. That is, we first compute the mean of the ten elements beginning with SECOND$ARRAY(0), then the mean of the ten elements beginning with SECOND$ARRAY(1), etc., through the mean of the ten elements beginning with SECOND$ARRAY(5). If we really wanted to compute moving averages, there are, of course, faster ways to do it, but this use of the procedure provides a nice illustration of another type of location reference. Looking at statement 44 we see that the parameter passed to the procedure this time is subscripted and is the location of element I in SECOND$ARRAY, where I is the index of the iterative DO in statement 43. The parameter passed to the procedure will thus be different on each invocation, just as we need for the moving-average computation.

```
PL/M-80 COMPILER    FIG. 6.2                                    PAGE   1


              /*******************************************************************************/
              /* A PROCEDURE TO GET THE MEAN OF THE VALUES OF AN ARRAY                        */
              /* THIS VERSION PLACES THE PROCEDURE IN A MODULE CONTAINING AN EXERCISER       */
              /*******************************************************************************/

  1           SIX$MEAN2:
              DO;
  2   1          DECLARE FIRST$ARRAY(10) ADDRESS DATA (1,6,2,9,2,8,0,7,4,1);
  3   1          DECLARE SECOND$ARRAY(*) ADDRESS DATA(1,1,1,1,1,1,21,12,34,45,67,78,0,1,109);
  4   1          DECLARE BUFFER(128) BYTE;
  5   1          DECLARE STATUS ADDRESS;
  6   1          DECLARE CRLF(2) BYTE DATA(0DH, 0AH);
  7   1          DECLARE I BYTE;
  8   1          DECLARE (MEAN$1, MEAN$2) ADDRESS;

              $INCLUDE(:F1:INOUT.SRC)
          =   $NOLIST

              /* A FIRST PROCEDURE TO GET THE MEAN OF THE VALUES OF AN ARRAY */
 29   1       MEAN$OF$ARRAY$VALUES$1:
              PROCEDURE (ARRAY$POINTER) ADDRESS;
 30   2          DECLARE ARRAY$POINTER ADDRESS;
 31   2          DECLARE (ARRAY BASED ARRAY$POINTER) (10) ADDRESS;
 32   2          DECLARE (I, TEMP) ADDRESS;

 33   2          TEMP = 0;
 34   2          DO I = 0 TO LAST(ARRAY);
 35   3             TEMP = TEMP + ARRAY(I);
 36   3          END;
 37   2          RETURN TEMP / LENGTH(ARRAY);

 38   2       END MEAN$OF$ARRAY$VALUES$1;

              /* A MAIN PROGRAM TO EXERCISE THE PROCEDURE */

 39   1          MEAN$1 = MEAN$OF$ARRAY$VALUES$1(.FIRST$ARRAY);
 40   1          CALL NUMOUT(MEAN$1, 10, ' ', .BUFFER, 4);
 41   1          CALL WRITE(0, .BUFFER, 4, .STATUS);
 42   1          CALL WRITE (0, .CRLF, 2, .STATUS);
 43   1          DO I = 0 TO 5;
 44   2             MEAN$2 = MEAN$OF$ARRAY$VALUES$1(.SECOND$ARRAY(I));
 45   2             CALL NUMOUT(MEAN$2, 10, ' ', .BUFFER, 4);
 46   2             CALL WRITE(0, .BUFFER, 4, .STATUS);
 47   2             CALL WRITE(0, .CRLF, 2, .STATUS);
 48   2          END;
 49   1          CALL EXIT;

 50   1       END SIX$MEAN2;
```

A SECOND PROCEDURE TO GET THE MEAN OF THE VALUES OF AN ARRAY

The procedure just shown is rather restricted in that it can deal only with arrays having ten elements, since we do not provide the procedure with a parameter giving the number of elements in the array. This is a rather serious limitation, imposed to keep the first illustration simple. Let us now remove this restriction, adding a parameter that gives the number of elements in the array of which we desire the mean. This adds no serious complications to the procedure, as shown in Fig. 6.3, but it does involve one aspect that may at first glance seem unusual.

In statement 32 we declare the two parameters to be of type ADDRESS. Statement 31 declares ARRAY to be a based variable just as before, but the dimensioning information seems to say that this array has only one element. We must recall, however, that no storage is allocated for a based variable. Whenever the procedure refers to ARRAY it actually processes whatever array in the main program is pointed to by ARRAY$POINTER. The arrays being processed may have any number of elements from one up to some practical limit imposed by memory size. Since no storage is allocated to the array in the procedure, it makes no difference how many elements we specify in the declaration.

However, it is essential that we do specify *some* size so that the PL/M compiler will know that we are dealing with an array and will therefore permit subscripts. It is actually completely immaterial what dimensioning information we give.

Since nothing in the procedure declares the size of the array, however, we may no longer use the PL/M procedures named LAST and LENGTH. This is no problem, however, since the necessary information is now provided by a procedure parameter.

The main program to exercise this procedure first gets the mean of FIRST$ARRAY as before (statements 39–42); next we have a loop to get moving averages of eight elements (statements 43–48). Finally (statements 49–54) we use the procedure to get averages of a varying number of elements of SECOND$ARRAY, ranging from the first element only up through all 15 elements. This requires only that the parameter specifying the number of elements in the array itself be variable depending on the index of the iterative DO.

A PROGRAM TO FIND BLANKS IN TEXT

Our next example is one that uses a procedure to process textual data looking for the first blank after the character pointed to by the procedure's first parameter.

The procedure is shown in statements 26–34 of Fig. 6.4. We see that the parameter POINTER is used as the base for the variable CHARACTER. The entire processing carried out by the procedure is to keep stepping this pointer until the character pointed to is blank, at which time the value of the pointer is returned. If the character pointed to by the actual parameter itself is blank, that value of the

```
PL/M-80 COMPILER    FIG. 6.3                                    PAGE   1


             /*************************************************************************/
             /* A SECOND PROCEDURE TO GET THE MEAN OF THE VALUES OF AN ARRAY             */
             /* WITH AN EXERCISER                                                        */
             /*************************************************************************/

  1          SIX$MEAN3:
             DO;
  2   1         DECLARE FIRST$ARRAY(10) ADDRESS DATA (1,6,2,9,2,8,0,7,4,1);
  3   1         DECLARE SECOND$ARRAY(*) ADDRESS DATA(1,1,1,1,1,1,21,12,34,45,67,78,0,1,109);
  4   1         DECLARE BUFFER(128) BYTE;
  5   1         DECLARE STATUS ADDRESS;
  6   1         DECLARE CRLF(2) BYTE DATA(0DH, 0AH);
  7   1         DECLARE (I, K) BYTE;
  8   1         DECLARE (MEAN$1, MEAN$2) ADDRESS;

             $INCLUDE(:F1:INOUT.SRC)
         =   $NOLIST

             /* A SECOND PROCEDURE TO GET THE MEAN OF THE VALUES OF AN ARRAY */
 29   1      MEAN$OF$ARRAY$VALUES$2:
             PROCEDURE (ARRAY$POINTER, N) ADDRESS;
 30   2         DECLARE (ARRAY$POINTER, N) ADDRESS;
 31   2         DECLARE (ARRAY BASED ARRAY$POINTER) (1) ADDRESS;
 32   2         DECLARE (I, TEMP) ADDRESS;

 33   2         TEMP = 0;
 34   2         DO I = 0 TO N - 1;
 35   3            TEMP = TEMP + ARRAY(I);
 36   3         END;
 37   2         RETURN TEMP / N;

 38   2      END MEAN$OF$ARRAY$VALUES$2;

             /* A MAIN PROGRAM TO EXERCISE THE PROCEDURE */

 39   1         MEAN$1 = MEAN$OF$ARRAY$VALUES$2(.FIRST$ARRAY, 10);
 40   1         CALL NUMOUT(MEAN$1, 10, ' ', .BUFFER, 4);
 41   1         CALL WRITE(0, .BUFFER, 4, .STATUS);
 42   1         CALL WRITE (0, .CRLF, 2, .STATUS);
 43   1         DO K = 0 TO 7;
 44   2            MEAN$2 = MEAN$OF$ARRAY$VALUES$2(.SECOND$ARRAY(K), 8);
 45   2            CALL NUMOUT(MEAN$2, 10, ' ', .BUFFER, 4);
 46   2            CALL WRITE(0, .BUFFER, 4, .STATUS);
 47   2            CALL WRITE(0, .CRLF, 2, .STATUS);
 48   2         END;
 49   1         DO K = 1 TO 15;
 50   2            MEAN$2 = MEAN$OF$ARRAY$VALUES$2(.SECOND$ARRAY(0), K);
 51   2            CALL NUMOUT(MEAN$2, 10, ' ',  .BUFFER, 4);
 52   2            CALL WRITE(0,  .BUFFER, 4, .STATUS);
 53   2            CALL WRITE(0, .CRLF, 2, .STATUS);
 54   2         END;

 55   1         CALL EXIT;

 56   1      END SIX$MEAN3;
```

pointer is returned unchanged. The procedure has no testing. If there are no blanks in the text pointed to, the procedure will run to the end of memory, then to location zero and keep hunting. This is why, in statement 2, a final blank is included as the last character of STRING. A realistic program would include passing a limit as a parameter.

Observe that the stepping of the pointer in statement 31 depends on the fact that we are working with a BYTE variable. If we wished to use this technique to step through an ADDRESS array, the pointer would have to be advanced by 2 each time.

The main program begins, in statements 35–37, by printing the first word of STRING, which was declared in statement 2. Statement 35 uses the NEXT$BLANK procedure to find the address of the first blank in STRING. Note that it is the *location* of the first character of STRING that is passed to the procedure; the procedure returns the *location* of the first blank. Subtracting the location of the first character of STRING from the location of the first blank gives the number of characters in the substring running from the first character of string up through the character before the first blank. This is what we wish to write out.

The CALL WRITE in statement 36 specifies to start writing at the first character of STRING and to write COUNT characters. It would have been possible to combine statements 35 and 36, eliminating the use of the intermediate variable COUNT, using this statement:

```
CALL WRITE(0, .STRING, NEXT$BLANK(.STRING) - .STRING, .STATUS);
```

The second usage of the procedure writes each word of the message on a separate line. To keep this process straight we need two pointers, here named START$PTR and END$PTR. The former always points to the first letter of a word and the latter points to the blank after the last letter of a word. The CALL WRITE in statement 41 thus writes the words of the message in succession.

The DO–WHILE in statement 39 stops the process when the end of the message has been reached *so long as there is at least one blank at the end of the message.* Here is the output when this program was run.

```
THE
THE
QUICK
BROWN
FOX
JUMPED
OVER
THE
LAZY
DOG
```

```
PL/M-80 COMPILER    FIG. 6.4                                    PAGE   1

             /*************************************************************************/
             /* A PROGRAM TO FIND BLANKS IN CHARACTER TEXT                             */
             /*************************************************************************/

 1           BLANKS:
             DO;
 2    1         DECLARE STRING(*) BYTE DATA('THE QUICK BROWN FOX JUMPED OVER THE LAZY DOG ');
 3    1         DECLARE (START$PTR, END$PTR) ADDRESS;
 4    1         DECLARE (COUNT, STATUS) ADDRESS;
 5    1         DECLARE CRLF(2) BYTE DATA(0DH, 0AH);

             $INCLUDE(:F1:INOUT.SRC)
         =   $NOLIST

26    1      NEXT$BLANK:
             PROCEDURE (POINTER) ADDRESS;
27    2         DECLARE POINTER ADDRESS;
28    2         DECLARE CHARACTER BASED POINTER BYTE;
29    2         DECLARE BLANK LITERALLY ''' ''';

30    2         DO WHILE CHARACTER <> BLANK;
31    3            POINTER = POINTER + 1;
32    3         END;
33    2         RETURN POINTER;

34    2      END NEXT$BLANK;

             /* A MAIN LINE ROUTINE */

             /* TEST 1: PRINT FIRST WORD OF STRING */
35    1         COUNT = NEXT$BLANK(.STRING) - .STRING;
36    1         CALL WRITE(0, .STRING, COUNT, .STATUS);
37    1         CALL WRITE(0, .CRLF, 2, .STATUS);

             /* TEST 2: PRINT ALL WORDS OF STRING, ONE TO A LINE */
38    1         START$PTR = .STRING;
39    1         DO WHILE START$PTR < .STRING(LAST(STRING));
40    2            END$PTR = NEXT$BLANK(START$PTR);
41    2            CALL WRITE(0, START$PTR, END$PTR - START$PTR, .STATUS);
42    2            CALL WRITE(0, .CRLF, 2, .STATUS);
43    2            START$PTR = END$PTR + 1;
44    2         END;

45    1         CALL EXIT;

46    1      END BLANKS;
```

A PROGRAM TO EXTRACT PL/M COMMENTS FROM A STRING

We continue with another example of text processing, which is slightly more complex and which illustrates some additional programming techniques. The task is to detect and print on separate lines any PL/M comments within a string of text. We recall that a PL/M comment is any string beginning with the characters /* and ending with the characters */.

The basic task is to find a way to keep track of where we are in relation to PL/M comments as we examine a string of characters one at a time from left to right. We need to have unambiguous answers to questions such as: Am I now inside a comment? Was the previous character an asterisk that is potentially the beginning of the end of a comment?

One good way to represent this logic is a technique known as a *state transition table*. We begin by defining four *states* as follows:

State 0: Not within a comment.

State 1: The previous character was a slash that may have been the start of a comment.

State 2: Inside a comment.

State 3: The previous character was an asterisk that may have been the beginning of the end of a comment.

For each of these states there are specific actions to be taken depending on whether the character now being examined is (1) a slash, (2) an asterisk, or (3) anything else. Combining the four states with the three possibilities, we get the *state transition table* shown in Fig. 6.5, which needs careful study.

	Current character		
	/	*	Anything else
State 0	1	0	0
State 1	1	2	0
State 2	2	3	2
State 3	0	3	2

Fig. 6.5. State transition table for a program to detect and print comments within a string of text. The state to go to next is found at the intersection of the row containing the current state and the column containing the current character.

The first line says that if we are in State 0—outside of a comment—and the current character is a slash, we move to State 1 for examining the next character. If we are in State 0 and the current character is an asterisk or anything else, we stay in State 0. Putting it another way, if we are not now in a comment, the only occurrence that can change that status is the detection of a slash.

The second line says that if we are in State 1, meaning that the previous character was a slash, then the detection of a slash means we stay in State 1. The detection of an asterisk means we move to State 2 and the detection of anything else puts us back into State 0. This expresses the meaning of the syntax rule which says that the beginning of a comment is marked by a slash and an asterisk, in that order, with nothing between.

The third line says that if we are inside a comment, then we continue to be inside a comment until detecting an asterisk.

The last line says that if the previous character was an asterisk that might mark the beginning of the end of the comment, then a slash means that we have, in fact, detected the end of the comment, so we move to State 0. An asterisk means we stay in State 3, still looking for the possibility of a terminating slash, and anything else means we are still inside the comment because the previous asterisk was not immediately followed by a slash.

This completely defines the way in which we move from one state to another. A further specification of what the program must do says that, for the first two entries in the first column, we need to set a pointer marking the possible beginning of a comment, and for the final entry in the first column we need to write the comment.

We can begin to study the program in Fig. 6.6 by looking first at the main program on the third page. The READ in statement 68 reads the first string and places it in BUFFER. BUFFER has been declared to have 128 bytes; in the CALL READ we specify that we will accept as many as 128 bytes but ask the READ procedure to place in COUNT the actual number of characters read. We now enter a DO–WHILE loop that repeats until detecting a *null line,* i.e., one that begins with a carriage return and thus contains no text characters. On each repetition of this loop we write the original string unaltered, call the procedure (which will print any PL/M comments), write a carriage return and line feed, and read the next string.

```
PL/M-80 COMPILER    FIG. 6.6                                          PAGE   1


              /*************************************************************************/
              /* A PROGRAM TO EXTRACT PL/M COMMENTS FROM AN INPUT STRING, USING        */
              /* A STATE TRANSITION TABLE IMPLEMENTED WITH A DO-CASE                   */
              /*                                                                       */
              /* THE INPUT STRING MAY BE AT MOST A LINE LONG, TERMINATED BY A          */
              /* CARRIAGE RETURN.  THE INPUT IS PRINTED, FOLLOWED BY ANY EMBEDDED      */
              /*  COMMENTS PRINTED ON SEPARATE LINES, FOLLOWED BY A BLANK LINE.        */
              /*************************************************************************/

  1           STRING$ANALYSIS:
              DO;
  2    1         DECLARE BUFFER(128) BYTE;
  3    1         DECLARE (COUNT, STATUS) ADDRESS;
  4    1         DECLARE CR BYTE DATA(0DH);
  5    1         DECLARE CRLF(2) BYTE DATA(0DH, 0AH);

              $INCLUDE(:F1:INOUT.SRC)
         =    $NOLIST
```

```
PL/M-80 COMPILER    FIG. 6.6                                              PAGE   2

                 $EJECT
      1          WRITE$COMMENTS:
                 PROCEDURE;
      2             DECLARE (CHAR$PTR, COMMENT$PTR) ADDRESS;
      2             DECLARE CHAR BASED CHAR$PTR BYTE;
      2             DECLARE STATE BYTE;
      2             DECLARE SLASH LITERALLY '''/''', ASTERISK LITERALLY '''*''', CR LITERALLY '0DH';

      2             STATE = 0;
      2             CHAR$PTR = .BUFFER;
      2             DO WHILE CHAR <> CR;
      3                DO CASE STATE;

                          /* STATE 0: NOT IN A COMMENT */
      4                   DO;
      5                      IF CHAR = SLASH THEN
      5                      DO;
      6                         STATE = 1;
      6                         COMMENT$PTR = CHAR$PTR;
      6                      END;
      5                   END;
                          /* STATE 1: PREVIOUS CHARACTER A SLASH; POSSIBLE START OF COMMENT */
      4                   DO;
      5                      IF CHAR = SLASH THEN
      5                         COMMENT$PTR = CHAR$PTR;
                             ELSE
      5                         IF CHAR = ASTERISK THEN
      5                            STATE = 2;
                                ELSE
      5                            STATE = 0;
      5                   END;
                          /* STATE 2: INSIDE A COMMENT */
      4                   DO;
      5                      IF CHAR = ASTERISK THEN
      5                         STATE = 3;
      5                   END;
                          /* STATE 3: PREVIOUS CHARACTER AN ASTERISK; POSSIBLE
                                   END OF COMMENT  */
      4                   DO;
      5                      IF CHAR = SLASH THEN
      5                      DO;
      6                         CALL WRITE(0, COMMENT$PTR, CHAR$PTR - COMMENT$PTR + 1, .STATUS);
      6                         CALL WRITE(0, .CRLF, 2, .STATUS);
      6                         STATE = 0;
      6                      END;
                             ELSE
      5                         IF CHAR = ASTERISK THEN
      5                            STATE = 3;
                                ELSE
      5                            STATE = 2;
      5                   END;

      4                END; /* OF DO CASE */
      3                CHAR$PTR = CHAR$PTR + 1;
      3             END; /* OF DO WHILE */
      2          END WRITE$COMMENTS;
```

```
PL/M-80 COMPILER    FIG. 6.6                                    PAGE   3

              $EJECT
                 /* MAIN PROGRAM LOOP */
68   1           CALL READ(1, .BUFFER, 128, .COUNT, .STATUS);
69   1           DO WHILE BUFFER(0) <> CR;
70   2              CALL WRITE(0, .BUFFER, COUNT, .STATUS);
71   2              CALL WRITE$COMMENTS;
72   2              CALL WRITE(0, .CRLF, 2, .STATUS);
73   2              CALL READ(1, .BUFFER, 128, .COUNT, .STATUS);
74   2           END;
75   1           CALL EXIT;

76   1        END STRING$ANALYSIS;
```

The procedure for finding and printing any comments in the string, WRITE$-COMMENTS, has no parameters and is untyped. The string that the main program reads is stored in BUFFER, which is a global variable, and processed there. The program declares a based variable named CHAR; the base of this variable, CHAR$-PTR, is set equal to the location of BUFFER in statement 32. In the rest of the procedure any reference to CHAR is a reference to whichever character in BUFFER is currently pointed at by CHAR$PTR. At the end of processing each character, statement 65 advances this pointer. For the purposes of this procedure as written —that is, with BUFFER being a global variable—it would also have been possible to use BUFFER directly, with a subscript.

The rest of the procedure is a direct translation of the rules in the state transition table. COMMENT$PTR points at the slash that begins a comment. CHAR$PTR always points at the current character, so that when the end of the comment is detected it is pointing at the terminating slash. The number of characters in the string pointed at by these two pointers is their difference plus one.

The rest of the program contains no surprises.

Here is the output produced when this program was run with some illustrative input strings.

```
/* THIS IS A PL/M COMMENT */ BUT THIS ISN'T
/* THIS IS A PL/M COMMENT */

/*** ALSO A COMMENT ***//*ALSO*/
/*** ALSO A COMMENT ***/
/*ALSO*/

COMMENTS DON'T HAVE TO HAVE ANY 'CONTENTS': /**//**//**/**//**//**//**/
/**/
/**/
/**/
/**/
/**/
/**/
```

```
THE SLASH AND THE ASTERISK MUST BE ADJACENT: /*A*//*B* // *C*/
/*A*/
/*B* // *C*/

*/ THE SLASH AND THE ASTERISK MUST APPEAR IN THE PRESCRIBED ORDER /*

/* AS AN EXERCISE, REVISE THE PROGRAM SO THAT '*/' IS THE OPENING BRACKET
/* AS AN EXERCISE, REVISE THE PROGRAM SO THAT '*/

AND '/*' THE CLOSING */
/*' THE CLOSING */

/* COMMENTS CANNOT BE /* 'NESTED' */ INSIDE OTHER COMMENTS */
/* COMMENTS CANNOT BE /* 'NESTED' */

(COULD YOU WRITE A STATE-TRANSITION TABLE TO PERMIT 'NESTED' COMMENTS?)

/*MISSING TERMINATIONS */ /* CAN MAKE FOR VERY CONFUSING SITUATIONS
/*MISSING TERMINATIONS */

THIS IS ESPECIALLY TRUE IN PROGRAMS, WHERE THE ABSENCE OF THE TERMINATION

PLACES ALL SUCCEEDING TEXT, UP TO THE NEXT TERMINATION, IN THE COMMENT, THUS

ELIMINATING INTERVENING PROGRAM TEXT.

COMMENTS DON'T HAVE TO 'MAKE SENSE': /*/*/*/*/*/*/*/*/*/*/*/*/*/*/*/*/*/*/*/
/*/*/
/*/*/
/*/*/
/*/*/
/*/*/
/*/*/
```

A PROCEDURE TO GET THE MEAN AND MEDIAN OF ARRAYS

We now return to the processing of numeric data in arrays, adding (to the requirements of the procedure studied earlier) that we must compute the *median* of the values as well as their mean. It is not guaranteed that the array values as presented to the procedure are in sequence, so the procedure must sort them. When this has been done, the median is the value in the middle position in the array, since half of the values in the array lie below and half above, which is the definition of a median. For an array having an even number of elements, we arbitrarily take the second of the two elements in the middle of the sorted array.

The procedure could be specified in various ways as regards passing parameters and returning values. We choose not to use any global variables, so we immediately have one new problem: A typed procedure can return only one value. Since a PL/M procedure call passes only values to the procedure, some new mechanism must be found for getting both the mean and the median back to the calling routine.

The solution we shall use is this: The new procedure will still be typed and the mean will be the value sent back by a RETURN statement. We shall pass to the procedure a value that points to the location of the median. This value can then be used as the base of a based variable. Thus, even though the only thing we can send to a PL/M procedure are the values of single variables, the procedure now knows where the median is located and can use that information however it may be useful. Before, we used this mechanism in order to obtain elements from arrays. Now we shall use it to send a value back from the procedure.

We shall assume that it is not permissible to sort the values in the array by rearranging the array itself. Therefore it will be necessary to move those values to a local array declared in the procedure and sort them there. (An alternative approach would be to use the address-sorting technique discussed toward the end of Chapter 4, which involves no movement of data.)

The program shown in Fig. 6.7 introduces no other new PL/M concepts, but we have taken advantage of the opportunity to refine the sorting method, so the program bears study.

The declarations at the beginning of the procedure, statements 31 and 32, establish ARRAY and MEDIAN as based variables. The values of their bases are supplied as parameters. This says that the names ARRAY and MEDIAN refer to whatever locations the calls in the main program specify.

The operations of moving the array values to temporary storage and summing them are combined in one loop in statements 38–41. We see, in the declaration in statement 34, that this procedure will not correctly process any array of more than 200 elements; if this procedure were to be widely used, it would be a good idea to test the value of N somewhere in the procedure and take appropriate action if it is too large.

The sorting method used this time is another type of exchange sorting, which takes some advantage of any ordering that may exist in the array as presented for processing. The scheme is that adjacent pairs of values are compared, moving from left to right through the array and exchanging where necessary. If at any time it is possible to move through the array without requiring any exchanges, then the job is done. A flag named EXCHANGE keeps track of whether any exchanges have been made on a given pass through the array.

It would be possible to set up the loop so that, in each pass through the array, all pairs are examined, but this is not actually necessary in passes after the first. The first pass guarantees that the largest element in the array is in the last position, the second pass guarantees that the next largest element is in next-to-last position, etc. It is a simple matter, therefore, to count the passes and use that number to reduce the limit value of the index of the iterative DO.

Note in statement 57 the subscript expression involving division, the first such that we have seen. The quotient will, of course, be an integer with the remainder dropped if N is odd. This implements the rule stating that the median is the element in the middle of the sorted array, "middle" being suitably defined for arrays with an even number of elements.

```
PL/M-80 COMPILER    FIG. 6.7                                                PAGE   1

           /*************************************************************************/
           /* A PROCEDURE TO FIND THE MEAN AND MEDIAN OF AN ARRAY, IN A MODULE      */
           /* THAT EXERCISES IT.                                                    */
           /*************************************************************************/

  1        SIX$MEAN$AND$MEDIAN$1:
           DO;
  2   1      DECLARE FIRST$ARRAY(10) ADDRESS DATA (1,6,2,9,2,8,0,7,4,1);
  3   1      DECLARE SECOND$ARRAY(*) ADDRESS DATA(9,0,45,12,1,1,21,12,34,45,8,78,0,1,99);
  4   1      DECLARE BUFFER(128) BYTE;
  5   1      DECLARE STATUS ADDRESS;
  6   1      DECLARE CRLF(2) BYTE DATA(0DH, 0AH);
  7   1      DECLARE I BYTE;
  8   1      DECLARE (MEAN$1, MEAN$2, MEDIAN$1, MEDIAN$2) ADDRESS;

           $INCLUDE(:F1:INOUT.SRC)
       =   $NOLIST

           /* A PROCEDURE TO GET MEAN AND MEDIAN OF THE VALUES OF AN ARRAY */
 29   1    MEAN$AND$MEDIAN:
           PROCEDURE (ARRAY$POINTER, MEDIAN$POINTER, N) ADDRESS;
 30   2      DECLARE (ARRAY$POINTER, MEDIAN$POINTER, N) ADDRESS;
 31   2      DECLARE (ARRAY BASED ARRAY$POINTER) (1) ADDRESS;
 32   2      DECLARE MEDIAN BASED MEDIAN$POINTER ADDRESS;
 33   2      DECLARE (I, TEMP, SUM) ADDRESS;
 34   2      DECLARE PROC$ARRAY(200) ADDRESS;
 35   2      DECLARE (EXCHANGE, PASS) BYTE;
 36   2      DECLARE TRUE LITERALLY '0FFH', FALSE LITERALLY '0';

             /* MOVE ARRAY VALUES TO TEMPORARY ARRAY; COMPUTE MEAN */
 37   2      SUM = 0;
 38   2      DO I = 0 TO N - 1;
 39   3        PROC$ARRAY(I) = ARRAY(I);
 40   3        SUM = SUM + ARRAY(I);
 41   3      END;

             /* SORT TEMPORARY ARRAY, TO GET MEDIAN; BUBBLE SORTING IS USED,
             WITH A PASS COUNTER TO PREVENT EXAMINING ITEMS AT END OF LIST THAT
             ARE ALREADY IN FINAL POSITION    */

 42   2      EXCHANGE = TRUE;
 43   2      PASS = 0;
 44   2      DO WHILE EXCHANGE;
 45   3        EXCHANGE = FALSE;
 46   3        DO I = 0 TO N - 2 - PASS;
 47   4          IF PROC$ARRAY(I) > PROC$ARRAY(I + 1) THEN
 48   4          DO;
 49   5            TEMP = PROC$ARRAY(I);
 50   5            PROC$ARRAY(I) = PROC$ARRAY(I + 1);
 51   5            PROC$ARRAY(I + 1) = TEMP;
 52   5            EXCHANGE = TRUE;
 53   5          END;
 54   4        END;
 55   3        PASS = PASS + 1;
 56   3      END;
 57   2      MEDIAN = PROC$ARRAY(N / 2);
 58   2      RETURN SUM / N;
 59   2    END MEAN$AND$MEDIAN;
```

```
PL/M-80 COMPILER    FIG. 6.7                                    PAGE   2

                  $EJECT
                  /* A MAIN PROGRAM TO EXERCISE THE PROCEDURE */

       1             MEAN$1 = MEAN$AND$MEDIAN(.FIRST$ARRAY, .MEDIAN$1, 10);
       1             CALL NUMOUT(MEAN$1, 10, ' ', .BUFFER, 4);
       1             CALL NUMOUT(MEDIAN$1, 10, ' ', .BUFFER(4), 4);
       1             CALL WRITE(0, .BUFFER, 8, .STATUS);
       1             CALL WRITE (0, .CRLF, 2, .STATUS);
       1             DO I = 0 TO 7;
       2                MEAN$2 = MEAN$AND$MEDIAN(.SECOND$ARRAY(I), .MEDIAN$2, 8);
       2                CALL NUMOUT(MEAN$2, 10, ' ', .BUFFER, 4);
       2                CALL NUMOUT(MEDIAN$2, 10, ' ', .BUFFER(4), 4);
       2                CALL WRITE(0, .BUFFER, 8, .STATUS);
       2                CALL WRITE(0, .CRLF, 2, .STATUS);
       2             END;
       1             CALL EXIT;

       1          END SIX$MEAN$AND$MEDIAN$1;
```

The main program exercises this procedure in two sections. The first finds the mean and median of the ten values of FIRST$ARRAY. It then moves through the fifteen values of SECOND$ARRAY, taking them in eight groups of eight each. Note, in both of these invocations of the procedure, that the first two parameters are written with dot operators. It is not the first *element* of FIRST$ARRAY that we want to pass to the procedure, but rather the *location* of the first element. And it is not the *median* that we want to pass to the procedure but rather the *location* at which the procedure should store the median.

Here is the printed output when this program was run.

```
   4   4
  12  12
  15  12
  21  21
  16  12
  25  21
  24  21
  24  21
  34  34
```

THE PROCEDURE NUMOUT

We have already made considerable use of the procedure NUMOUT, which converts from the binary form of a number to an ASCII string suitable for printing. This procedure, along with NUMIN, READ, WRITE, and EXIT, is incorporated in the program as a result of the line

```
$INCLUDE(:F1:INOUT.SRC)
```

which directs the compiler to obtain the file named INOUT from a diskette set up by the author for this purpose. (This obviously won't work on your system unless you also set up such a file!)

The program shown in Fig. 6.8 begins with a full page of descriptive material that fully documents how the program is to be used. This kind of description is indicative of what should be provided when a program is to be distributed and used by many programmers other than the original writer.

The actual processing described on the second page of Fig. 6.8 is fairly condensed and deserves careful study.

The declarations in statements 3 and 4 describe the five parameters and an index I. Statement 5 declares CHARS to be a based variable, based on the buffer address supplied as one of the parameters. This means that the ASCII characters that are the output of the program will be placed wherever the pointer in the parameter list says to put them. Statement 6 sets up a table of the 16 hexadecimal digits —not all of which will be used, of course, if the base is less than 16.

The loop in statements 7–10 does the actual conversion. Let us look carefully at statement 8. The expression

```
VALUE MOD BASE
```

returns the remainder on dividing VALUE by BASE; this is the least significant digit of the quantity represented by VALUE in the base represented by BASE. (See page 14 for a discussion of the MOD function.) For example, if we were converting 177_{10} to octal we would have

```
177 MOD 8 = 1
```

so the least significant digit of the octal representation of 177_{10} is 1.

The result of this computation is used as the subscript of the array named DIGITS, which picks up the ASCII representation of the appropriate digit. This digit is then placed in the rightmost position of the space designated by the combination of the parameters BUFADR and WIDTH.

Now we divide the value being converted by the base, using integer arithmetic as always, and place the result back in VALUE. Using the example earlier we would have

```
177/8 = 22
```

This reduced VALUE is what is used in the next execution of statement 8 as the

```
PL/M-80 COMPILER    FIG. 6.8                                    PAGE   1

1           SIX$NUMOUT:
            DO;

            /***********************************************************************/
            /*                                  NUMOUT                             */
            /***********************************************************************/
            /*
               ABSTRACT
               --------

                  'NUMOUT' CONVERTS A NUMBER FROM INTERNAL (BINARY) FORM
               TO AN ASCII STRING SUITABLE FOR PRINTING.

               PARAMETERS
               ----------

               VALUE         THE NUMBER WHOSE PRINTED REPRESENTATION IS DESIRED.
               BASE          AN INTEGER BETWEEN 2 AND 16, INCLUSIVE, SPECIFYING
                             IN WHAT NUMBER BASE 'VALUE' IS TO BE INTERPRETED.
               LC            (LEADING CHARACTER): LEADING ZEROES IN THE PRINTED
                             REPRESENTATION WILL BE DESIGNATED BY 'LC', WHICH
                             SHOULD BE AN ASCII CHARACTER.  USEFUL VALUES OF
                             'LC' ARE: 0(NULL), ' '(SPACE), AND '0'(ZERO).
               BUFADR        THE ADDRESS OF A BUFFER OF AT LEAST 'WIDTH' BYTES,
                             INTO WHICH THE PRINTED REPRESENTATION IS PLACED.
               WIDTH         THE NUMBER OF CHARACTER POSITIONS DESIRED IN THE
                             PRINTED REPRESENTATION.

               VALUE RETURNED
               ----- --------

                  THE ONLY RETURNED VALUE IS THE PRINTED REPRESENTATION WHICH
               IS PLACED IN THE BUFFER POINTED TO BY BUFADR.

               GLOBAL VARIABLES ACCESSED
               ------ --------- --------

               BYTES IN THE BUFFER (VIA A BASED VARIABLE, CHARS)

               GLOBAL VARIABLES MODIFIED
               ------ --------- --------

               BYTES IN THE BUFFER (VIA A BASED VARIABLE, CHARS)

               DESCRIPTION
               -----------

                  IF 'VALUE' IS TOO LARGE TO BE REPRESENTED IN 'WIDTH'
               CHARACTERS OF THE CHOSEN 'BASE', THEN ONLY THE LEAST
               SIGNIFICANT DIGITS WILL BE DISPLAYED.

                  THERE IS NO ERROR CHECKING.  INPUT VALUES MUST CONFORM TO THE
               RESTRAINTS:
                         BASE > 1 AND WIDTH > 0
            */
```

```
PL/M-80 COMPILER    FIG. 6.8                                    PAGE   2

                 $EJECT
  2   1          NUMOUT:
                 PROCEDURE(VALUE, BASE, LC, BUFADR, WIDTH);
  3   2             DECLARE (VALUE, BUFADR) ADDRESS;
  4   2             DECLARE (BASE, LC, WIDTH, I) BYTE;
  5   2             DECLARE (CHARS BASED BUFADR) (1) BYTE;
  6   2             DECLARE DIGITS(*) BYTE DATA('0123456789ABCDEF');

  7   2             DO I = 1 TO WIDTH;
  8   3                CHARS(WIDTH - I) = DIGITS(VALUE MOD BASE);
  9   3                VALUE = VALUE / BASE;
 10   3             END;
 11   2             I = 0;
 12   2             DO WHILE CHARS(I) = '0' AND I < WIDTH - 1;
 13   3                CHARS(I) = LC;
 14   3                I = I + 1;
 15   3             END;
 16   2          END NUMOUT;

 17   1          END SIX$NUMOUT;
```

loop continues. With the same example we would now have

```
22 MOD 8 = 6
```

This means that the second digit (from the right) of the octal representation of 177_{10} is 6. Continuing, we get

```
22/8 = 2
```

and

```
2 MOD 8 = 2
2/8 = 0
0 MOD 8 = 0
```

So $177_{10} = 0261_8$.

The value has now been converted to the base specified and the ASCII representation of the digits of the converted value are in BUFADR(0) through BUFADR(WIDTH−1). All that remains is to convert leading zeros to whatever character is specified by the parameter LC. This is done by the simple loop in statements 12–15.

Figure 6.9 is a program to generate some examples of how NUMOUT works.

```
PL/M-80 COMPILER    FIG. 6.9                                    PAGE   1

        /*************************************************************/
        /* A DRIVER TO PRODUCE EXAMPLES OF THE OPERATION OF NUMOUT */
        /*************************************************************/

        NUMOUT$DRIVER:
        DO;
           DECLARE BUFFER(128) BYTE;
           DECLARE STATUS ADDRESS;
           DECLARE CRLF(2) BYTE DATA(0DH, 0AH);

        $INCLUDE(:F1:INOUT.SRC)
        $NOLIST

           CALL NUMOUT (123, 2, ' ', .BUFFER, 8);
           CALL NUMOUT (123, 8, ' ', .BUFFER+8, 8);
           CALL NUMOUT (123, 10, ' ', .BUFFER+16, 8);
           CALL NUMOUT (123, 16, ' ', .BUFFER+24, 8);
           CALL WRITE (0, .BUFFER, 32, .STATUS);
           CALL WRITE (0, .CRLF, 2, .STATUS);
           CALL NUMOUT (123, 2, ' ', .BUFFER, 10);
           CALL WRITE (0, .BUFFER, 10, .STATUS);
           CALL WRITE (0, .CRLF, 2, .STATUS);
           CALL NUMOUT (123, 2, '0', .BUFFER, 10);
           CALL WRITE (0, .BUFFER, 10, .STATUS);
           CALL WRITE (0, .CRLF, 2, .STATUS);
           CALL NUMOUT (123, 2, 'X', .BUFFER, 10);
           CALL WRITE (0, .BUFFER, 10, .STATUS);
           CALL WRITE (0, .CRLF, 2, .STATUS);
           CALL NUMOUT (123, 2, 0, .BUFFER, 10);
           CALL WRITE (0, .BUFFER, 10, .STATUS);
           CALL WRITE (0, .CRLF, 2, .STATUS);

           CALL EXIT;

        END NUMOUT$DRIVER;
```

When the program was run, it produced these results:

```
 1111011      173     123     7B
   1111011
0001111011
XXX1111011
1111011
```

The last line demonstrates the use of the *null character,* the result of sending a binary zero to the output device. This character is not written, and takes no space. The result is to place the first nonzero character in the leftmost position of the space assigned.

Note that NUMOUT does not produce any identification of the number base in its output.

THE PROCEDURE NUMIN

Just as we need a procedure to convert from internal binary to external ASCII, we also need a procedure to make the reverse conversion. The techniques for carrying out this operation are instructive.

The input procedure is more complex than the output because we do not know until reaching the end of the input string what the number base is. We must accordingly convert the input string on the assumption that it might be in any of four possible bases and then decide upon reaching the end of the string which of the four to return. The problem is complicated by the fact that, as we process the input characters, we don't know whether the letters B and D represent hexadecimal digits or denote the base for binary and decimal. Which they are becomes known only upon reaching the end of the input string, which is signaled by detecting some character other than a hexadecimal digit.

The only input to the procedure is the address of a pointer to the string of bytes giving the ASCII representations of an input number. The declarations in Fig. 6.10 include four variables where we will build up the four possible converted values, and the sixteen hexadecimal digits as an array.

Processing begins by setting the variables for the binary, octal, decimal, and hexadecimal converted values to zero. A simple loop next moves CURRENT$CHAR-$PTR past all leading blanks. Now comes a longer loop that makes the conversions of successive characters until finding one that is not a hexadecimal digit. The variable MORE$STRING controls this loop. Immediately after we enter the unit controlled by the DO–WHILE, at statement 13, we set MORE$STRING false and then set it back to true if we do find a digit pointed at by CURRENT$CHAR$PTR.

The actual conversion from the ASCII representation of a character to its value in binary—considered as a digit in one of the four possible number systems—is carried out by statements 14–26. I is an index that identifies which (if any) of the 16 hexadecimal digits we are dealing with. For example, if a digit currently being processed is the ASCII representation of 7, which is 37H, then I will be a 7, in pure binary. Likewise, if the digit currently being processed is the ASCII representation of a hexadecimal F, which is 46H, then I will be 15 in pure binary. If we succeed in comparing the input character with all 16 ASCII representations in the array named DIGITS without finding a match, then statement 24 will never be executed and the DO–WHILE will terminate; we have found the end of the digits in the input string.

The actual conversion from binary, octal, decimal, or hexadecimal to internal binary is carried out by a process of repeatedly multiplying the value of the digits so far converted by the number base and adding the value of the current digit. To summarize the method with an example, suppose we are converting the number 469_{10} to binary. Examining the digits from left to right, we would first get the binary representation of 4 in base 2. We would then multiply that value by 10 and add the binary representation of 6. We would finally multiply that sum by 10 and add the binary representation of 9.

```
PL/M-80 COMPILER    FIG. 6.10                                    PAGE   1


1          SIX$NUMIN:
           DO;

           /*****************************************************************************/
           /*                                  NUMIN                                   */
           /*****************************************************************************/
           /*
              ABSTRACT
              --------

                 'NUMIN' CONVERTS AN ASCII STRING INTO AN INTERNAL (BINARY) NUMBER
              SUITABLE FOR COMPUTATION.

              PARAMETERS
              ----------

              BUFFER$PTR$ADDRESS    THE ADDRESS OF A POINTER TO A BUFFER AREA WHICH
                                    CONTAINS THE ASCII STRING.

              VALUE RETURNED
              ----- --------

              1.  THE VALUE OF THE ASCII STRING IN BINARY FORMAT

              GLOBAL VARIABLES ACCESSED
              ------ --------- --------

              POINTER TO THE BUFFER AREA (VIA A BASED VARIABLE, BUFFER$PTR)
              BYTES IN THE BUFFER AREA (VIA A BASED VARIABLE, CURRENT$CHAR)

              GLOBAL VARIABLES MODIFIED
              ------ --------- --------

              POINTER TO THE BUFFER AREA (VIA A BASED VARIABLE, BUFFER$PTR)

              DESCRIPTION
              -----------

                 LEADING BLANKS ARE IGNORED.  THE STRING SHOULD BE IN THE COMMON
              PL/M FORMAT FOR NUMERIC CONSTANTS, WHICH IS:
                                 <STRING> [<BASE INDICATOR>]
              IF THE <BASE INDICATOR> IS NOT PRESENT, BASE 10 (D) IS ASSUMED.
              THE VALID BASE INDICATORS ARE "D" FOR DECIMAL, "B" FOR BINARY,
              "O" OR "Q" FOR OCTAL, AND "H" FOR HEXADECIMAL.

                 NO ERROR CHECKING IS PERFORMED.  IF AN INVALID <BASE INDICATOR>
              IS ENCOUNTERED, DECIMAL (D) IS ASSUMED.  IF NO NUMERIC CONSTANT
              IS ENCOUNTERED, ZERO IS RETURNED.

                 THE POINTER POINTED TO BY THE PARAMETER IS UPDATED TO POINT TO
              THE CHARACTER IMMEDIATELY FOLLOWING <BASE INDICATOR>.

                 A NUMERIC CONSTANT GREATER THAN 65535D WILL RETURN AN
              UNPREDICTABLE RESULT.
           */
```

```
PL/M-80 COMPILER    FIG. 6.10                                                          PAGE    2

                $EJECT
  2    1        NUMIN:
                PROCEDURE(BUFFER$PTR$ADDRESS) ADDRESS;
  3    2           DECLARE (BUFFER$PTR$ADDRESS, CURRENT$CHAR$PTR, BASE2, BASE8, BASE10, BASE16) ADDRESS,
                           BUFFER$PTR BASED BUFFER$PTR$ADDRESS ADDRESS,
                           CURRENT$CHAR BASED CURRENT$CHAR$PTR BYTE,
                           (I, MORE$STRING) BYTE;
  4    2           DECLARE DIGITS (*) BYTE DATA ('0123456789ABCDEF');
  5    2           DECLARE TRUE  LITERALLY '0FFH',
                           FALSE LITERALLY '0';

  6    2           BASE2, BASE8, BASE10, BASE16 = 0;
  7    2           CURRENT$CHAR$PTR = BUFFER$PTR;
  8    2           DO WHILE CURRENT$CHAR = ' ';
  9    3              CURRENT$CHAR$PTR = CURRENT$CHAR$PTR + 1;
 10    3           END;
 11    2           MORE$STRING = TRUE;
 12    2           DO WHILE MORE$STRING;
 13    3              MORE$STRING = FALSE;
 14    3              DO I = 0 TO LAST(DIGITS);
 15    4                 IF CURRENT$CHAR = DIGITS(I) THEN
 16    4                 DO;
 17    5                    IF I < 2 THEN
 18    5                       BASE2 = BASE2 + BASE2 + I;
 19    5                    BASE8 = SHL(BASE8, 3) + I;
 20    5                    IF I < 10 THEN
 21    5                       BASE10 = BASE10 * 10 + I;
 22    5                    BASE16 = SHL(BASE16, 4) + I;
 23    5                    CURRENT$CHAR$PTR = CURRENT$CHAR$PTR + 1;
 24    5                    MORE$STRING = TRUE;
 25    5                 END;
 26    4              END;
 27    3           END;
 28    2           BUFFER$PTR = CURRENT$CHAR$PTR + 1;
 29    2           IF CURRENT$CHAR = 'H' THEN
 30    2              RETURN BASE16;
 31    2           IF CURRENT$CHAR = 'O' OR CURRENT$CHAR = 'Q' THEN
 32    2              RETURN BASE8;
 33    2           BUFFER$PTR = CURRENT$CHAR$PTR;
 34    2           CURRENT$CHAR$PTR = CURRENT$CHAR$PTR - 1;
 35    2           IF CURRENT$CHAR = 'B' THEN
 36    2              RETURN BASE2;
 37    2           RETURN BASE10;
 38    2        END NUMIN;


 39    1        END SIX$NUMIN;
```

Statements 17–22 do this conversion for the four number bases, taking into account special problems with binary and decimal. The problem is that B in a string can be either the hexadecimal digit for decimal 11 or the designator of a binary number. Since it cannot be both, we make the multiplication by 2 in converting to binary only if I is less than 2, meaning that we may actually have a binary digit. The multiplication is done by addition, which is faster than actual multiplication. In the case of octal, we multiply by 8 with a left shift of three positions. This does not have to be in an IF statement because the O or Q that marks an octal number is not one of the hexadecimal digits. If what we have later turns out to be a hexadecimal number, then we will be discarding the value of BASE8 anyway. For conversion to decimal we have a potential problem with the D that may be used to mark a decimal number. This time the multiplication is done by an explicit multiply. Finally, the multiplication by 16 for a potential hexadecimal number is done by a left shift of 4. In any event, we advance the character pointer and set MORE$STRING to true.

Eventually we will find a character other than a hexadecimal digit. If that character is H, O, or Q, then CURRENT$CHAR$PTR is pointing at the last character of the string and, therefore, is pointing at the character immediately to the right of the last digit of the number. If the string ended with B or D, then we do not get out of the loop until detecting the next character after that. In these cases CURRENT$-CHAR$PTR is therefore pointing at the character two positions to the right of the last digit. Finally, if the character that got us out of the loop was any other character, such as a blank or a comma but, in fact, *anything* else, then CURRENT$CHAR$-PTR is also pointing at the character immediately following the last digit of the number.

One of the requirements of the procedure is that after it is completed, BUFFER-$PTR should be pointing to the next character after the end of the string. In finishing the processing, we must take this requirement into account and also consider that in some cases CURRENT$CHAR$PTR is pointing at the last character of the string and in some cases at the character after the last character of the string.

Statements 28–37 take all this into account. Statement 28 sets BUFFER$PTR (the pointer outside the procedure, whose address was passed as BUFFERPTR-ADDRESS) to one more than the location of the last character of the string. It is thus correct if statement 30 or 32 causes an exit from the procedure. If we reach statement 33, then CURRENT$CHAR$PTR was already pointing at the last character after the end of the string and BUFFER$POINTER is set equal to this value. Now in order to find out whether the last character of the string was a B, for binary, we have to decrement CURRENT$CHAR$PTR. This lets us exit if what we had was a binary number. If the number was not hexadecimal, octal, or binary, it is assumed to have been decimal, whether or not followed by the letter D, and we return that value.

It is the necessity here at the very end to set the outside pointer whose address is the parameter of the procedure to one value and then look at some other character, that makes it necessary to set up the variable named BUFFER$PTR.

CASE STUDY: FIRST VERSION OF AN INDEXING PROGRAM

Our case study for this chapter and the next will be to develop a program to print the index for this book, which will let us put the topics studied in this chapter to good use. We shall also take advantage of this opportunity to demonstrate an approach to the process of program development.

The input to the program will be a file on diskette containing all of the index entries for the book. This file will have been prepared in advance from page proofs, using conventional paper-and-pencil techniques, and placed on disk using the ISIS text editor described briefly in Chapter 9. There will be a record in this file for each index entry. The basic task of the program is to print these lines in a format that satisfies the publisher's requirements as to the maximum number of characters in each line and the number of lines in each column. Whenever an entry is too long to fit on one line, the program must find an appropriate place to break the line and then continue on the next line with an indentation of four spaces. Furthermore, any line that begins with the greater-than sign (>) is thus signaled to be a subheading that is to be indented two spaces after deleting the "indent marker." Finally, the full-scale version of the program, shown in the next chapter, is required to handle some additional features having to do with hyphenation of long words and error checking, as well as an optional preliminary editing phase.

Figure 6.11 shows a sample input file to the program as far as we shall take it in this chapter, that is, not including the hyphenation considerations. (These are entries from another of the author's books; it is not possible, of course, to know at the time of writing this chapter what the page numbers will be for entries in *this* book.)

THE PROGRAM DEVELOPMENT PROCESS

We shall develop the program in three stages. The first will be a highly preliminary version that focuses on the top-level logic of the program and largely ignores the details of processing. In particular, it will take no account of the need to break long lines and will instead simply print each line as read. Once we have written and checked out this skeletal version of the program, satisfying ourselves that its high-level logic is correct, we can begin to elaborate the detailed processing that is required. The second version of the program, at the end of this chapter, will deal with the breaking of long lines. Once we have that version written and have satisfied ourselves that the added features correctly interact with the top-level logic worked out in the first version, then we shall be able to go on, in the next chapter, to add the final set of requirements having to do with hyphenation and error checking.

This case study thus illustrates the process of *top-down program development*. This is a strategy that concentrates on the top-level logic—which could also be described as the most abstract formulation of the program—and then works down through more and more detailed aspects of the complete task. This approach has a

```
Minor control, 158
Minus sign, in PICTURE, 102-105, 193
>in arithmetic expression, 348
Mnemonic name, 9, 122, 123
MOVE, 5, 32, 40, 82, 99, 195
MOVE CORRESPONDING, 203, 204, 215, 318
MULTIPLY, 32, 33, 38, 39, 42, 349

Name, data, 5, 9, 25, 82, 83, 255
>paragraph, 5, 16, 121, 147, 255, 298-300
Naming convention, 25, 83, 121, 299
Negative data, 40, 98, 103-105
Nested IF, 114, 158-169
NEXT SENTENCE, 64, 65, 165, 178, 206, 292, 295
New master, 231
NOMINAL KEY, 324, 327
Nonnumeric item, 29, 74, 77, 97, 107, 154
Nonnumeric literal, 5, 74
NOT, 68, 77, 158, 181, 206-208
NUMERIC, 77
Numeric bit, 193
Numeric item, 29, 74, 77, 97, 107
Numeric literal, 5, 74

Object, of relation, 67, 207
Object program, 98, 99, 149, 154, 190, 277, 289
OCCURS, 279, 280, 282, 284, 285, 290
Old master, 231
ON SIZE ERROR, 36-41, 43, 114, 121, 125, 215, 348, 351
One-level control total example, 144-157, 335-338
OPEN, 5, 15, 255, 259, 260, 312, 327
Operational sign, 98, 102-105, 194, 200
Operator precedence rule, 205, 349
Optional word, 34, 153
OR, 78, 204-208, 214
Order validation, 320-327
Overflow area, 315, 331
Out-of-line code, 110
Oval, in flowchart, 56

Packed decimal, 191, 193-195, 318
Page heading, 114, 124, 337
Page number, 114, 337
Paragraph, 5, 16, 21, 147, 156, 255, 355
Paragraph name, 5, 16, 121, 147, 255, 298-300
Parallelogram, in flowchart, 56
Parentheses, 206, 214, 350
Parity bit, 190, 259
Pay calculation example, 69-77, 79-84, 111-126
PERFORM, 64, 121, 164, 267, 272, 299
PERFORM UNTIL, 16-20, 59, 60, 109, 110, 112, 271, 355
PERFORM VARYING, 287-289
Period, 3, 4, 10, 15, 32, 62, 66, 67, 90, 110, 152, 156, 160
PICTURE, 4, 14, 25, 28-32, 74, 97-109, 120
Plus sign, in PICTURE, 104, 105
>in arithmetic expression, 267, 348
Positive data, 103-105
```

Fig. 6.11. Illustrative input text to the program to produce a book index.

number of advantages compared with trying to write the whole program at once (before checking any of it):

- It puts the most testing on the critical top-level logic of the program.
- It tends to localize errors, since whenever we begin testing the next version of the program, there is some hope that most of the errors will be in the new material.
- It facilitates projects in which several programmers work on separate sections of large programs. Once the top-level part is running, programmers working on lower-level sections can utilize the top-level section to check out their work. This not only supports the work of the programmers doing the detailed processing, but also gives further testing to the top-level sections.

THE SKELETON VERSION OF THE INDEXING PROGRAM

Figure 6.12 shows the output required of our first version of the program, given the input that was shown in Fig. 6.11. We see that all lines have been printed exactly as they were except that any line beginning with a greater-than symbol has been indented two spaces and has had that symbol removed. We see also that, where the input file had about 60 entries, only 51 have been printed by the program, 51 being a guess at what the publisher will require as the number of lines in each column. One of the requirements of the full-scale version of the program is that it be able to accept this parameter—called MAX$LINES in the programs—from the console, permitting the publisher to make last-minute decisions on the format of the index. In our first version we shall ignore such details and use 51 as a fixed number.

Figure 6.13 is an outline of the top-level logic of the program. It presents—in the simplest possible form, without any distracting details—what the program is to do. This kind of outline is often called *pseudocode,* to indicate that it is related to the code that we shall write but that it is not subject to the same syntax rules.

We see that the program is designed to print the specified number of lines and then stop. This reflects a decision to deal with only one column of the index at a time. After each column has been printed, the input file on diskette will be modified to remove the material already printed and the program will be run again. It would be possible to write a program that would print the entire index, but it turns out that there are a number of decisions that must be made as one goes along. For example, it is not acceptable to begin a column with the continuation of a line that was begun at the bottom of a previous column. When this occurs, either the main entry at the bottom of the previous column must be repeated, or some way must be found to modify the input to alter the length of the previous column. This is a cut-and-try process that it has not proved worthwhile (in past book projects) to try to automate.

The program in Fig. 6.14 is a direct elaboration of the pseudocode in Fig. 6.13. The procedure named SETUP gives a value to MAX$LINES and opens three files that will be used by the program. The operation of the ISIS routine named OPEN

```
Minor control, 158
Minus sign, in PICTURE, 102-105, 193
  in arithmetic expression, 348
Mnemonic name, 9, 122, 123
MOVE, 5, 32, 40, 82, 99, 195
MOVE CORRESPONDING, 203, 204, 215, 318
MULTIPLY, 32, 33, 38, 39, 42, 349

Name, data, 5, 9, 25, 82, 83, 255
  paragraph, 5, 16, 121, 147, 255, 298-300
Naming convention, 25, 83, 121, 299
Negative data, 40, 98, 103-105
Nested IF, 114, 158-169
NEXT SENTENCE, 64, 65, 165, 178, 206, 292, 295
New master, 231
NOMINAL KEY, 324, 327
Nonnumeric item, 29, 74, 77, 97, 107, 154
Nonnumeric literal, 5, 74
NOT, 68, 77, 158, 181, 206-208
NUMERIC, 77
Numeric bit, 193
Numeric item, 29, 74, 77, 97, 107
Numeric literal, 5, 74

Object, of relation, 67, 207
Object program, 98, 99, 149, 154, 190, 277, 289
OCCURS, 279, 280, 282, 284, 285, 290
Old master, 231
ON SIZE ERROR, 36-41, 43, 114, 121, 125, 215, 348, 351
One-level control total example, 144-157, 335-338
OPEN, 5, 15, 255, 259, 260, 312, 327
Operational sign, 98, 102-105, 194, 200
Operator precedence rule, 205, 349
Optional word, 34, 153
OR, 78, 204-208, 214
Order validation, 320-327
Overflow area, 315, 331
Out-of-line code, 110
Oval, in flowchart, 56

Packed decimal, 191, 193-195, 318
Page heading, 114, 124, 337
Page number, 114, 337
Paragraph, 5, 16, 21, 147, 156, 255, 355
Paragraph name, 5, 16, 121, 147, 255, 298-300
Parallelogram, in flowchart, 56
Parentheses, 206, 214, 350
Parity bit, 190, 259
Pay calculation example, 69-77, 79-84, 111-126
PERFORM, 64, 121, 164, 267, 272, 299
PERFORM UNTIL, 16-20, 59, 60, 109, 110, 112, 271, 355
```

Fig. 6.12. Output of the first version of a program to produce a book index. This version does not break long lines.

```
Initialize

Line counter = 0

DO WHILE line counter < max lines

    Print a line, increment line counter

END

Wrapup
```

Fig. 6.13. Pseudocode of the basic program structure of a program to print a properly spaced index for this book.

```
PL/M-80 COMPILER    FIG. 6.14                                                         PAGE   1


            /* PRELIMINARY VERSION OF A PROGRAM TO PRINT A PROPERLY-SPACED INDEX FOR THIS BOOK */

            /*****************************************************************************
            * THE PROGRAM ACCEPTS, FROM DISK, RECORDS THAT WERE PREPARED USING THE TEXT    *
            * EDITOR.  EACH RECORD REPRESENTS ONE COMPLETE ENTRY IN AN INDEX, WITH ONE     *
            * EDITING CONTROL OPTIONALLY PRESENT: ANY LINE THAT BEGINS WITH > IS TO BE     *
            * INDENTED TWO SPACES.                                                         *
            *                                                                              *
            * THIS VERSION OF THE PROGRAM PRINTS EACH LINE JUST AS IT READS IT, NO MATTER  *
            * HOW LONG IT IS, AND PRINTS 51 LINES PER COLUMN.                              *
            *                                                                              *
            * THERE IS NO ERROR CHECKING.                                                  *
            *                                                                              *
            *****************************************************************************/

  1         SIMPLEST$INDEX:
            DO;
  2    1       DECLARE TEXT(128) BYTE;
  3    1       DECLARE (MAX$LINES, MAX$CHARS, LINE$CTR) BYTE;
  4    1       DECLARE (DISK$AFTN, ECHO$AFTN, TO$AFTN) ADDRESS; /* AFTN = ACTIVE FILE TABLE NUMBER */

            $INCLUDE(:F1:INOUT.SRC)
         =  $NOLIST


 25    1    SETUP:
            PROCEDURE;
 26    2       DECLARE STATUS ADDRESS;

 27    2       MAX$LINES = 51;   /* WILL BE READ FROM CONSOLE IN LATER VERSIONS */

 28    2       CALL OPEN(.ECHO$AFTN, .(':F1:SCRTCH '), 2, 0, .STATUS);
 29    2       CALL OPEN(.DISK$AFTN, .(':F1:INDEXS.TXT '), 1, ECHO$AFTN, .STATUS);
 30    2       CALL OPEN(.TO$AFTN, .(':TO: '), 2, 0, .STATUS);

 31    2    END SETUP;
```

```
PL/M-80 COMPILER    FIG. 6.14                                          PAGE   2


                 $EJECT
32    1          PRINT$LINES$FROM$TEXT$RECORD:
                 PROCEDURE;
33    2             DECLARE (BP, EP) ADDRESS;  /* BEGINNING AND ENDING TEXT POINTERS */
34    2             DECLARE CHAR BASED BP BYTE;
35    2             DECLARE LEADING$BLANKS BYTE;
36    2             DECLARE (COUNT, STATUS) ADDRESS;
37    2             DECLARE BLANK LITERALLY ''' ''', INDENT LITERALLY '''>''';

38    2             CALL READ(DISK$AFTN, .TEXT, 128, .COUNT, .STATUS);
39    2             BP = .TEXT;
40    2             IF CHAR = INDENT THEN
41    2             DO;
42    3                LEADING$BLANKS = 2;
43    3                BP = BP + 1;
44    3             END;
                    ELSE
45    2                LEADING$BLANKS = 0;

46    2             EP = .TEXT(COUNT - 1);

47    2             CALL WRITE(TO$AFTN, .('    '), LEADING$BLANKS, .STATUS);
48    2             CALL WRITE(TO$AFTN, BP, EP - BP + 1, .STATUS);
49    2             LINE$CTR = LINE$CTR + 1;

50    2          END PRINT$LINES$FROM$TEXT$RECORD;
                 $EJECT
51    1          WRAPUP:
                 PROCEDURE;
52    2             DECLARE STATUS ADDRESS;

53    2             CALL CLOSE(ECHO$AFTN, .STATUS);
54    2             CALL CLOSE(DISK$AFTN, .STATUS);
55    2             CALL CLOSE(TO$AFTN, .STATUS);

56    2          END WRAPUP;


                 /*****************************************************************
                  *                                                               *
                  *                         MAIN PROGRAM                          *
                  *                                                               *
                  *****************************************************************/


57    1             CALL SETUP;

58    1             LINE$CTR = 0;
59    1             DO WHILE LINE$CTR < MAX$LINES;
60    2                CALL PRINT$LINES$FROM$TEXT$RECORD;
61    2             END;

62    1             CALL WRAPUP;

63    1             CALL EXIT;

64    1          END SIMPLEST$INDEX;
```

is discussed briefly in Chapter 9 and more fully in appropriate manuals. For now we simply say that the OPEN operation must be carried out before we can read or write any file with the exception of the console—which (by no accident) is the only file we have used up to this point.

The procedure named PRINT$LINES$FROM$TEXT$RECORD does what its name implies. It begins by reading an input line from the diskette; the fact that the diskette is the source of the file is communicated by the action of the OPEN in giving a value to the parameter DISK$AFTN. After the READ, the array named TEXT contains a line from the input file of index entries and COUNT gives the total number of bytes in the line, including the line feed and the carriage return.

In the later version of this program we shall be doing considerable processing of the characters in the array named TEXT, making it very convenient to work with pointers to based variables. CHAR was accordingly declared as based variable (line 34) with the base being an address variable named BP (for beginning pointer).

The first thing we do after the READ is to set this pointer to the first character of the array named TEXT. Now we can ask whether this character is the greater-than symbol marking a line that must be indented. If it is, we give the variable named LEADING$BLANKS a value of 2 and add 1 to BP so that it is pointing at the first character of TEXT, not at the greater-than symbol. In the normal case where the first character is not a greater-than symbol, we set LEADING$BLANKS to zero. Now (line 46) we set a variable named EP (for ending pointer) so that it points at the last character of the text, which will be the line feed. We subtract 1 from COUNT to take into consideration that arrays are numbered from zero, not one.

Now we write either zero or two leading blanks and then the output line before adding 1 to the line counter.

The WRAPUP procedure has only to close the files, which is an operation we can postpone considering until Chapter 9.

The main program is an almost literal restatement of the pseudocode.

THE SECOND VERSION OF THE INDEXING PROGRAM

With a rudimentary version of the program running, we now attack the central activity at the next level of detail, which is finding a place to break input records that are too long to fit on one line. This is a moderately complex operation that can best be worked out with its own pseudocode, as shown in Fig. 6.15. As before, we get an input line and set up to handle indents. Then we go into a DO–WHILE that will print as many lines as necessary, each no longer than the parameter MAX$CHARS that will be read from the console. If the entire input line fits to begin with, the operation is quite simple. Otherwise we must "back up" until we find a blank at which the line can be broken. If there is no blank, then we wish to return to the calling program with an error indication. This will be done by returning a value of 1 in such a case, whereas zero will be returned in the normal case. (The procedure must, of course, be typed to make this possible.) If we are able to break the line,

```
PRINT$LINES$FROM$TEXT$RECORD

    Get a text record
    Set up to handle indents
    DO WHILE not finished with line
       IF rest of line fits in available space THEN
          Print it
       ELSE
          Find a blank, print as much as possible, and
          set up to continue on next line.  If no space
          at which to break, RETURN 1.
       Write carriage return and line feed
       Add 1 to line counter
    END
    RETURN 0

END
```

Fig. 6.15. Pseudocode of a method for printing a line of index, including finding places to break long lines.

we print as much as possible and then set up for the printing of the next line. Regardless of whether a continuation will be required, we now write a carriage return and a line feed and add 1 to the line counter.

This pseudocode is intermediate in detail between the quite abstract pseudocode of the main program that was shown in Fig. 6.13 and the actual details of the program itself. This is the way it ought to be if the pseudocode is really needed at all—that is, if we are not able to write the program directly. Putting it another way, we need a pseudocode in those situations where the logic of a module is too complex to permit us to concentrate on that logic at the same time as we try to write the details of the code correctly.

The second version of the program is shown in Fig. 6.16. The first change from the earlier version is seen in the procedure named SETUP, where we now read from the console two numbers, separated by a blank, giving the maximum number of lines per column and the maximum number of characters per line. If values for these parameters are not entered, they are defaulted to 51 and 25, reasonable guesses as to what might be needed.

The first change we see in PRINT$LINES$FROM$TEXT$RECORD is in line 58. We see that 3 has been subtracted from COUNT, not 1, so that the ending pointer points at the last character of TEXT, not at the line feed. Since we will be printing long input lines on more than one output line, we shall have to arrange for the carriage return and line feed separately.

A long DO–WHILE prints lines so long as the beginning pointer is less than the ending pointer. A simple test (line 60) establishes whether the line—or what is left of it if we have already been around the loop before—can be printed in the

```
PL/M-80 COMPILER    FIG. 6.16                                                    PAGE   1

          /* A PROGRAM TO PRINT A PROPERLY-SPACED INDEX FOR THIS BOOK */

          /*****************************************************************************
          *                                                                             *
          * THE PROGRAM ACCEPTS, FROM DISK, RECORDS THAT WERE PREPARED USING THE TEXT   *
          * EDITOR.  EACH RECORD REPRESENTS ONE COMPLETE ENTRY IN AN INDEX, WITH ONE    *
          * EDITING CONTROL OPTIONALLY PRESENT: ANY LINE THAT BEGINS WITH > IS TO BE    *
          * INDENTED TWO SPACES.                                                        *
          *                                                                             *
          * THE PROGRAM ACCEPTS TWO PARAMETERS FROM THE CONSOLE:                        *
          *  1. MAX$LINES: THE MAXIMUM NUMBER OF LINES PER COLUMN--DEFAULT 51           *
          *  2. MAX$CHARS: THE MAXIMUM NUMBER OF CHARACTERS PER LINE--DEFAULT 25        *
          *                                                                             *
          * AN ERROR IS REPORTED IF A BREAK IS REQUIRED IN A LINE THAT DOES NOT         *
          * HAVE A SPACE WHERE NEEDED.                                                  *
          * WHEN A LINE MUST BE CONTINUED ON A FOLLOWING LINE, THE CONTINUATION IS      *
          * INDENTED FOUR SPACES.  A BLANK LINE OF INPUT PRODUCES A BLANK LINE OF       *
          * OUTPUT; THIS IS USED TO PLACE A BLANK LINE BETWEEN LETTER-GROUPS.           *
          *                                                                             *
          *****************************************************************************/

          INDEX:
          DO;
             DECLARE TEXT(128) BYTE;
             DECLARE (MAX$LINES, MAX$CHARS, LINE$CTR, COMPLETION$CODE) BYTE;
             DECLARE (DISK$AFTN, ECHO$AFTN, TO$AFTN) ADDRESS;
                          /* AFTN = ACTIVE FILE TABLE NUMBER */

          $INCLUDE(:F1:INOUT.SRC)
     =    $NOLIST
          $EJECT
          SETUP:
          PROCEDURE;
             DECLARE TEMPORARY BYTE;
             DECLARE BUFFER(30) BYTE;
             DECLARE BUFFPTR ADDRESS;
             DECLARE (COUNT, STATUS) ADDRESS;

             /* GET MAX LINES AND MAX CHARS PER LINE (FROM CONSOLE), UNLESS DEFAULTED */
             CALL READ(1, .BUFFER, 128, .COUNT, .STATUS);
             BUFFPTR = .BUFFER;
             TEMPORARY = NUMIN(.BUFFPTR);
             IF TEMPORARY = 0 THEN
                MAX$LINES = 51;
             ELSE
                MAX$LINES = TEMPORARY;
             TEMPORARY = NUMIN(.BUFFPTR);
             IF TEMPORARY = 0 THEN
                MAX$CHARS = 25;
             ELSE
                MAX$CHARS = TEMPORARY;

             CALL OPEN(.ECHO$AFTN, .(':F1:SCRTCH '), 2, 0, .STATUS);
             CALL OPEN(.DISK$AFTN, .(':F1:INDEX.TXT '), 1, ECHO$AFTN, .STATUS);
             CALL OPEN(.TO$AFTN, .(':TO: '), 2, 0, .STATUS);

          END SETUP;
```

```
PL/M-80 COMPILER    FIG. 6.16                                     PAGE   2


               $EJECT
 44   1        PRINT$LINES$FROM$TEXT$RECORD:
               PROCEDURE BYTE;
 45   2           DECLARE (BP, EP) ADDRESS;  /* BEGINNING AND ENDING TEXT POINTERS */
 46   2           DECLARE (CHAR BASED BP, CHAR$CHECK BASED EP) BYTE;
 47   2           DECLARE LEADING$BLANKS BYTE;
 48   2           DECLARE (COUNT, STATUS) ADDRESS;
 49   2           DECLARE BLANK LITERALLY ''' ''', INDENT LITERALLY '''>''';

 50   2           CALL READ(DISK$AFTN, .TEXT, 128, .COUNT, .STATUS);
 51   2           BP = .TEXT;
 52   2           IF CHAR = INDENT THEN
 53   2           DO;
 54   3              LEADING$BLANKS = 2;
 55   3              BP = BP + 1;
 56   3           END;
                 ELSE
 57   2              LEADING$BLANKS = 0;

 58   2           EP = .TEXT(COUNT - 3);

 59   2           DO WHILE BP < EP;
 60   3              IF LEADING$BLANKS + (EP - BP) < MAX$CHARS THEN
 61   3              DO;
 62   4                 CALL WRITE(TO$AFTN, .('    '), LEADING$BLANKS, .STATUS);
 63   4                 CALL WRITE(TO$AFTN, BP, EP - BP + 1, .STATUS);
 64   4                 BP = EP;   /* TO STOP DO WHILE */
 65   4              END;
                    ELSE
 66   3              DO;
 67   4                 EP = BP + MAX$CHARS - LEADING$BLANKS;
 68   4                 DO WHILE CHAR$CHECK <> BLANK AND EP > BP;
 69   5                    EP = EP - 1;
 70   5                 END;
 71   4                 IF EP = BP THEN
 72   4                    RETURN 1;   /* THERE WAS NO BLANK AT WHICH TO BREAK LINE */
 73   4                 CALL WRITE(TO$AFTN, .('    '), LEADING$BLANKS, .STATUS);
 74   4                 CALL WRITE(TO$AFTN, BP, EP - BP, .STATUS);
 75   4                 LEADING$BLANKS = 4;  /* PREPARE TO INDENT SUBSEQUENT LINES */
 76   4                 BP = EP + 1;
 77   4                 EP = .TEXT(COUNT - 3);
 78   4              END;

 79   3              CALL WRITE(TO$AFTN, .(0DH, 0AH), 2, .STATUS);   /* CRLF */
 80   3              LINE$CTR = LINE$CTR + 1;

 81   3           END;

 82   2           RETURN 0;   /* NORMAL PROCESSING COMPLETED */

 83   2        END PRINT$LINES$FROM$TEXT$RECORD;
```

```
PL/M-80 COMPILER    FIG. 6.16                                                    PAGE   3

                $EJECT
 84    1        WRAPUP:
                PROCEDURE;
 85    2           DECLARE STATUS ADDRESS;
 86    2           DECLARE BUFFER(30) BYTE;

 87    2           IF COMPLETION$CODE = 1 THEN
 88    2              CALL WRITE(0, .('NO BLANK AT WHICH TO BREAK LINE'), 31, .STATUS);
                   ELSE
 89    2           DO;
 90    3              CALL NUMOUT(LINE$CTR, 10, ' ', .BUFFER, 3);
 91    3              CALL WRITE(0, .BUFFER, 3, .STATUS);
 92    3              CALL WRITE(0, .('  LINES IN THIS COLUMN'), 22, .STATUS);
 93    3           END;
 94    2           CALL WRITE(0, .(0DH, 0AH), 2, .STATUS);  /* CRLF */
 95    2           CALL CLOSE(ECHO$AFTN, .STATUS);
 96    2           CALL CLOSE(DISK$AFTN, .STATUS);
 97    2           CALL CLOSE(TO$AFTN, .STATUS);

 98    2        END WRAPUP;


                /***************************************************************
                 *                                                             *
                 *                        MAIN PROGRAM                         *
                 *                                                             *
                 ***************************************************************/


 99    1           CALL SETUP;

100    1           LINE$CTR, COMPLETION$CODE = 0;
101    1           DO WHILE LINE$CTR < MAX$LINES AND COMPLETION$CODE = 0;
102    2              COMPLETION$CODE = PRINT$LINES$FROM$TEXT$RECORD;  /* A PROCEDURE CALL */
103    2           END;

104    1           CALL WRAPUP;

105    1           CALL EXIT;

106    1        END INDEX;
```

available number of characters. If so, we print the required number of blanks and the characters from the beginning pointer to the ending pointer, and set the beginning pointer to be equal to the ending pointer to terminate repetition of the DO–WHILE.

If the line will not fit, we must search for a blank at which to break the line. The search should begin with the character after the last one that can be printed in the available space; this is given by the formula shown in line 67. Then, using EP as the base for a new based variable named CHAR$CHECK, we back up, looking for a blank. The DO–BLANK that controls the backing up must not only ask whether the current character is a blank but also test that the ending pointer is still greater than the beginning pointer. If the two pointers ever become equal, it means we have searched through all of the characters to be printed without finding a blank; i.e., the line cannot be broken. This possibility is tested for and if it is found, then in line 72 we RETURN a value of 1 and get out of the procedure. If this has not happened, we again write the specified number of blanks and write all the characters from the one pointed at by BP up to but not including the one pointed at by EP, which is a blank.

Now we must set leading blanks to 4 so that the continuation in the next line will be indented four spaces from the margin. BP must be set so that it points at the character after the blank where we broke, and EP must be reset to the last character of the text. The rest of this procedure is as shown in the pseudocode.

The procedure named WRAPUP has been modified so that it writes (at the console) either a comment that a line could not be broken or the number of lines in the column. We shall see, in examining the main program logic, that the number of lines in a column can actually be greater than MAX$LINES, by deliberate design. The design consideration is that, in running the indexing program, if continuation lines in the last entry cause a column to have more lines than specified by MAX$-LINES, some cut-and-try operations will be required, and we wish all the continuation lines to be written. If this is a lefthand column, we may let it run one line longer and make the righthand column an extra line long also. Or perhaps we will choose to modify one of the earlier entries so that it takes an extra line, thus pushing the last entry to the top of the next column. A variety of strategems is available, all of which require us to know how many lines the program produced in order to rework the column.

The main program is modified from that of the preliminary version of the program in that PRINT$LINES$FROM$TEXT$RECORD, which, as noted before, is a typed procedure, gives a value to the variable named COMPLETION$CODE that is tested in WRAPUP. We now see how it is that the number of lines can exceed MAX$-LINES: LINE$CTR is tested only after returning from the procedure. An input line requiring several output lines could push LINE$CTR past MAX$LINES within the procedure, before reaching the DO–WHILE test again.

Figure 6.17 shows a number of columns of output from this program, using the same input shown in Fig. 6.11. For each column, the values for MAX$CHARS that were entered from the console have been written in by hand.

Defaults:
51 lines
25 chars

```
Minor control, 158
Minus sign, in PICTURE,
    102-105, 193
  in arithmetic
    expression, 348
Mnemonic name, 9, 122,
    123
MOVE, 5, 32, 40, 82, 99,
    195
MOVE CORRESPONDING, 203,
    204, 215, 318
MULTIPLY, 32, 33, 38, 39,
    42, 349

Name, data, 5, 9, 25, 82,
    83, 255
  paragraph, 5, 16, 121,
    147, 255, 298-300
Naming convention, 25,
    83, 121, 299
Negative data, 40, 98,
    103-105
Nested IF, 114, 158-169
NEXT SENTENCE, 64, 65,
    165, 178, 206, 292,
    295
New master, 231
NOMINAL KEY, 324, 327
Nonnumeric item, 29, 74,
    77, 97, 107, 154
Nonnumeric literal, 5, 74
NOT, 68, 77, 158, 181,
    206-208
NUMERIC, 77
Numeric bit, 193
Numeric item, 29, 74, 77,
    97, 107
Numeric literal, 5, 74

Object, of relation, 67,
    207
Object program, 98, 99,
    149, 154, 190, 277,
    289
OCCURS, 279, 280, 282,
    284, 285, 290
Old master, 231
ON SIZE ERROR, 36-41, 43,
    114, 121, 125, 215,
    348, 351
One-level control total
    example, 144-157,
    335-338
```

"53 lines in this column"

30 lines
20 chars

```
Minor control, 158
Minus sign, in
    PICTURE,
    102-105, 193
  in arithmetic
    expression, 348
Mnemonic name, 9,
    122, 123
MOVE, 5, 32, 40, 82,
    99, 195
MOVE CORRESPONDING,
    203, 204, 215,
    318
MULTIPLY, 32, 33,
    38, 39, 42, 349

Name, data, 5, 9,
    25, 82, 83, 255
  paragraph, 5, 16,
    121, 147, 255,
    298-300
Naming convention,
    25, 83, 121, 299
Negative data, 40,
    98, 103-105
Nested IF, 114,
    158-169
NEXT SENTENCE, 64,
    65, 165, 178,
    206, 292, 295
```

"30 lines in this column"

20 lines
15 chars

```
Minor control,
    158
Minus sign, in
    PICTURE,
    102-105,
    193
  in arithmetic
    expression,
    348
Mnemonic name,
    9, 122, 123
MOVE, 5, 32,
    40, 82, 99,
    195
MOVE
```

"no blank at which to break line"

35 lines
35 chars

```
Minor control, 158
Minus sign, in PICTURE, 102-105,
    193
  in arithmetic expression, 348
Mnemonic name, 9, 122, 123
MOVE, 5, 32, 40, 82, 99, 195
MOVE CORRESPONDING, 203, 204, 215,
    318
MULTIPLY, 32, 33, 38, 39, 42, 349

Name, data, 5, 9, 25, 82, 83, 255
  paragraph, 5, 16, 121, 147, 255,
    298-300
Naming convention, 25, 83, 121, 299
Negative data, 40, 98, 103-105
Nested IF, 114, 158-169
NEXT SENTENCE, 64, 65, 165, 178,
    206, 292, 295
New master, 231
NOMINAL KEY, 324, 327
Nonnumeric item, 29, 74, 77, 97,
    107, 154
Nonnumeric literal, 5, 74
NOT, 68, 77, 158, 181, 206-208
NUMERIC, 77
Numeric bit, 193
Numeric item, 29, 74, 77, 97, 107
Numeric literal, 5, 74

Object, of relation, 67, 207
Object program, 98, 99, 149, 154,
    190, 277, 289
OCCURS, 279, 280, 282, 284, 285,
    290
Old master, 231
```

"35 lines in this column"

Fig. 6.17. The output of the indexing program shown in Fig. 6.16. The same input text was used in each case, but the values of MAX$LINES and MAX$CHARS were varied, as shown above each column. Written in at the bottom of each column is the console message produced.

A COMMENT ON PROGRAM DEVELOPMENT

We would not wish to leave the reader with the impression that top-down development and pseudocode solve all the problems of program development. It still takes skill and experience to know how best to break a program into procedures; one level of program development must often be partially redone when the details of the next lower level are better understood; coding errors still happen; communication between programmers working on the same project is still a major concern. All of this is true even given program specifications that are stable; in real life the specifications usually change to some degree along the way.

Nevertheless, the experience of many programmers in a wide variety of projects has shown that the severity of the various problems noted above is diminished when top-down development is followed. We recommend the practice.

EXERCISES

*1. Find any errors in the following sets of declarations. (The four parts are independent.)

a)
```
DECLARE POINTER BYTE;
DECLARE CHARACTER BASED POINTER BYTE;
```

b)
```
DECLARE A ADDRESS;
DECLARE B(20) BASED A;
```

c)
```
DECLARE RST ADDRESS;
DECLARE (ABC, XYZ) BASED RST BYTE;
```

d)
```
DECLARE ATLANTA ADDRESS;
DECLARE SALESMAN BASED ATLANTA;
```

*2. In the program of Fig. 6.2:

a) What is the difference between ARRAY(0) and .ARRAY(0)?

b) What would this statement do?

```
MEAN$3 = MEAN$OF$ARRAY$VALUES(.SECOND$ARRAY);
```

c) What is the difference between .ARRAY(0) and .ARRAY?

d) What would this statement do?

```
MEAN$4 = MEAN$OF$ARRAY$VALUES(.FIRST$ARRAY(9));
```

3. Modify the program of Fig. 6.3 so that the procedure MEANOFARRAY$-VALUES$2 returns a value of zero, without attempting any other processing, if the value of N is zero.

***4.** How would the operation of the program of Fig. 6.3 be affected if the declaration in statement 31 were changed to the following?

```
DECLARE (ARRAY BASED ARRAY$POINTER) (10000) ADDRESS;
```

***5.** A student suggests changing the program of Fig. 6.3 so that the declaration in statement 32 reads

```
DECLARE I ADDRESS, TEMP ADDRESS INITIAL(0);
```

and then removing the initialization of TEMP in statement 33. Would the modified program work?

6. Modify the program of Fig. 6.4 to remove the requirement that there be a blank at the end of the string of text.

7. Modify the program of Fig. 6.4 so that it regards commas and periods, as well as blanks, as word separators. Also, modify the main program so that it inspects for successive separators in a string, such as two blanks or a comma followed by a blank, and prints only the words of the string.

8. Write the main program statements to make the program of Fig. 6.4 replace all blanks in the string by slashes.

9. Revise the state transition table of Fig. 6.5 and the program of Fig. 6.6 so that a comment is any string enclosed between revised brackets */ and /*.

10. Suppose that STRING is a string of characters, and that COUNT is an ADDRESS variable giving the number of bytes in STRING, including two bytes at the end of STRING containing a carriage return and a line feed. Write a program that moves all the characters of STRING, not including the carriage return and the line feed and not including any dollar signs, to another string named CONDENSED$STRING. The space occupied by any dollar signs is to be "closed up," as though the dollar signs had not been there.

11. Modify the program of Fig. 6.7 so that the location of the mean is also a parameter; the modified procedure should be untyped.

***12.** In the main program of Fig. 6.7, what would this statement do, assuming appropriate declarations for the variables?

```
MEAN$3 = MEAN$AND$MEDIAN(THIRD$ARRAY, MEDIAN$3, .NUMBER);
```

13. Modify NUMOUT so that it places B, Q, D, H, or X after the converted number, to indicate that the new base is binary, octal, decimal, hexadecimal, or none of these, respectively.

14. Modify the program of Fig. 6.14 so that it deletes blanks at the beginning of the line. This will require only a simple loop after the READ, with no modification of what follows.

15. Modify the program of Fig. 6.16 so that if the first character of the input is the indent marker, any continuation lines for that string are indented six spaces from the margin rather than four.

16. Modify the program of Fig. 6.16 so that it can handle two levels of subordination, as follows:
    - If the input does not begin with an indent marker, print that line starting at the left margin and indent continuations four spaces.
    - If the input line begins with one indent marker, begin that line two spaces from the left margin and indent continuations six spaces.
    - If the input line begins with two indent markers, begin that line four spaces from the left margin and indent continuations eight spaces.

17. Modify the program of Fig. 4.12 so that reserved words are in an array (not a structure), with no blanks between words, and so that there is an auxiliary BYTE array containing in element *i* the number of letters in reserved word *i*.

18. Write a program to produce justified printing from a string named TEXT. You might approach the development in the following steps:
    a) The program prints lines of no more than 48 characters on a line and no more than 54 lines on a page, with no user options. The right margin is "ragged," i.e., not justified, which means that as many complete words are printed on each line as possible, with no attempt to place the last letter on each line in a specified position.
    b) The program asks the user for MAX$CHARS and MAX$LINES, and somehow handles text strings that do not fill a line or a page.
    c) The program determines the maximum possible words on a line, then inserts as many blanks between words in the line as necessary to place the last letter of the line in the position specified by the user with the parameter MAX$-CHARS.
    d) The program asks for the *running head* that is to be printed at the top center of each page, and the starting page number; it prints the running head and consecutive page numbers.

CHAPTER 7

BLOCK STRUCTURE

INTRODUCTION

A PL/M program is composed of blocks. A DO block consists of the words DO and END and whatever is enclosed between them; a PROCEDURE block consists of the words PROCEDURE and END and everything enclosed between them. Blocks may be nested in any way: DO blocks may contain other DO blocks; DO blocks may contain PROCEDURE blocks and vice versa; and procedures may contain other procedures.

There are a number of motivations for providing a language with consistent block structuring.

- Program organization is facilitated, since proper usage of blocks clearly displays the relationship of the parts of a program.
- The design of the compiler is greatly facilitated.
- The *scope* of variables—that is, the part of a program in which they are known—is precisely defined. This offers advantages in that the scope of variables can be localized to the smallest part of the program where they need to be known. It is sometimes said that variables should be "hidden" in the smallest block where they are needed, to avoid unwanted interactions between blocks.

The primary goal of the effective use of block structuring, as with most other aspects of programming, is to write programs that are very easy for *people* (including the original programmer) to understand. Doing so improves the probability that the program will be correct when first written, simplifies program checkout, makes it much easier for several programmers to work on a large project, and materially reduces the problems in changing a program in response to new specifications, new equipment, or the detection of old program errors.

We have already used block structuring heavily for organization of program control, so that an entire group of statements can be treated as a unit for control purposes. We have also already had an introduction to the question of scope of variables in connection with procedures, where we spoke about local and global variables. The purpose of this chapter is to formalize the definitions of these matters, introduce some related new topics, and then see the entire subject area worked out in a case study, which will be a further elaboration of the program to produce an index, which we considered in the previous chapter.

INCLUSIVE AND EXCLUSIVE EXTENTS

Discussions of scope of variables and other objects will be facilitated by the following two definitions:

> The *inclusive extent* of a block is everything from the DO or PROCEDURE statement that begins the block to the END statement that terminates it. The DO or PROCEDURE statement and the END statement *are* considered to be part of the inclusive extent of a block. Any label on a DO statement, or the procedure name in a PROCEDURE statement, is *not* part of the inclusive extent.
>
> The *exclusive extent* of a block is the inclusive extent of that block *minus* the inclusive extents of all blocks, if any, nested within it.

In a nutshell, the inclusive extent includes nested blocks and the exclusive extent excludes them. Alternative terminology for the exclusive extent of a block is the *outer level* of the block.

For an example of the meanings of these terms, consider the program of Fig. 7.1, which is a slight revision of the program of Fig. 6.7 to find the mean and median of the values in an array. The modification is that the sorting operation has been made into a DO block with its own label and with its own declarations. Let us examine the block structure of this program.

The entire program is, of course, a block. Since the program is not nested within any other block, it is a module. Since it has executable statements at the module level, that is, since statements 63–75 are not nested within any block except the DO in statement 1 and the END in statement 76, this is a main-program module. The program contains a PROCEDURE block having its own declarations. Within the procedure there is a small block (statements 36–39) used for control purposes. Then the block with the label SORT in statements 40–59 has its own declarations; within it are three DO blocks used for control. Finally, the main program at the module level contains an iterative DO for control.

```
PL/M-80 COMPILER    FIG. 7.1                                    PAGE   1


              /* MEAN AND MEDIAN OF ARRAYS, WITH EXERCISER */
 1            SIX$MEAN$AND$MEDIAN$1:
              DO;
 2   1          DECLARE FIRST$ARRAY(10) ADDRESS DATA (1,6,2,9,2,8,0,7,4,1);
 3   1          DECLARE SECOND$ARRAY(*) ADDRESS DATA(9,0,45,12,1,1,21,12,34,45,8,78,0,1,99);
 4   1          DECLARE BUFFER(128) BYTE;
 5   1          DECLARE STATUS ADDRESS;
 6   1          DECLARE CRLF(2) BYTE DATA(0DH, 0AH);
 7   1          DECLARE I BYTE;
 8   1          DECLARE (MEAN$1, MEAN$2, MEDIAN$1, MEDIAN$2) ADDRESS;

              $INCLUDE(:F1:INOUT.SRC)
         =    $NOLIST

              /* A PROCEDURE TO GET MEAN AND MEDIAN OF THE VALUES OF AN ARRAY */
29   1        MEAN$AND$MEDIAN:
              PROCEDURE (ARRAY$POINTER, MEDIAN$POINTER, N) ADDRESS;
30   2          DECLARE (ARRAY$POINTER, MEDIAN$POINTER, N) ADDRESS;
31   2          DECLARE (ARRAY BASED ARRAY$POINTER) (1) ADDRESS;
32   2          DECLARE MEDIAN BASED MEDIAN$POINTER ADDRESS;
33   2          DECLARE (I, SUM) ADDRESS;
34   2          DECLARE PROC$ARRAY(200) ADDRESS;

                /* MOVE ARRAY VALUES TO TEMPORARY ARRAY; COMPUTE MEAN */
35   2          SUM = 0;
36   2          DO I = 0 TO N - 1;
37   3             PROC$ARRAY(I) = ARRAY(I);
38   3             SUM = SUM + ARRAY(I);
39   3          END;

                /* SORT TEMPORARY ARRAY, TO GET MEDIAN; BUBBLE SORTING IS USED,
                WITH A PASS COUNTER TO PREVENT EXAMINING ITEMS AT END OF LIST THAT
                ARE ALREADY IN FINAL POSITION    */

40   2        SORT:
                DO;
41   3             DECLARE TEMP ADDRESS;
42   3             DECLARE (EXCHANGE, PASS) BYTE;
43   3             DECLARE TRUE LITERALLY '0FFH', FALSE LITERALLY '0';

44   3             EXCHANGE = TRUE;
45   3             DO WHILE EXCHANGE;
46   4                PASS = 0;
47   4                EXCHANGE = FALSE;
48   4                DO I = 0 TO N - 2 - PASS;
49   5                   IF PROC$ARRAY(I) > PROC$ARRAY(I + 1) THEN
50   5                   DO;
51   6                      TEMP = PROC$ARRAY(I);
52   6                      PROC$ARRAY(I) = PROC$ARRAY(I + 1);
53   6                      PROC$ARRAY(I + 1) = TEMP;
54   6                      EXCHANGE = TRUE;
55   6                   END;
56   5                END;
57   4                PASS = PASS + 1;
58   4             END;
59   3          END;
60   2          MEDIAN = PROC$ARRAY(N / 2);
61   2          RETURN SUM / N;
62   2        END MEAN$AND$MEDIAN;
```

```
PL/M-80 COMPILER    FIG. 7.1                                        PAGE    2

                 $EJECT
                 /* A MAIN PROGRAM TO EXERCISE THE PROCEDURE */

63    1            MEAN$1 = MEAN$AND$MEDIAN(.FIRST$ARRAY, .MEDIAN$1, 10);
64    1            CALL NUMOUT(MEAN$1, 10, ' ', .BUFFER, 4);
65    1            CALL NUMOUT(MEDIAN$1, 10, ' ', .BUFFER(4), 4);
66    1            CALL WRITE(0, .BUFFER, 8, .STATUS);
67    1            CALL WRITE (0, .CRLF, 2, .STATUS);
68    1            DO I = 0 TO 7;
69    2               MEAN$2 = MEAN$AND$MEDIAN(.SECOND$ARRAY(I), .MEDIAN$2, 8);
70    2               CALL NUMOUT(MEAN$2, 10, ' ', .BUFFER, 4);
71    2               CALL NUMOUT(MEDIAN$2, 10, ' ', .BUFFER(4), 4);
72    2               CALL WRITE(0, .BUFFER, 8, .STATUS);
73    2               CALL WRITE(0, .CRLF, 2, .STATUS);
74    2            END;
75    1            CALL EXIT;

76    1         END SIX$MEAN$AND$MEDIAN$1;
```

The inclusive extent of the program is the entire program. The exclusive extent of the program is its inclusive extent minus any blocks nested within it, namely, MEANANDMEDIAN. The exclusive extent of the total program, in other words, consists of statements 1–8 and 63–76. The inclusive extent of MEANANDMEDIAN is statements 29–62; its exclusive extent is statements 29–35 and 60–62.

SCOPE OF PL/M PROGRAM OBJECTS

The concept of scope applies to every object in a program that can be declared. So far we have declared variables, procedures, and macros, the last being the usual name for the LITERALLY feature. It is also possible to declare *labels,* which we shall consider in more detail later in the chapter.

The scope of an object is the part of the program in which the object's identifier is "known." Within this part of the program the object is handled as specified by its declaration. Outside of this part of the program, the object is treated as unknown; in the case of a variable, for instance, it would be reported by the compiler to be undefined.

The declaration of any object will be in the exclusive extent of some block. The scope of the object is the inclusive extent of that block minus the inclusive extent of any nested blocks in which the same identifier is declared.

As we have seen throughout the book, the scope of most objects is restricted by the rule that they may not be referred to until after they have been declared. The exceptions to this rule are labels, considered later in this chapter, and reentrant procedures, which we shall consider in the next chapter.

Consider these rules in connection with the program of Fig. 7.1. The array FIRST$ARRAY is at the module level; that is, it is in the exclusive extent of the entire module. The scope of this variable is the entire program, since no variable of the same name is declared within the blocks named MEANANDMEDIAN and SORT that are nested within the program. The same remark applies to all of the other variables at the module level except the variable I. Since a variable of the same name is declared within the nested procedure, the scope of the variable declared in statement 7 does not include any part of the procedure. The reference to I in statements 68 and 69 will be to the variable declared in statement 7. Within the procedure, the variable declared in statement 7 is simply unknown; the variable I declared in statement 33 is an altogether different object. The scope of the variable I declared in statement 33 is the entire procedure, since the block named SORT nested within the procedure does not declare another variable of the same name. The references to I in statements 36–53 are to the variable declared in statement 33. The scope of all other variables declared in statements 30–34 is also the entire procedure. The block nested within this procedure contains other declarations to be sure, but these additional declarations do not "interrupt" the scope of those declared earlier.

The scope of the variables and macros declared in statements 41–43 is just the SORT block. If these objects were referred to elsewhere in the procedure or in the main program, the compiler would report them to be unknown in these other places.

The program we are considering illustrates one of the motivations for using block structure. The variables EXCHANGE, PASS, and TEMP and the macros TRUE and FALSE are not needed anywhere else in the program. By declaring them at the lowest level we simplify understanding of the program organization. If that assertion does not seem self-evident in this example, bear in mind that most applications programs are very much larger than anything seen in this book. When a program can run dozens of pages, with declarations necessarily scattered throughout it, limiting the scope of variables and other objects to the lowest possible level distinctly improves program understandability.

A SKELETON PROGRAM TO ILLUSTRATE THE SCOPE OF VARIABLES

In working with large programs that rely on effective use of block structure to clarify organization, it will be important to have a clear understanding of the scope of identifiers that are declared in more than one place and therefore refer to different objects in different places. The rule is clear: The scope of an object is the inclusive extent of the block in which it is defined minus any nested blocks containing declarations of the same identifier. But the meaning of this definition may need further examples for full comprehension.

Consider the skeleton program shown in Fig. 7.2. We wish to concentrate only on block structure and declarations, so executable statements are indicated only by dots. Let us explore the scope of all the variables here.

The variable named VAR$1, declared at the module level in statement 2, is known everywhere except in BLOCK$A, where it is unknown because another

```
1           PROGRAM:
            DO;
2    1          DECLARE VAR$1 BYTE;
3    1          BLOCK$A:
                DO;
4    2              DECLARE (VAR$1, VAR$2) BYTE;
                    .
                    .
                    .
5    2          END BLOCK$A;
6    1          BLOCK$B:
                DO;
7    2              DECLARE VAR$3 BYTE;
8    2              BLOCK$C:
                    DO;
9    3                  DECLARE VAR$2 BYTE;
                        .
                        .
                        .
10   3              END BLOCK$C;
                    .
                    .
                    .
11   2          END BLOCK$B;
                .
                .
                .
12   1      END PROGRAM;
```

Fig. 7.2. Skeleton program illustrating the scope of variables.

object having the same identifier is declared there, in statement 4. The variables named VAR$1 and VAR$2 declared in BLOCK$A, statement 4, are known only within that block. The first of these is an entirely different variable from the variable having the same identifier declared at the module level. The declaration in statement 4 of VAR$2 establishes its scope as the inclusive extent of BLOCK$A; this declaration can have no connection with the declaration of another variable of the same name inside of BLOCK$C since BLOCK$C is not nested within BLOCK$A. VAR$3, declared in statement 7, is known within BLOCK$B including the nested BLOCK$C. VAR$2 as declared (statement 9) in BLOCK$C is known only there.

Now consider some possible changes in this program. Suppose we wanted VAR$2 as declared in BLOCK$C to be known not just in BLOCK$C but throughout BLOCK$B. Simple! Just move the declaration to the beginning of BLOCK$B. Suppose we then decided we wanted VAR$2 to be the same object in both BLOCK$A and BLOCK$B. This time it would be necessary only to place a single declaration of VAR$2 at the module level. Suppose we wanted to be able to refer to VAR$1 within BLOCK$B and have that be a reference to the variable declared in BLOCK$A. This could be done by reorganizing the program so that BLOCK$B is nested within BLOCK$A or by creating an entirely new block in which both BLOCK$A and BLOCK$B are nested, and declaring VAR$1 in the exclusive extent of the new block. Finally, suppose that we wanted to refer to VAR$3 from within BLOCK$A without using any of the strategems employed in the other examples, such as moving declarations, nesting blocks or creating new blocks. The answer this time is that it cannot be done. This is what scope is all about: An object is known only within the inclusive extent of the block in which it is declared.

Once one is familiar with the meaning of block structure as it applies to scope, it rapidly becomes an ally rather than an adversary. Variables that need to be known throughout the program are declared at the module level. Everything else is "hidden" in the smallest simple DO or PROCEDURE block that contains all references to it. Within nested blocks one may devise identifiers freely, knowing that any identifier that happens to be the same as that of an object declared at a higher level will be a reference to an entirely different object. Naturally, trouble can be created in this process if we define an object twice and then become confused as to which object an identifier refers to. This is another argument for using as few global variables as possible.

LABELS AND THEIR SCOPE

Labels may be used to identify any statement in a program. This is sometimes done for understandability reasons, to add a bit of explanation about the program other than with a comment. They are also used to permit checking by the compiler, when the label on a DO is placed in what is intended as the matching END. Finally, labels may be used for *transfers of control.*

Transfer of control is done with the GO TO statement, which may also be written GOTO. The statement consists of the words GO TO (or the word GOTO) followed by a label. When such a statement is executed, the flow of control—as otherwise defined by the sequence of statements, IF statements and DO groups—is broken. The next statement executed after the GO TO is the one to which the label in the statement is attached.

For an example of how GO TO statements can be used, consider the program shown in Fig. 7.3. This is a modification of the program in Fig. 5.5 for finding a square root. The program here is designed to accept numbers from the console, find the square roots, and send the square roots back to the console. A zero acts as a sentinel: when the program is asked to take the square root of zero, it will terminate.

The square-root procedure is the same as before. In the main program we have a DO WHILE 1 to create a deliberate "infinite loop" from which we will escape with a GO TO when the sentinel is detected. This test is made immediately after reading a number and converting it to binary; if it is zero, the statement

```
GO TO ABORT;
```

is executed, transferring control out of the loop. Normal sequential execution of statements is stopped and control transfers to the statement named ABORT. If the number just read is not zero, then we go on and compute its square root. At the end of these operations the loop repeats.

When used in this particular way, that is, to implement the escape from a main-

```
PL/M-80 COMPILER    FIG. 7.3                                        PAGE   1

        /* A SQUARE ROOT PROCEDURE, AND A PROGRAM TO EXERCISE IT */
        /* THE MAIN LINE ROUTINE IN THIS VERSION USES GO TO STATEMENTS */

        SQUARE$ROOT$PROGRAM:
        DO;
           DECLARE (N, ROOT, BUFFPTR) ADDRESS;
           DECLARE BUFFER(128) BYTE;
           DECLARE (COUNT, STATUS) ADDRESS;

        $INCLUDE (:F1:INOUT.SRC)
        $NOLIST

        SQRT:
        PROCEDURE (N) ADDRESS;
           DECLARE (N, X, X$NEW) ADDRESS;
           X = N;
           X$NEW = SHR(N + 1, 1);
           DO WHILE X <> X$NEW;
              X = X$NEW;
              X$NEW = SHR(N/X + X + 1, 1);
           END;
           RETURN X$NEW;
        END SQRT;

        /* A PROGRAM TO EXERCISE THE SQUARE ROOT ROUTINE */

        DO WHILE 1;
           CALL READ(1, .BUFFER, 128, .COUNT, .STATUS);
           BUFFPTR = .BUFFER;
           N = NUMIN(.BUFFPTR);
           IF N = 0 THEN
              GO TO ABORT;
           ROOT = SQRT(N);
           CALL NUMOUT(ROOT, 10, ' ', .BUFFER, 5);
           CALL WRITE(0, .BUFFER, 5, .STATUS);
           CALL WRITE(0, .(0DH, 0AH, 0AH), 3, .STATUS);
        END;

        ABORT:
           CALL EXIT;

        END SQUARE$ROOT$PROGRAM;
```

program reading-and-processing loop, the GO TO may seem to be a reasonable programming-language feature. We shall see in the case study that there are *occasionally* situations where the careful and disciplined use of the GO TO statement can lead to improved program clarity. However, undisciplined use of the GO TO statement can lead to programs that are extremely difficult to understand.

This is not the place for an extended debate on "the GO TO question." We prefer to show the reader the techniques that we consider to be good programming practice, and let it go at that. However, to give just one example of the difficulty of understanding a program written with casual use of GO TOs, we may exhibit the program in Fig. 7.4. This carries out the same functions as the program in Fig. 4.13

```
PL/M-80 COMPILER    FIG. 7.4                                    PAGE    1

        /* A THIRD SORTING ROUTINE - USES ADDRESS SORTING TO SORT A STRUCTURE */
        /* MODIFIED VERSION OF PROGRAM IN FIGURE 4.13: USES GO TO STATEMENTS */

        SORT$7:
        DO;
            DECLARE RECORD(10) STRUCTURE (KEY BYTE, CONTENTS ADDRESS)
                DATA('D',429,'N',20881,'F',560,'B',1201,'X',500,'7',12300,'Q',
                1292,'C',9810,'A',300,'G',0);
            DECLARE RANK(10) BYTE;
            DECLARE (I, J, TEMP$BYTE) BYTE;
            DECLARE LAST$RECORD$NUMBER LITERALLY '9';

            DECLARE BUFFER(5) BYTE;
            DECLARE (COUNT, STATUS) ADDRESS;
            DECLARE CRLF(2) BYTE DATA (0DH, 0AH);

        $INCLUDE(:F1:INOUT.SRC)
        $NOLIST

            I = 0;
        LABEL$1:
            RANK(I) = I;
            I = I + 1;
            IF I <= LAST$RECORD$NUMBER THEN GO TO LABEL$1;
            I = 0;
        LABEL$2:
            J = I + 1;
        LABEL$3:
            IF RECORD(RANK(I)).KEY <= RECORD(RANK(J)).KEY THEN GO TO LABEL$4;
            TEMP$BYTE = RANK(I);
            RANK(I) = RANK(J);
            RANK(J) = TEMP$BYTE;
        LABEL$4:
            J = J + 1;
            IF J <= LAST$RECORD$NUMBER THEN GO TO LABEL$3;
            I = I + 1;
            IF I <= LAST$RECORD$NUMBER - 1 THEN GO TO LABEL$2;
            I = 0;
        LABEL$5:
            CALL WRITE(0, .RECORD(RANK(I)).KEY, 1, .STATUS);
            CALL NUMOUT(RECORD(RANK(I)).CONTENTS, 10, '0', .BUFFER, 5);
            CALL WRITE(0, .BUFFER, 5, .STATUS);
            CALL WRITE(0, .CRLF, 2, .STATUS);
            I = I + 1;
            IF I <= 9 THEN GO TO LABEL$5;
            CALL EXIT;
        END SORT$7;
```

and uses the same data names. No attempt has been made to make it deliberately obscure. The reader will presumably agree that it is more difficult to understand than the earlier version.

The reason it is more difficult to understand is that, to comprehend its operation, we must know in detail the order in which different statements are executed. In the style of programming used elsewhere in the book, which may be referred to as *struc-*

tured programming, the relationships of program segments are clearly displayed by such techniques as indentation of units controlled by IF statements and DO blocks. Putting it another way, it is possible to understand what a statement in a structured program does by looking at its relationship to the statements around it and no more. Its subordination to control elements is displayed in a graphic two-dimensional form by the use of indentation. With declarations being placed as close as possible to the "working level," most of what one needs to know about how a given statement operates is physically close by that statement on the page.

With the GO TO style, on the other hand, to understand a statement requires knowing in detail the sequence of statement execution by which a given point in the program was reached. Worse, when GO TOs are used in an undisciplined way, it is possible that there are many different paths—all extremely complex—by which it is possible to reach a given statement in the program. The human brain is in many ways an amazing instrument, but it is actually not very good at keeping track of that kind of detail. Programs have been constructed—unintentionally, for the most part—that are, for all practical purposes, incomprehensible to anyone except the original writer. And even the original writer, after a period of not working at the program, might also find it incomprehensible. This is a highly undesirable state of affairs, from numerous points of view. In our attempt to write understandable programs we prefer to use GO TOs only in the very special kind of situations that will be sketched in the case study.

MORE ON THE SCOPE OF LABELS

Labels are subject to the same rules of scope as are other objects. The application of those rules, however, has some implications that are special.

It is necessary to clarify something that was mentioned in passing before: The inclusive extent of a DO block does not include any label on the DO statement that begins the block. This means that the same identifier used as a label on the DO statement can be used within that block, in which case it will interrupt the scope of the label on the DO statement and constitute a different label. It is *strongly* recommended that this capability not be used. No benefits can be suggested for doing so and the potential for confusion is entirely unacceptable.

It is possible for labels to be mentioned in DECLARE statements, which is called *explicit label declaration.* The normal method of simply writing a label attached to a statement is called *implicit declaration.* Explicit label declaration is provided solely for use with the PUBLIC and EXTERNAL attributes discussed in Chapter 9; we shall have no other occasion to use it. It does permit us, however, to express a consideration about the scope of labels. The scope of an implicitly declared label is the same as the scope of an explicit declaration at the beginning of the smallest block that encloses the implicit declaration. This means that the scope of a label cannot extend beyond the smallest block enclosing it.

This means, in a word, that it is not possible for a GO TO to transfer control from an outer block to a labeled statement in a nested block. It also means that a transfer from a nested block to an outer block must be entirely within one outer block.

In fact, the only possible GO TO transfers are the following:

- From a point in the exclusive extent of a block to a statement in the exclusive extent of the same block.
- From an inner block to a statement in the exclusive extent of an enclosing block, not necessarily the smallest enclosing block. However, if the inner block is a procedure block, the transfer may only be to a labeled statement in the outer level of the main program module.

(One other type of GO TO will be considered in Chapter 9 in connection with the EXTERNAL and PUBLIC attributes.)

For an example of the application of these rules, consider the skeleton program in Fig. 7.5. The first transfer is legal, since the GO TO and the label are in the exclusive extent of the same block. The second transfer is illegal, since it is an attempt

```
PROGRAM:
DO;
   DECLARE . . .
   PROCEDURE$A:
      DECLARE . . .
      . . .
      GO TO LABEL$A;          /* TRANSFER 1: LEGAL */
      . . .
   LABEL$A:
      . . .
      GO TO LABEL$B;          /* TRANSFER 2: ILLEGAL */
      . . .
      DO;
      LABEL$B:
      . . .
         GO TO LABEL$A;       /* TRANSFER 3: LEGAL */
         . . .
      END;

      PROCEDURE$B:
         DECLARE . . .
         . . .
         GO TO LABEL$A;       /* TRANSFER 4: ILLEGAL */
         . . .
         GO TO LABEL$C;       /* TRANSFER 5: LEGAL */
         . . .
      END PROCEDURE$B;
   END PROCEDURE$A;

/* MAIN PROGRAM */
   LABEL$C:
   . . .
END PROGRAM;
```

Fig. 7.5. Skeleton program illustrating legal and illegal transfers of control.

to transfer from an outer block to a nested block; LABEL$B is not known outside of the block that encloses it. The third transfer is legal since it goes from a nested block to an enclosing block. The fourth transfer is illegal, because it is an attempt to go from a nested procedure to a target other than a statement at the module level. The fifth transfer is to a target at the module level and is legal.

LABELS VS. PROCEDURE NAMES

Labels and procedure names have strong superficial similarities: Both are followed by colons, both precede statements, and both are used to identify a statement from elsewhere in the program. But the two are not the same; there are two important differences:

- It is possible to transfer to a labeled statement, using a GO TO; a GO TO with a procedure name as its target is illegal.
- A rule of the language says that most objects may not be referred to until after they have been declared. Procedure names are subject to this requirement; labels are the only exception to it, whether declared implicitly or explicitly.

CASE STUDY: THE FINAL VERSION OF THE INDEXING PROGRAM

We wish to add several capabilities to the program shown at the end of the previous chapter. The most important of these is the ability to handle input records in which long words have been entered with indications of where they may be hyphenated. When a long line has to be broken, we look either for a blank or for a hyphenation point.

The second new feature is the ability to recognize a number of errors in the input, such as a line that begins with a hyphen, or one that has an indent marker other than at the beginning of a line, or several others.

A third requirement is that multiple blanks are to be replaced by a single blank.

Finally, we wish to be able to specifiy that the program is to examine enough entries to fill a column even though it finds errors. This is to be done conditionally in what will be called *edit mode,* if a third value entered along with MAX$LINES and MAX$CHARS is nonzero. This facility will be used in a preliminary operation in which the entire input file will be inspected for errors.

THE MAIN PROGRAM

The main program shown on page 7 of the listing in Fig. 7.6 begins by calling for the setup operations. Then, after initializing the line counter, it goes into a DO–WHILE loop to produce as many lines of output as specified by MAX$LINES. This DO–WHILE has a label since, as we shall see, a GO TO in a procedure named ERROR can transfer to it. For the same reason, there is a label on the CALL WRAPUP statement.

```
PL/M-80 COMPILER    FIG. 7.6                                     PAGE   1

            /* FINAL VERSION OF A PROGRAM TO PRINT A PROPERLY-SPACED INDEX FOR THIS BOOK */

            /****************************************************************************
            *                                                                           *
            * THE PROGRAM ACCEPTS, FROM DISK, RECORDS THAT WERE PREPARED USING THE TEXT *
            * EDITOR.  EACH RECORD REPRESENTS ONE COMPLETE ENTRY IN AN INDEX, WITH TWO  *
            * EDITING CONTROLS OPTIONALLY PRESENT:                                      *
            *   1. ANY LINE THAT BEGINS WITH > IS TO BE INDENTED TWO SPACES             *
            *   2. A HYPHEN FOLLOWED BY A SPACE IS A 'CONDITIONAL HYPHEN': IF NECESSARY *
            *      THE LINE CAN BE BROKEN AT THIS POINT; THE HYPHEN AND SPACE MUST BE   *
            *      REMOVED IF A BREAK IS NOT NEEDED                                     *
            *                                                                           *
            *  THE PROGRAM ACCEPTS THREE PARAMETERS FROM THE CONSOLE:                   *
            *   1. MAX$LINES: THE MAXIMUM NUMBER OF LINES PER COLUMN--DEFAULT 51        *
            *   2. MAX$CHARS: THE MAXIMUM NUMBER OF CHARACTERS PER LINE--DEFAULT 25     *
            *   3. EDIT$MODE: IF NON-ZERO, A COLUMN IS TO BE CHECKED FOR ERRORS,        *
            *      WITHOUT STOPPING WHEN ERRORS ARE DETECTED.  HOWEVER, PROGRAM REPORTS *
            *      ONLY THE FIRST ERROR IT DETECTS IN ANY ONE LINE.                     *
            *                                                                           *
            *  SEVERAL ERRORS ARE DETECTED:                                             *
            *   1. A LINE CANNOT BEGIN WITH A HYPHEN                                    *
            *   2. THE INDENT SYMBOL IS ALLOWED ONLY AT THE BEGINNING OF A LINE         *
            *   3. TWO CONSECUTIVE HYPHENS ARE NOT PERMITTED                            *
            *   4. A HYPHEN FOLLOWING A SPACE IS NOT PERMITTED                          *
            *   5. A BREAK IS REQUIRED IN A LINE THAT DOES NOT HAVE A SPACE OR A
            *      CONDITIONAL HYPHEN                                                   *
            *                                                                           *
            * WHEN A LINE MUST BE CONTINUED ON A FOLLOWING LINE, THE CONTINUATION IS     *
            * INDENTED FOUR SPACES. A BLANK LINE OF INPUT PRODUCES A BLANK LINE OF      *
            * OUTPUT; THIS IS USED TO PLACE A BLANK LINE BETWEEN LETTER-GROUPS.         *
            * IN TEXT, TWO OR MORE BLANKS ARE REPLACED BY ONE BLANK.                    *
            *                                                                           *
            ****************************************************************************/


  1         FINAL$INDEX:
            DO;
  2   1        DECLARE TEXT(128) BYTE;    /* THE INPUT RECORD TO BE PROCESSED */
  3   1        DECLARE (MAX$LINES, MAX$CHARS, LINE$CTR, EDIT$MODE) BYTE;
  4   1        DECLARE (DISK$AFTN, ECHO$AFTN, LP$AFTN) ADDRESS;
                              /* AFTN = ACTIVE FILE TABLE NUMBER */
  5   1        DECLARE BUFFER(30) BYTE;
  6   1        DECLARE (COUNT, STATUS) ADDRESS;
  7   1        DECLARE WRITE$CRLF LITERALLY 'WRITE(LP$AFTN, .(0DH,0AH), 2, .STATUS)';

            $INCLUDE(:F1:INOUT.SRC)
        =   $NOLIST
```

THE SETUP PROCEDURE

This procedure is very similar to what we saw before, the only addition being the assignment of a value to a variable named EDIT$MODE.

```
PL/M-80 COMPILER    FIG. 7.6                                        PAGE   2


             $EJECT
28    1      SETUP:
             PROCEDURE;
29    2        DECLARE TEMPORARY BYTE;
30    2        DECLARE BUFFER(30) BYTE;
31    2        DECLARE BUFFPTR ADDRESS;
32    2        DECLARE (COUNT, STATUS) ADDRESS;

               /* GET MAX LINES AND MAX CHARS PER LINE (FROM CONSOLE), UNLESS DEFAULTED */
33    2        CALL READ(1, .BUFFER, 128, .COUNT, .STATUS);
34    2        BUFFPTR = .BUFFER;
35    2        TEMPORARY = NUMIN(.BUFFPTR);
36    2        IF TEMPORARY = 0 THEN
37    2          MAX$LINES = 51;
               ELSE
38    2          MAX$LINES = TEMPORARY;
39    2        TEMPORARY = NUMIN(.BUFFPTR);
40    2        IF TEMPORARY = 0 THEN
41    2          MAX$CHARS = 25;
               ELSE
42    2          MAX$CHARS = TEMPORARY;
43    2        TEMPORARY = NUMIN(.BUFFPTR);
44    2        IF TEMPORARY = 0 THEN
45    2          EDIT$MODE = 0;
               ELSE
46    2          EDIT$MODE = 0FFH;

47    2        CALL OPEN(.ECHO$AFTN, .(':F1:SCRTCH '), 2, 0, .STATUS);
48    2        CALL OPEN(.DISK$AFTN, .(':F1:INDEX.TXT '), 1, ECHO$AFTN, .STATUS);
49    2        CALL OPEN(.LP$AFTN, .(':LP: '), 2, 0, .STATUS);

50    2      END SETUP;
```

THE ERROR PROCEDURE

Any time an error is detected anywhere within the procedure PROCESSONE-TEXT$RECORD, we call another procedure named ERROR, passing it an error number as a parameter. This parameter is used to control a DO CASE that selects the writing of an appropriate error description. These error messages are written on the console unconditionally, whether they occur in edit mode or not. If we are in edit mode, we wish also to write the offending line of text so that it can be corrected. Then if we have not yet filled up a column, we would like to go back to editing again. This is most directly done by a GO TO that returns control to the DO–WHILE in the main program labelled RESUME. If we are not in edit mode, a transfer to TERMINATE stops program execution without writing any more lines.

```
PL/M-80 COMPILER    FIG. 7.6                                PAGE   3

            $EJECT
            /*************************************************************************
             * THE FOLLOWING PROCEDURE REPORTS ERRORS AND TRANSFERS TO THE MAIN PROGRAM *
             *                                                                        *
             * NOTE CAREFULLY: THIS PROCEDURE DOES **NOT** RETURN TO CALLING POINT    *
             *                                                                        *
             *************************************************************************/

 51   1     ERROR:
            PROCEDURE (ERROR$NUMBER);
 52   2        DECLARE ERROR$NUMBER BYTE;
 53   2        DO CASE ERROR$NUMBER - 1;
 54   3           CALL WRITE(0, .('HYPHEN CANNOT BEGIN LINE'), 24, .STATUS);
 55   3           CALL WRITE(0, .('INDENT PERMITTED ONLY AT BEGINNING'), 34, .STATUS);
 56   3           CALL WRITE(0, .('TWO CONSECUTIVE HYPHENS NOT PERMITTED'), 37, .STATUS);
 57   3           CALL WRITE(0, .('HYPHEN FOLLOWING BLANK NOT PERMITTED'), 36, .STATUS);
 58   3           CALL WRITE(0, .('NO BLANK AT WHICH TO BREAK LINE'), 31, .STATUS);
 59   3        END; /* DO CASE */

 60   2        CALL WRITE$CRLF;

 61   2        IF EDIT$MODE THEN
 62   2        DO;
 63   3           CALL WRITE(0, .TEXT, COUNT, .STATUS);
 64   3           CALL WRITE$CRLF;
 65   3           GO TO RESUME;
 66   3        END;
               ELSE
 67   2           GO TO TERMINATE;

 68   2     END ERROR;



            /*********************************************************************
             *  THE FOLLOWING PROCEDURE CONTAINS TWO OTHER PROCEDURES, AS WELL AS  *
             *  EXECUTABLE STATEMENTS NOT CONTAINED IN THE TWO PROCEDURES         *
             *********************************************************************/

 69   1     PROCESS$ONE$TEXT$RECORD:
            PROCEDURE;
 70   2        DECLARE CODE(128) BYTE;    /* CODES DESCRIBING TEXT CHARACTERS */
 71   2        DECLARE (BP, EP) ADDRESS;  /* BEGINNING AND ENDING TEXT POINTERS */
 72   2        DECLARE (CHAR BASED BP, CHAR$CHECK BASED EP) BYTE;
 73   2        DECLARE LEADING$BLANKS BYTE;
 74   2        DECLARE BLANK LITERALLY ''' ''',
                        HYPHEN LITERALLY '''-''',
                        INDENT LITERALLY '''>''';
 75   2        DECLARE BLANK$CODE LITERALLY '0',
                        BREAK$CODE LITERALLY '1',
                        ALL$OTHERS$CODE LITERALLY '2';
```

```
PL/M-80 COMPILER    FIG. 7.6                                                    PAGE   4


         $EJECT
         /*************************************************************************
          *  THE FOLLOWING PROCEDURE IS NESTED WITHIN PROCESS$ONE$TEXT$RECORD    *
          *************************************************************************/
  76 2     ANALYZE:
           PROCEDURE;
  77 3        DECLARE AP ADDRESS;    /* ANALYZER POINTER */
  78 3        DECLARE CHAR BASED AP BYTE; /* SAME NAME AS BEFORE, BUT DIFFERENT BASE */
  79 3        DECLARE (SENDING$PTR, RECEIVING$PTR) ADDRESS; /* FOR SHIFT OPERATIONS */
  80 3        DECLARE (SENDING$CHAR BASED SENDING$PTR,
                       RECEIVING$CHAR BASED RECEIVING$PTR) BYTE;
  81 3        DECLARE STATE BYTE;

  82 3        STATE = 0;
  83 3        AP = BP;
  84 3        DO WHILE AP <= EP;

  85 4           IF NOT (CHAR = INDENT OR CHAR = HYPHEN OR CHAR = BLANK) THEN
  86 4           DO;  /* SAME ACTION FOR ALL STATES; NEED NOT BE PART OF DO CASE */
  87 5              STATE = 1;
  88 5              CODE(AP - .TEXT) = ALL$OTHERS$CODE;
  89 5           END;
                 ELSE
  90 4              DO CASE STATE;

                    /* STATE 0: 1ST CHARACTER OF RECORD */
  91 5              DO;
  92 6                 IF CHAR = INDENT THEN
  93 6                 DO;
  94 7                    LEADING$BLANKS = 2;
  95 7                    BP = BP + 1;
  96 7                 END;
  97 6                 ELSE IF CHAR = HYPHEN THEN
  98 6                    CALL ERROR(1);        /* HYPHEN CANNOT BEGIN LINE */
  99 6                 ELSE IF CHAR = BLANK THEN
 100 6                    CODE(AP - .TEXT) = BLANK$CODE;
                    END;  /* STATE 0 */

                    /* STATE 1: PREVIOUS CHARACTER WAS NOT INDENT, HYPHEN, OR BLANK */
 102 5              DO;
 103 6                 IF CHAR = INDENT THEN
 104 6                    CALL ERROR(2);        /* INDENT PERMITTED ONLY AT BEGINNING */
 105 6                 ELSE IF CHAR = HYPHEN THEN
 106 6                 DO;
 107 7                    STATE = 2;
 108 7                    CODE(AP - .TEXT) = ALL$OTHERS$CODE;
 109 7                 END;
 110 6                 ELSE IF CHAR = BLANK THEN
 111 6                 DO;
 112 7                    STATE = 3;
 113 7                    CODE(AP - .TEXT) = BLANK$CODE;
 114 7                 END;
                    END; /* STATE 1 */
```

```
PL/M-80 COMPILER    FIG. 7.6                                      PAGE   5


       $EJECT
                 /* STATE 2: PREVIOUS CHARACTER A HYPHEN FOLLOWING A TEXT CHARACTER */
                 DO;
                    IF CHAR = INDENT THEN
                       CALL ERROR(2);        /* INDENT PERMITTED ONLY AT BEGINNING */
                    ELSE IF CHAR = HYPHEN THEN
                       CALL ERROR(3);        /*; TWO CONSECUTIVE HYPHENS NOT PERMITTED */
                    ELSE IF CHAR = BLANK THEN    /* A CONDITIONAL HYPHEN */
                    DO;
                       STATE = 1;
                       DO SENDING$PTR = AP + 1 TO EP;
                          RECEIVING$PTR = SENDING$PTR - 2;
                          RECEIVING$CHAR = SENDING$CHAR;
                       END;
                       AP = AP - 2;
                       EP = EP - 2;
                       CODE(AP - .TEXT) = BREAK$CODE; /* MARK WHERE BREAK IS POSSIBLE */
                    END;
                 END; /* STATE 2 */

                 /* STATE 3: PREVIOUS CHARACTER BLANK, NOT PART OF CONDITIONAL HYPHEN */
                 DO;
                    IF CHAR = INDENT THEN
                       CALL ERROR(2);        /* INDENT PERMITTED ONLY AT BEGINNING */
                    ELSE IF CHAR = HYPHEN THEN
                       CALL ERROR(4);        /* HYPHEN FOLLOWING BLANK NOT PERMITTED */
                    ELSE IF CHAR = BLANK THEN
                    DO;
                       DO SENDING$PTR = AP + 1 TO EP;
                          RECEIVING$PTR = SENDING$PTR - 1;
                          RECEIVING$CHAR = SENDING$CHAR;
                       END;
                       AP = AP - 1;
                       EP = EP - 1;
                    END;
                 END; /* STATE 3 */

                 END;  /* DO CASE */

             AP = AP + 1;

         END; /* DO WHILE */

     END ANALYZE;
```

```
PL/M-80 COMPILER    FIG. 7.6                                                      PAGE   6

             $EJECT
             /*************************************************************************
             *  THE FOLLOWING PROCEDURE IS NESTED WITHIN PROCESS$ONE$TEXT$RECORD    *
             *************************************************************************/
152    2        PRINT$ONE$LINE:
                PROCEDURE;
153    3           IF LEADING$BLANKS + (EP - BP) < MAX$CHARS THEN
154    3           DO;
155    4              CALL WRITE(LP$AFTN, .('    '), LEADING$BLANKS, .STATUS);
156    4              CALL WRITE(LP$AFTN, BP, EP - BP + 1, .STATUS);
157    4              BP = EP;  /* TO STOP DO WHILE */
158    4           END;
                   ELSE
159    3           DO;
160    4              DECLARE EP$SAVE ADDRESS;

161    4              EP$SAVE = EP;
162    4              EP = BP + MAX$CHARS - LEADING$BLANKS;
163    4              DO WHILE CODE(EP - .TEXT) = ALL$OTHERS$CODE AND EP > BP;
164    5                 EP = EP - 1;
165    5              END;
166    4              IF EP = BP THEN
167    4                 CALL ERROR(5);              /* NO PLACE AT WHICH TO BREAK LINE */
168    4              CALL WRITE(LP$AFTN, .('    '), LEADING$BLANKS, .STATUS);
169    4              IF CODE(EP - .TEXT) = BLANK$CODE THEN     /* EP POINTS AT A BLANK */
170    4              DO;
171    5                 CALL WRITE(LP$AFTN, BP, EP - BP, .STATUS);
172    5              END;
                      ELSE         /* EP POINTS AT CHARACTER BEFORE HYPHENATION POINT */
173    4              DO;
174    5                 CALL WRITE(LP$AFTN, BP, EP - BP + 1, .STATUS);
175    5                 CALL WRITE(LP$AFTN, .('-'), 1, .STATUS);
176    5              END;
177    4              LEADING$BLANKS = 4;
178    4              BP = EP + 1;
179    4              EP = EP$SAVE;
180    4           END;

181    3           CALL WRITE$CRLF;
182    3           LINE$CTR = LINE$CTR + 1;

183    3        END PRINT$ONE$LINE;

             /*************************************************************************
              *   THE EXECUTABLE STATEMENTS FOR PROCESS$ONE$TEXT$RECORD FOLLOW    *
              *************************************************************************/
184    2        CALL READ(DISK$AFTN, .TEXT, 128, .COUNT, .STATUS);
185    2        BP = .TEXT;
186    2        EP = .TEXT(COUNT - 3);
187    2        LEADING$BLANKS = 0;
188    2        CALL ANALYZE;
189    2        DO WHILE BP < EP;
190    3           CALL PRINT$ONE$LINE;
191    3        END;

192    2     END PROCESS$ONE$TEXT$RECORD;
```

```
PL/M-80 COMPILER    FIG. 7.6                                        PAGE   7

                $EJECT
193   1         WRAPUP:
                PROCEDURE;

194   2            CALL NUMOUT (LINE$CTR, 10, ' ', .BUFFER, 3);
195   2            CALL WRITE(0, .BUFFER, 3, .STATUS);
196   2            CALL WRITE(0, .(' LINES IN THIS COLUMN'), 22, .STATUS);
197   2            CALL WRITE$CRLF;

198   2            CALL CLOSE(ECHO$AFTN, .STATUS);
199   2            CALL CLOSE(DISK$AFTN, .STATUS);
200   2            CALL CLOSE(LP$AFTN, .STATUS);

201   2         END WRAPUP;


                /****************************************************************
                 *                                                              *
                 *                        MAIN PROGRAM                          *
                 *                                                              *
                 ****************************************************************/


202   1            CALL SETUP;

203   1            LINE$CTR = 0;

204   1         RESUME:
                   DO WHILE LINE$CTR < MAX$LINES;
205   2               CALL PROCESS$ONE$TEXT$RECORD;
206   2            END;

207   1         TERMINATE:
                   CALL WRAPUP;
208   1            CALL EXIT;

209   1         END FINAL$INDEX;
```

This kind of GO TO—i.e., one that implements an abort exit on finding a serious data error—is one of the few kinds of GO TO that can be defended as promoting understandability. The program could assuredly be written to carry out the same functions without any GO TO statements, but only at the expense of rather complex logic in the processing procedures, logic that would have no purpose except to skip over remaining functions upon detecting an error. The way we have shown is preferable, even though it too has traps for the unwary, such as the fact that, when ERROR is invoked, control does not return to the next statement after the CALL.

THE PROCEDURE FOR PROCESSING ONE TEXT RECORD

This procedure has a good deal more to do than the corresponding procedure in the program of the previous chapter. In fact, this procedure now contains two other procedures as well as executable code that is not within either of these *nested* procedures. The general outline of this part of the program is shown in the pseudocode of Fig. 7.7. Looking at the end of the pseudocode, we see that it gets one line of text from the diskette, carries out some preliminary operations, then calls one of the nested procedures—the one named ANALYZE. This does most of the error checking as well as setting up the values in an array named CODE that specifies where it is possible to break the text. We shall see how it operates when we inspect the program.

Once ANALYZE has been called, we invoke the nested procedure named PRINTONELINE as many times as necessary to print all the text in the input line.

The scheme for indicating in the input text where words may be hyphenated is to enter a hyphen followed by a blank. We take it that it would never be necessary to print such a combination of characters, so the combination can safely be used to specify a possible hyphenation point. A hyphen not followed by a space represents itself. Hyphenation points could have been indicated in other ways, the most obvious of which would have been to use some special character that can never appear otherwise in the input text. Doing so would not have greatly simplified the program, however; and doing it this way lets us illustrate some useful information-processing techniques. Figure 7.8 shows a sample of input text for this program; this sample contains no errors.

Most of the procedure named ANALYZE consists of a long DO CASE implementing a state transition table (like that in Chapter 6, page 134) for the analysis of our text. The four states are as shown in the comments at the beginning of the code for the respective cases.

The basic functions of ANALYZE, besides detecting errors, are to remove the conditional hyphens and to set up the values in the array named CODE that shows where the blanks and hyphenation points are. For each character of the input record, we place into the corresponding position of CODE either a zero to indicate that the character was a blank, a 1 to indicate that the word can be broken after that character, or a 2 to indicate "all other." Actually, these codes apply not to the input text *as read,* but to its *compressed* form after the removal of conditional hyphens and after the replacement of multiple blanks by single blanks.

With this much introduction it should be possible to read the rest of the procedure. Note in state 2 the loop to move everything after a conditional hyphen two places to the left, and in state 3 the loop to move everything after a second consecutive blank one place to the left.

The procedure named PRINTONELINE is quite similar to the procedure named PRINT$LINES$FROM$TEXT$RECORD in the program of Fig. 6.16. If the entire line can be printed in the space available, the program does so; otherwise

```
PROCESS$ONE$TEXT$RECORD:
PROCEDURE . . .
   Declarations


ANALYZE:
PROCEDURE . . .
   Declarations

   Use a state-transition CASE structure to check for the
   various errors; remove "conditional hyphens"; set up a
   table in CODE showing where blanks and hyphenation
   points are.

END ANALYZE


PRINT$ONE$LINE:
PROCEDURE . . .
   Declarations

   Print line(s) from one input record, breaking lines
   at blanks or where conditional hyphens appear

END PRINT$ONE$LINE


/* executable statements for PROCESS$ONE$TEXT$RECORD  */

   Read a line of input

   Set pointers

   CALL ANALYZE

   DO WHILE more characters of line remain to be printed
      CALL PRINT$ONE$LINE
   END

END PROCESS$ONETEXT$RECORD
```

Fig. 7.7. Pseudocode of the logic of the module to process one line of index text.

it looks for a blank or a conditional hyphen, and prints as much of the line as possible. In the latter operation it is necessary to save the ending pointer (EP) in order to restore it after backing up through the text looking for a point at which to break. In the earlier program we restored this pointer simply by recomputing its value from the count of characters returned by the READ operation. This time we cannot do that because the elimination of conditional hyphens and multiple blanks will have shortened the line. This little problem could be solved in several ways; the way chosen here is to set up a variable in which to save the value of EP. Since this variable is never needed outside of this one DO block, we are able to declare it within

```
Minor control, 158
Minus sign, in PIC- TURE, 102-105,                   193
>in arith- metic ex- pres- sion, 348
Mnemonic                 name, 9, 122, 123
MOVE, 5,  32, 40, 82,   99, 195
MOVE COR- RES- PON- DING, 203, 204, 215, 318
MULTIPLY, 32, 33, 38, 39, 42, 349

Name, data, 5, 9, 25, 82, 83, 255
>paragraph, 5, 16, 121, 147, 255, 298-300
Naming con- ven- tion, 25, 83, 121, 299
Negative data, 40, 98, 103-105
Nested IF, 114, 158-169
NEXT SEN- TENCE, 64, 65, 165, 178, 206, 292, 295
New master, 231
NOMINAL KEY, 324, 327
Nonnumeric item, 29, 74, 77, 97, 107, 154
Nonnumeric lit- eral, 5, 74
NOT, 68, 77, 158, 181, 206-208
NUMERIC, 77
Numeric bit, 193
Numeric item, 29, 74, 77, 97, 107
Numeric lit- eral, 5, 74

Object, of re- la- tion, 67, 207
Object pro- gram, 98, 99, 149, 154, 190, 277, 289
OCCURS, 279, 280, 282, 284, 285, 290
Old master, 231
ON SIZE ERROR, 36-41, 43, 114, 121,  125,   215, 348, 351
One-level con- trol total ex- ample, 144-157, 335-338
OPEN, 5, 15, 255,      259, 260, 312, 327
Operational   sign, 98, 102-105, 194,   200
Operator pre- ced- ence rule, 205, 349
Optional word, 34, 153
```

Fig. 7.8. Sample input to the indexing program of this chapter.

the DO block itself. We thus have an example of declaration other than at the beginning of a program or of a procedure.

The search for a place at which to break is now done not by looking at the text itself, but by looking at the values in the CODE array. If we cannot find such a place, we have an error exit; if we can, we must determine whether the break was at a blank or at a hyphenation point. If it was at a blank, we do just what we did before, which was to print all the characters up to but not including the blank. If the break was at a hyphenation point, we print all the characters up to and including the one after which we are able to hyphenate, and then a hyphen.

THE WRAPUP PROCEDURE

In our earlier program, the WRAPUP procedure included the writing of an error message when there was no place to break a line. Now, with all of the error handling being done by a separate procedure, all that is required of WRAPUP is to write the number of lines in the column and close the files.

Figure 7.9 shows the columns printed by this program with several values of MAX$CHARS and MAX$LINES, using the input shown earlier in Fig. 7.8. The program was also tested separately with input containing a variety of errors, on which it also operated correctly.

SUMMARY

This is the longest program we shall see in this book. We have tried to facilitate your understanding of it by presenting it in three stages of successive refinement. We venture to suggest that the program of Fig. 7.6 would be significantly harder to understand if one were to approach it without the benefit of having studied the earlier versions.

This is not to suggest that program documentation has to include simpler versions of the final program. The emphasis here is on good practice in program development. The real point of this discussion is that if a student *understands* a program better when he sees a sequence of increasingly more detailed versions, then the *development* of such a program will be aided even more.

EXERCISES

***1.** In the program of Fig. 7.6, what statements are in the inclusive and exclusive extents of the procedure PROCESSONETEXT$RECORD?

***2.** In the program of Fig. 7.6, what statements are in the inclusive and exclusive extents of the procedure ANALYZE?

3. In the program of Fig. 8.10, what statements are in the inclusive and exclusive extents of the procedure SETUP?

***4.** In the program of Fig. 6.7, what is the scope of the variable I declared in statement 7? What is the scope of MEAN$1 declared in statement 8?

5. In the program of Fig. 7.6, what is the scope of the variable LEADING$BLANKS declared in statement 73?

***6.** In the program of Fig. 7.3, what is the scope of the label ABORT that appears in statement 46?

7. In the program of Fig. 7.6, what is the scope of the labels RESUME and TERMINATE in the main program?

8. What would the program of Fig. 7.1 do if statements 45 and 46 were reversed?

9. Modify the program of Fig. 7.1 so that TEMP is declared at the lowest possible level, instead of where it is.

Default
51 lines
25 chars

```
Minor control, 158
Minus sign, in PICTURE,
     102-105, 193
  in arithmetic expres-
     sion, 348
Mnemonic name, 9, 122,
     123
MOVE, 5, 32, 40, 82, 99,
     195
MOVE CORRESPONDING, 203,
     204, 215, 318
MULTIPLY, 32, 33, 38, 39,
     42, 349

Name, data, 5, 9, 25, 82,
     83, 255
  paragraph, 5, 16, 121,
     147, 255, 298-300
Naming convention, 25,
     83, 121, 299
Negative data, 40, 98,
     103-105
Nested IF, 114, 158-169
NEXT SENTENCE, 64, 65,
     165, 178, 206, 292,
     295
New master, 231
NOMINAL KEY, 324, 327
Nonnumeric item, 29, 74,
     77, 97, 107, 154
Nonnumeric literal, 5, 74
NOT, 68, 77, 158, 181,
     206-208
NUMERIC, 77
Numeric bit, 193
Numeric item, 29, 74, 77,
     97, 107
Numeric literal, 5, 74

Object, of relation, 67,
     207
Object program, 98, 99,
     149, 154, 190, 277,
     289
OCCURS, 279, 280, 282,
     284, 285, 290
Old master, 231
ON SIZE ERROR, 36-41, 43,
     114, 121, 125, 215,
     348, 351
One-level control total ex-
     ample, 144-157,
     335-338
```

30 lines
20 chars

```
Minor control, 158
Minus sign, in PIC-
     TURE, 102-105,
     193
  in arithmetic ex-
     pression, 348
Mnemonic name, 9,
     122, 123
MOVE, 5, 32, 40, 82,
     99, 195
MOVE CORRESPONDING,
     203, 204, 215,
     318
MULTIPLY, 32, 33,
     38, 39, 42, 349

Name, data, 5, 9,
     25, 82, 83, 255
  paragraph, 5, 16,
     121, 147, 255,
     298-300
Naming convention,
     25, 83, 121, 299
Negative data, 40,
     98, 103-105
Nested IF, 114,
     158-169
NEXT SENTENCE, 64,
     65, 165, 178,
     206, 292, 295
```

20 lines
15 chars

```
Minor control,
     158
Minus sign, in
     PICTURE,
     102-105,
     193
  in arithmetic
     expression,
     348
Mnemonic name,
     9, 122, 123
MOVE, 5, 32,
     40, 82, 99,
     195
MOVE CORRESPON-
     DING, 203,
     204, 215,
     318
MULTIPLY, 32,
     33, 38, 39,
     42, 349
```

35 lines
35 chars

```
Minor control, 158
Minus sign, in PICTURE, 102-105,
     193
  in arithmetic expression, 348
Mnemonic name, 9, 122, 123
MOVE, 5, 32, 40, 82, 99, 195
MOVE CORRESPONDING, 203, 204, 215,
     318
MULTIPLY, 32, 33, 38, 39, 42, 349

Name, data, 5, 9, 25, 82, 83, 255
  paragraph, 5, 16, 121, 147, 255,
     298-300
Naming convention, 25, 83, 121, 299
Negative data, 40, 98, 103-105
Nested IF, 114, 158-169
NEXT SENTENCE, 64, 65, 165, 178,
     206, 292, 295
New master, 231
NOMINAL KEY, 324, 327
Nonnumeric item, 29, 74, 77, 97,
     107, 154
Nonnumeric literal, 5, 74
NOT, 68, 77, 158, 181, 206-208
NUMERIC, 77
Numeric bit, 193
Numeric item, 29, 74, 77, 97, 107
Numeric literal, 5, 74

Object, of relation, 67, 207
Object program, 98, 99, 149, 154,
     190, 277, 289
OCCURS, 279, 280, 282, 284, 285,
     290
Old master, 231
```

Fig. 7.9. Output of the program of Fig. 7.6, all using the input shown in Fig. 7.8, but with different values of MAX$LINES and MAX$CHARS entered from the console.

10. In the program of Fig. 7.6, the declarations in statements 71 and 73 must be where they are, rather than in the procedures ANALYZE and PRINTONELINE, because they are used in the executable statements for PROCESSONETEXT$RECORD. How about the declarations in statements 74 and 75, which declare variables not used in the executable statements for PROCESSONETEXT$RECORD? Could they be placed in both of the included procedures to "hide" the variables at the lowest possible level?

11. Modify the program of Fig. 7.6 so that the operations following the label TERMINATE appear in WRAPUP, thus eliminating one GO TO.

CHAPTER 8

INTERRUPT PROCESSING

INTRODUCTION

In this chapter we shall consider the handling of *interrupts,* which make it possible to break into the sequence of execution of a running program to carry out other tasks and then resume execution of the program that was interrupted, as though nothing had happened. This facility makes it possible to respond immediately to external events. Sometimes the external events are of a repetitive nature, such as a clock pulse, which we simply wish to count whenever it arrives, and then go back to the other processing. Other times the external event is a signal that data is ready to be read or that some process variable has exceeded allowable limits. There are many other examples. Most microcomputer applications involve processing of interrupts to some degree.

The simplest examples of interrupt processing are fairly uncomplicated and easy to understand. At the other end of the scale, the more involved interrupt programs can be very complex indeed, especially when several interrupt routines have to interact under critical timing conditions.

In this chapter we shall study the fundamentals, enough to do significant applications programming. The first set of examples will involve one level of interrupt, ending with a real-time clock that presents the time of day on the CRT of an Intellec system. Then, after considering the concepts of *reentrancy* and *recursion,* we shall look into a case study involving the numerical control of a machine tool, using a program having two levels of interrupts.

PL/M INTERRUPT-PROCESSING FUNDAMENTALS

The 8080 CPU can respond to eight different interrupt signals, numbered 0 through 7. Most microcomputer systems contain hardware (external to the 8080) that gives different priorities to the different signals, interrupt 0 having the highest priority. Accordingly, it is customary to speak of eight *levels* of interrupts. If we wish to process an interrupt at level n, then we must provide an *interrupt procedure,* which is a procedure containing the attribute INTERRUPT n. This procedure must be untyped, have no parameters, and must be declared at the outer level of a program module. The effect of providing a procedure with this attribute, subject to certain conditions to be discussed shortly, is as follows. When an interrupt at level n occurs, execution of the instruction then under way is completed; the interrupt service routine for level n is activated; when it is completed, control returns to the instruction after the one that was interrupted.

The main qualification to what has just been stated is that the Intel 8080 processor contains a bit specifying whether interrupts are *enabled* or *disabled.* If an interrupt arrives at a time when interrupts have been disabled, then that interrupt is not processed until interrupts have again been enabled. The 8080 always starts with interrupts disabled.

Interrupts can be disabled during program execution in two ways. The first is automatic: They are always disabled when an interrupt is processed. The second is through execution of a statement called DISABLE. We shall see, in the examples that follow, where the statement is needed.

Corresponding to the DISABLE statement we have the ENABLE statement, which can be used to reverse the effect of a DISABLE. It can also be placed in the beginning of an interrupt procedure if we wish the procedure itself to be interruptable, which will occasionally be useful. Without such an ENABLE statement, interrupts are disabled throughout the execution of an interrupt procedure, but are automatically enabled upon exiting from the procedure, either by reaching the end or by executing a RETURN.

INTERRUPT PROCESSING IN AN INTELLEC SYSTEM

The Intellec interrupt system is fairly typical of microcomputer interrupt systems in that it contains a priority scheme, which works as follows: If an interrupt arrives at a time when another interrupt procedure is being executed (with interrupts having been enabled at the beginning of the procedure), the new interrupt will not be processed unless it has a higher priority than the one then being processed. (Higher priority means a smaller interrupt number.) This lets us set up priority interrupt systems in which, for example, a brief action like counting a clock pulse can interrupt a lower-priority operation like the servicing of normal data arrival, but not vice versa. Although the 8080 always starts with interrupts disabled, the Intellec system does an ENABLE before any programs are executed.

When working with interrupts on the Intellec system, we must take into account a third consideration that is special to it but which would be implemented in many applications as well. That is the presence of an *interrupt mask,* which makes it possible to specify which interrupts are to be serviced and which are to be ignored. In the Intellec system we send a byte to output port 0FCH; only those interrupt levels corresponding to zeros in this byte will be accepted.

A final factor relating to the development of programs on an Intellec system is that interrupts 0, 1, and 2 have functions associated with the ISIS-II system. In program development we would ordinarily avoid these three interrupt levels in order to be able to use the functions associated with them in the ISIS-II operating system. However, interrupt level 1 is the one that the real-time clock built into the Intellec system activates. In order to use the real-time clock, as we shall in the examples, it is necessary to relinquish use of the functions associated with interrupt 1 and also take certain actions in the program to override this normal usage.

Throughout this chapter we shall assume an Intellec environment for all examples. Bear in mind that some details of programming would be different in an actual application, since the application hardware might handle interrupts differently.

A TIMER IMPLEMENTED WITH A REAL-TIME CLOCK INTERRUPT

To see some of these ideas in operation, consider a program to produce output to the Intellec CRT at regular intervals.

The program is based on the existence in the Intellec hardware of a real-time clock that produces pulses at a 1.024-kHz rate. After appropriate initializing operations have been carried out by the program, pulses from this clock cause an interrupt at level 1 and a procedure set up to service these interrupts can increment a counter and thus keep track of time. A main-program loop can continuously interrogate the value of this counter, and when it reaches specified values, take actions appropriate to the amount of time that has passed.

We shall examine a sequence of four programs, starting with a simple interval timer and working up to a time-of-day routine.

THE SIMPLEST TIMER PROGRAM

The first version of the program does nothing more than write an X on the CRT of the Intellec console every quarter-second. The basic logic of the program is shown in the pseudocode of Fig. 8.1. We see an interrupt service routine named CLOCK that simply adds 1 to the value of a byte variable named CLOCK$PULSES, each

```
CLOCK:
PROCEDURE INTERRUPT 1;
   CLOCK$PULSES = CLOCK$PULSES + 1;      /* BYTE VARIABLE 'ROLLS' FROM 255 TO 0 */
END CLOCK;

/* MAIN PROGRAM */

INITIALIZE
DO FOREVER;
   IF CLOCK$PULSES = 0 THEN
   DO;
      CLOCK$PULSES = 1;
      WRITE AN X TO CRT, TO MARK PASSAGE OF 0.25 SEC
   END;
END;
```

Fig. 8.1. Pseudocode of the logic of a program to produce an output every quarter-second.

time a pulse from the Intellec real-time clock causes an interrupt. When this is done with the value of CLOCK$PULSES having been 255, the counter "rolls over" to zero.

The main program begins with some initialization operations and then goes into a DO FOREVER loop that continuously tests the value of CLOCK$PULSES. Whenever that value is zero we want to send an X to the CRT. At the same time, however, we must change CLOCK$PULSES to some nonzero value. If we did not do so, the program would write an X on the CRT and come back to test CLOCK$PULSES again, well within the approximate 1-millisecond interval before the next real-time clock pulse, leading to a shorter interval than desired.

This program logic will send an X to the CRT for every 255 pulses from the real-time clock. The frequency of this clock being approximately 1024 pulses per second, the X's will thus appear about every quarter-second.

The program in Fig. 8.2 implements this logic in a straightforward way but also includes some additional operations to get things started and to account for details of the way the Intellec system deals with interrupts. Heavy vertical lines identify statements the details of which the reader may safely skim over, since they deal only with things we must do to make the program run on an Intellec system. In an ordinary application, things of a similar nature would sometimes be required, but the details would vary. We may, however, sketch what is going on.

Lines 33–38 carry out initialization operations. Since it would be potentially disastrous to the program if an interrupt could occur while we were carrying out these operations, we begin in line 32 with a DISABLE. This operation prevents any interrupt from being recognized. The OUTPUT operations in lines 33–34 have to do with functions of the Intellec interrupt logic, the details of which are not important to us. These values must be sent to these ports in order to run an interrupt program on the Intellec; beyond that we don't care, for our purposes here. The OUTPUT operation in line 35 sets a mask that determines which interrupts will be accepted; those interrupt levels corresponding to zero bits in the byte sent to the port will be accepted. Finally we send a value to the port associated with the real-

```
PL/M-80 COMPILER    FIG. 8.2                                        PAGE    1

                $NOINTVECTOR

                /****************************************************************************/
                /* FIRST VERSION OF TIMER; USES THE INTELLEC 1.024 KHZ CLOCK TO PRODUCE */
                /* TICKS TO CRT AT 1/4 SEC INTERVALS                                     */
                /****************************************************************************/

  1             INTERRUPT$1:
                DO;
  2    1           DECLARE CLOCK$PULSES BYTE INITIAL(0);
  3    1           DECLARE LOC$8 BYTE AT (8);
  4    1           DECLARE LOC$9 ADDRESS AT (9);
  5    1           DECLARE STATUS ADDRESS;
  6    1           DECLARE FOREVER LITERALLY 'WHILE 1';

                $INCLUDE(:F1:INOUT.SRC)
           =    $NOLIST

 27    1        CLOCK$1:
                PROCEDURE INTERRUPT 1;
 28    2           CLOCK$PULSES = CLOCK$PULSES + 1;    /* BYTE VALUE 'ROLLS' FROM 255 TO 0 */
 29    2           OUTPUT(0FFH) = 2;                 /* ENABLE REAL-TIME CLOCK */
 30    2           OUTPUT(0FDH) = 20H;               /* RESTORE INTELLEC INTERRUPT LOGIC */
 31    2        END CLOCK$1;

                /*  MAIN PROGRAM  */

 32    1           DISABLE;

 33    1           OUTPUT(0FDH) = 12H;     /* INITIALIZE INTELLEC INTERRUPT LOGIC */
 34    1           OUTPUT(0FCH) = 0;       /* DITTO */
 35    1           OUTPUT(0FCH) = 0F8H;    /* ACCEPT INTERRUPTS 0, 1, AND 2 */
 36    1           OUTPUT(0FFH) = 2;       /* ENABLE REAL-TIME CLOCK */

 37    1           LOC$8 = 0C3H;           /* SET UP JUMP TO INTERRUPT 1 SERVICE ROUTINE */
 38    1           LOC$9 = .CLOCK$1;       /* DITTO */

 39    1           ENABLE;

 40    1           DO FOREVER;
 41    2              IF CLOCK$PULSES = 0 THEN
 42    2              DO;
 43    3                 CLOCK$PULSES = 1;
 44    3                 CALL WRITE(0, .('X'), 1, .STATUS);
 45    3              END;
 46    2           END;

 47    1        END INTERRUPT$1;
```

time clock, telling it to start sending pulses as soon as interrupts are enabled. Before enabling them, however, we must set up a jump instruction so that an interrupt at level 1 will cause a transfer to our interrupt service routine rather than to the ISIS routine normally associated with that interrupt. This takes a bit of trickery since the ISIS system is set up to "protect itself," so to speak, against attempts to load things into areas used by ISIS.

The problem to be solved is this: An interrupt on level 1 causes a transfer of control (after the completion of the current instruction) to location 8. (Interrupt zero causes a transfer to location zero, interrupt 2 causes a transfer to 16, interrupt 3 causes a transfer to 24, etc.) What we would like to have at location 8 is the instruction code for JUMP, which is 0C3H, followed by the address of our interrupt procedure for level 1. Since we cannot directly load such an instruction as part of the program, we set up the object program to do it after loading. This is the function of statements 37 and 38, combined with the declarations on lines 3 and 4. The AT attributes in the latter force the variables to be assigned to the specified locations but do not place anything in them.

The compiler control option NOINTVECTOR, at the beginning of the program, is needed to prevent the compiler from setting up a normal "interrupt vector" for interrupt 1. ISIS would not permit such an interrupt vector to be loaded into memory.

With all the preliminary operations taken care of, we execute an ENABLE that permits interrupts to be processed. From now on, any time a pulse from the real-time clock appears—no matter what else is going on—other processing will stop and the interrupt service routine will be executed.

The DO FOREVER loop is as shown in the pseudocode. We must constantly be aware that *anything* in this loop, including the WRITE routine that it invokes, can be interrupted. It could very well happen, for example, that the interrupt could arrive while the comparison in line 41 is being made. After the completion of that instruction, the interrupt service routine would then be carried out. In such a case, even though the value of CLOCK$PULSES had been zero at the time of the comparison, by the time line 43 is reached, it will already have been incremented by 1 by the interrupt service routine. This happens not to cause any trouble with this program logic, but does make the timing slightly uncertain. If this mattered, there are things we could do about it, as we shall see.

A SECOND TIMER ROUTINE

The previous program is obviously of rather limited generality. For the next step in the sequence, let us investigate what can be done to produce pulses at an arbitrary rate—within certain limits. The limit on the high end is that we can't get longer than a quarter of a second so long as we are restricted to a BYTE variable for the counter; we shall remove that restriction in the third version of the program. At the low end, we are restricted by the rate at which the CRT can accept characters, which is about every 4 ms.

Let us write a program to send an X to the CRT every 0.1 second. The modifications required, as shown in the program in Fig. 8.3, are quite simple. The only changes required are in the interrupt service routine. Instead of simply letting the byte variable "roll over," we test it each time to see whether it has reached 103, which is the number of pulses corresponding to approximately 0.1 second. If it has reached that value, we reset it to zero; otherwise we increment it.

A ONE-SECOND TIMER

Let us now modify the program so that it will time an interval of 1 second. The most obvious way to do this is to extend CLOCK$PULSES to an address variable

```
PL/M-80 COMPILER    FIG. 8.3                                   PAGE   1

          $NOINTVECTOR
          /*************************************************************************/
          /* SECOND VERSION OF TIMER; USES THE INTELLEC 1.024 KHZ CLOCK TO PRODUCE  */
          /* TICKS TO CRT AT 1/10 SEC INTERVALS                                     */
          /*************************************************************************/

          INTERRUPT$2:
          DO;
             DECLARE CLOCK$PULSES BYTE;
             DECLARE LOC$8 BYTE AT (8);
             DECLARE LOC$9 ADDRESS AT (9);
             DECLARE STATUS ADDRESS;
             DECLARE FOREVER LITERALLY 'WHILE 1';

          $INCLUDE(:F1:INOUT.SRC)
      =   $NOLIST

          CLOCK$2:
          PROCEDURE INTERRUPT 1;
             IF CLOCK$PULSES = 103 THEN
                CLOCK$PULSES = 0;
             ELSE
                CLOCK$PULSES = CLOCK$PULSES + 1;
             OUTPUT(0FFH) = 2;              /* ENABLE REAL-TIME CLOCK */
             OUTPUT(0FDH) = 20H;            /* RESTORE INTELLEC INTERRUPT LOGIC */
          END CLOCK$2;

          /*  MAIN PROGRAM  */

             DISABLE;

             OUTPUT(0FDH) = 12H;     /* INITIALIZE INTELLEC INTERRUPT LOGIC */
             OUTPUT(0FCH) = 0;       /* DITTO */
             OUTPUT(0FCH) = 0F8H;    /* ACCEPT INTERRUPTS 0, 1, AND 2 */
             OUTPUT(0FFH) = 2;       /* ENABLE REAL-TIME CLOCK */

             LOC$8 = 0C3H;           /* SET UP JUMP TO INTERRUPT 1 SERVICE ROUTINE */
             LOC$9 = .CLOCK$2;       /* DITTO */

             ENABLE;

             DO FOREVER;
                IF CLOCK$PULSES = 0 THEN
                DO;
                   CLOCK$PULSES = 1;
                   CALL WRITE(0, .('X'), 1, .STATUS);
                END;
             END;

          END INTERRUPT$2;
```

and count it up to 1024. This can be done as a trivial modification to the program just shown, but let us take a different approach that will let us deal with another issue in interrupt handling.

The change is to put the testing of CLOCK$PULSES back into the main program loop, where it was in the first version of the clock program in Fig. 8.2. Now, however, instead of looking for a zero value as the BYTE value "rolls over," we shall test an ADDRESS value against a termination value and reset it to zero when that value is reached.

To use this approach safely, however, we must deal with a problem that can arise in the testing of CLOCK$PULSES in this manner. The issue is instructive and fundamental to proper interrupt processing.

The problem is that it is possible for the testing of the address variable in the DO FOREVER loop to be interrupted in the middle. Depending on the details of the 8080 machine instructions that the compiler produces from this IF statement, there may be as many as four instructions involved in determining whether CLOCK$PULSES is equal to 1024. The danger is that the program might be set up to access the two bytes of this ADDRESS variable with separate instructions. Then if the process were interrupted between these two instructions, one byte of CLOCK$PULSES could contain the value before the interrupt and the other byte the value after the interrupt. Under certain circumstances this could cause the program to be seriously in error. If this error caused the interval to be, say, 65 seconds instead of 1 second, there is a decent chance it would be caught during checkout even if it didn't happen very often. On the other hand, if the error was such that it caused the interval to be 0.7 seconds instead of 1 second and if this happened on the average only once every thousand times, it might *never* be caught.

But there is more. Whether this problem occurs at all depends on how the compiler sets up the object code. We could perhaps inspect the object code and satisfy ourselves that in a given program the problem could not arise. This would be an undesirable solution, however, since recompilation a year or two later, with a modified version of the compiler, might create the problem where there had been none before.

The solution is actually quite simple: Disable interrupts during this testing. This should be done whenever the program is in a *critical region,* which is defined as a part of the program in which a data structure is potentially processable by two different routines. In this case the "data structure" is simply an ADDRESS variable and the two routines are the main program and the interrupt service routine. Since serious repercussions could result from modification of this variable while the main program is trying to process it, we simply disable interrupts during this period. (This approach assumes latched interrupts, which will still be available after leaving the critical region; pulsed interrupts would have to be handled differently.)

The program in Fig. 8.4 incorporates these modifications. We see in line 41, just before the IF statement that tests CLOCK$PULSES, a DISABLE. In the case

```
PL/M-80 COMPILER    FIG. 8.4                                        PAGE   1

                $NOINTVECTOR
                /*************************************************************************/
                /* THIRD VERSION OF TIMER: PRODUCES TICKS TO CRT AT 1 SEC INTERVALS      */
                /* THIS VERSION PROTECTS A CRITICAL REGION                               */
                /*************************************************************************/

 1              INTERRUPT$4:
                DO;
 2    1            DECLARE CLOCK$PULSES ADDRESS INITIAL(0);
 3    1            DECLARE LOC$8 BYTE AT (8);
 4    1            DECLARE LOC$9 ADDRESS AT (9);
 5    1            DECLARE STATUS ADDRESS;
 6    1            DECLARE FOREVER LITERALLY 'WHILE 1';

                $INCLUDE(:F1:INOUT.SRC)
           =    $NOLIST

27    1         CLOCK$1:
                PROCEDURE INTERRUPT 1;
28    2            CLOCK$PULSES = CLOCK$PULSES + 1;
29    2            OUTPUT(0FFH) = 2;              /* ENABLE REAL-TIME CLOCK */
30    2            OUTPUT(0FDH) = 20H;            /* RESTORE INTELLEC INTERRUPT LOGIC */
31    2         END CLOCK$1;

                /*  MAIN PROGRAM  */

32    1            DISABLE;

33    1            OUTPUT(0FDH) = 12H;      /* INITIALIZE INTELLEC INTERRUPT LOGIC */
34    1            OUTPUT(0FCH) = 0;        /* DITTO */
35    1            OUTPUT(0FCH) = 0F8H;     /* ACCEPT INTERRUPTS 0, 1, AND 2 */
36    1            OUTPUT(0FFH) = 2;        /* ENABLE REAL-TIME CLOCK */

37    1            LOC$8 = 0C3H;            /* SET UP JUMP TO INTERRUPT 1 SERVICE ROUTINE */
38    1            LOC$9 = .CLOCK$1;        /* DITTO */

39    1            ENABLE;

40    1            DO FOREVER;
41    2               DISABLE;                       /* START OF CRITICAL REGION */
42    2               IF CLOCK$PULSES = 1024 THEN
43    2               DO;
44    3                  CLOCK$PULSES = 0;
45    3                  ENABLE;   /* END OF CRITICAL REGION WHEN CLOCK$PULSES = 1024 */
46    3                  CALL WRITE(0, .('X'), 1, .STATUS);
47    3               END;
48    2               ENABLE;    /* END OF CRITICAL REGION WHEN CLOCK$PULSES NOT = 1024 */
49    2            END;

50    1         END INTERRUPT$4;
```

where the test establishes that CLOCK$PULSES is 1024, we want the critical region to extend just past resetting CLOCK$PULSES to zero. Therefore we place an ENABLE at line 45. Naturally this ENABLE will be executed only when the condition is true, whereas the DISABLE on line 41 was unconditional. We therefore need an ENABLE in line 48 also.

One might ask: Why not simply omit the ENABLE in line 45, thus including the CALL WRITE in the critical region also? The answer has to do with the time required by the main-program processing compared with the time available between real-time clock pulses. If the main-program processing is guaranteed to be well under one millisecond, there is no problem; it will be finished before the next clock pulse comes along. As it happens that is the case here. Suppose, however, that when the clock rolled over, the required processing took a good deal longer than this, say 10 milliseconds. If we were to disable interrupts during the entire period, we would obviously lose all the clock pulses during that time and the clock would run slow. This program does not have that problem since the critical region in fact extends over only a few ten's of *micro*seconds. If the processing represented by CALL WRITE did take ten *milli*seconds, however, the program as written would be interrupted periodically by the interrupt service routine, which would cause no problems.

A TIME-OF-DAY CLOCK

The final program in this sequence, shown in Fig. 8.5, produces the time of day on the Intellec CRT: Each second it writes the time in hours, minutes, and seconds. The time of day at which the program is started is entered from the CRT keyboard.

The main new feature of this program is a somewhat more elaborate interrupt service procedure. It counts clock pulses to 1024 to get seconds; then it selectively rolls counters containing seconds, minutes, and hours. The main program includes new operations in lines 62–66 to get, from the keyboard, the time of day at which the program is started. The comment about the "command tail" refers to the fact that the time of day is entered on the same line with the command that calls the program from disk and into operation. The DO FOREVER loop contains the operations needed to write the time onto the CRT screen.

Provision of a critical region in this DO FOREVER loop is good practice and strongly recommended. As it happens *in this program,* however, the problem it is designed to prevent could not arise. Let us be clear on what the problem is and see why it could not happen here.

The problem is that, after determining in statement 70 that CLOCK$PULSES is equal to zero, the clock routine could interrupt the conversion of the three values for output, thus creating a false time. Suppose, for example, that the time is 12:34:59, and that, after obtaining minutes in statement 76, the clock rolls over. The 12 and the 34 have already been obtained so that the old value of minutes will

```
PL/M-80 COMPILER    FIG. 8.5                                      PAGE   1

              $NOINTVECTOR

              /*********************************************************************/
              /* A CLOCK PROGRAM: ACCEPTS TIME OF DAY IN HOURS, MINUTES, AND SECONDS, */
              /* THEN CONTINUOUSLY DISPLAYS TIME EVERY SECOND                        */
              /*********************************************************************/

 1            CLOCK:
              DO;
 2    1          DECLARE (HOUR, MIN, SEC) BYTE INITIAL(0, 0, 0);
 3    1          DECLARE CLOCK$PULSES ADDRESS INITIAL(0);
 4    1          DECLARE LOC$8 BYTE AT (8);
 5    1          DECLARE LOC$9 ADDRESS AT (9);
 6    1          DECLARE BUFFER(100) BYTE;
 7    1          DECLARE BUFFPTR ADDRESS;
 8    1          DECLARE (COUNT, STATUS) ADDRESS;
 9    1          DECLARE CRLF(2) BYTE DATA(0DH, 0AH);
10    1          DECLARE FOREVER LITERALLY 'WHILE 1';

              $INCLUDE(:F1:INOUT.SRC)
          =   $NOLIST

31    1       CLOCK$3:
              PROCEDURE INTERRUPT 1;
32    2          CLOCK$PULSES = CLOCK$PULSES + 1;
33    2          IF CLOCK$PULSES = 1024 THEN
34    2          DO;
35    3             CLOCK$PULSES = 0;
36    3             SEC = SEC + 1;
37    3             IF SEC = 60 THEN
38    3             DO;
39    4                SEC = 0;
40    4                MIN = MIN + 1;
41    4                IF MIN = 60 THEN
42    4                DO;
43    5                   MIN = 0;
44    5                   HOUR = HOUR + 1;
45    5                   IF HOUR = 24 THEN
46    5                   DO;
47    6                      HOUR = 0;
48    6                   END;
49    5                END;
50    4             END;
51    3          END;
52    2          OUTPUT(0FFH) = 2;        /* ENABLE REAL-TIME CLOCK */
53    2          OUTPUT(0FDH) = 20H;      /* RESTORE INTELLEC INTERRUPT LOGIC */
54    2       END CLOCK$3;
```

be written. But when statement 77 is executed, it is the new value of seconds that will be obtained. The time written will therefore be written incorrectly as 12:34:00.

However, in this program the problem cannot arise. Let us see why:

The DO FOREVER loop repeats constantly. Almost all of the time CLOCK$-PULSES is not equal to zero and the loop simply repeats without having done any other operations. The total number of instructions executed in this normal case is

```
PL/M-80 COMPILER    FIG. 8.5                                                              PAGE    2

                $EJECT
                /* MAIN PROGRAM */

     1             DISABLE;

     1             OUTPUT(0FDH) = 12H;
     1             OUTPUT(0FCH) = 0;
     1             OUTPUT(0FCH) = 0F8H;
     1             OUTPUT(0FFH) = 2;
     1             LOC$8 = 0C3H;
     1             LOC$9 = .CLOCK$3;

     1             CALL READ(1, .BUFFER, 100, .COUNT, .STATUS);   /* GET TIME FROM COMMAND TAIL */
     1             BUFFPTR = .BUFFER;
     1             HOUR = NUMIN(.BUFFPTR);
     1             MIN = NUMIN(.BUFFPTR);
     1             SEC = NUMIN(.BUFFPTR);

     1             ENABLE;

     1             DO FOREVER;
     2                DISABLE;            /* ENTER CRITICAL REGION */
     2                IF CLOCK$PULSES = 0 THEN
     2                DO;
     3                   CLOCK$PULSES = 1;
     3                   ENABLE;  /* EXIT CRITICAL REGION WHEN CLOCK$PULSES = 0 */
     3                   BUFFER(0) = 0DH;
     3                   CALL NUMOUT(HOUR, 10, ' ', .BUFFER+1, 2);
     3                   CALL NUMOUT(MIN, 10, ' ', .BUFFER+3, 3);
     3                   CALL NUMOUT(SEC, 10, ' ', .BUFFER+6, 3);
     3                   CALL WRITE(0, .BUFFER, 9, .STATUS);
     3                END;
     2                ENABLE;      /* EXIT CRITICAL REGION WHEN CLOCK$PULSES NOT = 0 */
     2             END;  /* DO FOREVER */

     1          END CLOCK;
```

so small that one time through the entire loop may take no more than perhaps 20 microseconds. When the interrupt service routine eventually sets CLOCK$PULSES to zero, the DO FOREVER loop will therefore know it within at most a few microseconds after it happens. At this point the conversion of the three time values and writing them to the CRT is carried out immediately, which takes only a few milliseconds, and once again the DO FOREVER loop goes back to waiting for CLOCK$-PULSES to reach zero. Under these circumstances the interrupt service routine cannot cause the problem of changing one of the time values during the conversion process.

If this routine were incorporated into a larger program with many other things going on, some of which could sometimes take around a second, then we would have to reconsider this matter. The best solution would be to move hours, minutes, and seconds, within the critical region, to three other variables and then use the values from these other variables in the calls to NUMOUT.

REENTRANCY

Consider the program skeleton shown in Fig. 8.6, the crucial feature of which is that PROC$A is called both by an interrupt service routine and by the main program. Now consider the following scenario: The main program has called PROC$A, with interrupts enabled, and PROC$A is in the middle of execution. At this point the interrupt service routine is activated, during the course of which it also calls PROC$A. PROC$A now has a problem: How does it keep separate the variables that it was working on during the first invocation, from those it will work on during the second invocation? Furthermore, when it is completed, how does it know where to go back to?

```
PROC$A:
   PROCEDURE . . .   REENTRANT
   . . .
END PROC$A;

INTERRUPT$PROCESSOR:
   PROCEDURE INTERRUPT 4;
   . . .
   CALL PROC$A;
   . . .
END INTERRUPT$PROCESSOR;

/* MAIN PROGRAM */
   . . .
   CALL PROC$A;
   . . .
```

Fig. 8.6. Skeleton pseudocode of a program requiring reentrancy.

The answer is *reentrancy*: PROC$A must be declared to have the attribute REENTRANT. Now, additional measures are taken such that the program structure shown will be handled without any trouble. (For those who know the Intel 8080 operation, the answer is that all variables in PROC$A are allocated on the stack; at each reinvocation of PROC$A the stack is pushed and the variables for the new invocation are allocated to the top of the stack. When this second invocation is completed, the stack is popped. Everything is in good order when the first invocation is eventually resumed.)

If PROC$A calls any other procedure, then those other procedures should also be reentrant since it could be their execution that is interrupted just as easily as that of PROC$A. In the Intellec environment this means that PROC$A should not call any ISIS routines since these are not reentrant. In particular, CALL READ and CALL WRITE should not be used.

RECURSIVE PROCEDURES

Reentrancy deals with any situation where a procedure can be invoked a second time before it has returned from the first invocation. We have seen how this can happen with interrupts but there are other situations as well where this can arise. The most common of these is a *recursive procedure,* which is one that calls itself.

A very simple example of a recursive procedure is one to compute factorials. In point of fact, no one would ever compute factorials this way in an applications program, but the concept of recursion is so cleanly illustrated that the example is very widely used.

```
PL/M-80 COMPILER    FIG. 8.7                                        PAGE   1

/***********************************************************************/
/* A RECURSIVE FACTORIAL PROGRAM                                        */
/***********************************************************************/

FACTORIAL$PROGRAM:
DO;
   DECLARE N ADDRESS INITIAL(1);
   DECLARE N$FACTORIAL ADDRESS;
   DECLARE BUFFER(128) BYTE;
   DECLARE (COUNT, STATUS, BUFFPTR) ADDRESS;

$INCLUDE(:F1:INOUT.SRC)
$NOLIST

FACTORIAL:
PROCEDURE (N) ADDRESS REENTRANT;
   DECLARE (N, X) ADDRESS;

   IF N = 1 THEN
      X = 1;
   ELSE
      X = N * FACTORIAL(N - 1);
   RETURN X;
END FACTORIAL;

/*  MAIN PROGRAM  */
   DO WHILE N <> 0;
      CALL READ(1, .BUFFER, 10, .COUNT, .STATUS);
      BUFFPTR = .BUFFER;
      N = NUMIN(.BUFFPTR);
      N$FACTORIAL = FACTORIAL(N);
      CALL NUMOUT(N$FACTORIAL, 10, ' ', .BUFFER + 1, 9);
      BUFFER(1) = 21H;      /* EXCLAMATION = FACTORIAL SIGN */
      BUFFER(3) = 3DH;      /* EQUAL SIGN */
      BUFFER(10) = 0DH;     /* CARRIAGE RETURN */
      BUFFER(11) = 0AH;     /* LINE FEED */
      CALL WRITE(0, .BUFFER, 12, .STATUS);
   END;

   CALL EXIT;

END FACTORIAL$PROGRAM;
```

The program in Fig. 8.7 uses a recursive procedure to compute factorials. The main program is a straightforward matter of reading numbers from the console and printing the results. In line 37 we call for the factorial of N to be computed, using the procedure named FACTORIAL.

Looking at that procedure we see that it is typed, having the attribute ADDRESS, and it has been designated as REENTRANT. The heart of the program is the IF statement. This says that if N equals 1, the value of X—the number we shall return—is equal to 1. Otherwise X is equal to N times the factorial of N − 1; we get the factorial of N − 1 by invoking this same procedure again—from within itself. Naturally the multiplication that is indicated in line 30 cannot be carried out until we get back from the call of this procedure. When this procedure is invoked a second time, the IF statement will again be executed. If the argument in the second invocation is 1, i.e., if the original value of N was 2, then the second invocation can return the value 1 without invoking the procedure a third time. But if the argument on the second invocation is not 1, then the procedure will have to be invoked a third time, etc. Eventually the procedure will have been invoked enough times to reduce the argument to 1, at which point we come back through the nested calls carrying out the multiplications. The final result is RETURNed.

Without going into all the details, we can say that when a reentrant procedure is invoked, a number of bytes of information must be placed "on the stack" to permit correct resumption of execution. The number of bytes per invocation is eight plus the number of bytes of variable storage declared by the procedure.

There is no way that the compiler or other components of the ISIS operating system can know how deep the recursive calls will go since that depends on run-time data. There is, therefore, no way the operating system can know how much space to allocate for the stack. This we must do by using the STACKSIZE control on the LOCATE program, which will be discussed in Chapter 9.

The output when this program was run is shown below. The incorrect value for 9 is the result of trying to produce a number too large for the space available in an ADDRESS variable.

```
1
1! =      1
2
2! =      2
3
3! =      6
5
5! =    120
7
7! =   5040
8
8! =  40320
9
9! =  35200
```

INDIRECT RECURSION

Recall that reentrancy involves any situation where a procedure can be invoked a second time before completing the work of its first invocation. *Direct recursion* is a procedure that calls itself. *Indirect recursion* involves a procedure that calls some other procedure which then calls the first one, or a first procedure that calls a second procedure which calls a third procedure which then calls the first one, and so on. The REENTRANT attribute must be used for every procedure in an indirect recursion chain.

CASE STUDY: A NUMERICALLY CONTROLLED MACHINE TOOL

In the case study for this chapter we consider a program using two levels of interrupts to control a machine tool. The application, as far as we shall take it, is very rudimentary, but it will nevertheless let us explore some interesting issues in interrupt handling and would actually be a reasonable way to approach the development of a full-scale program. We shall continue the discussion of the program development into the case study of the next chapter.

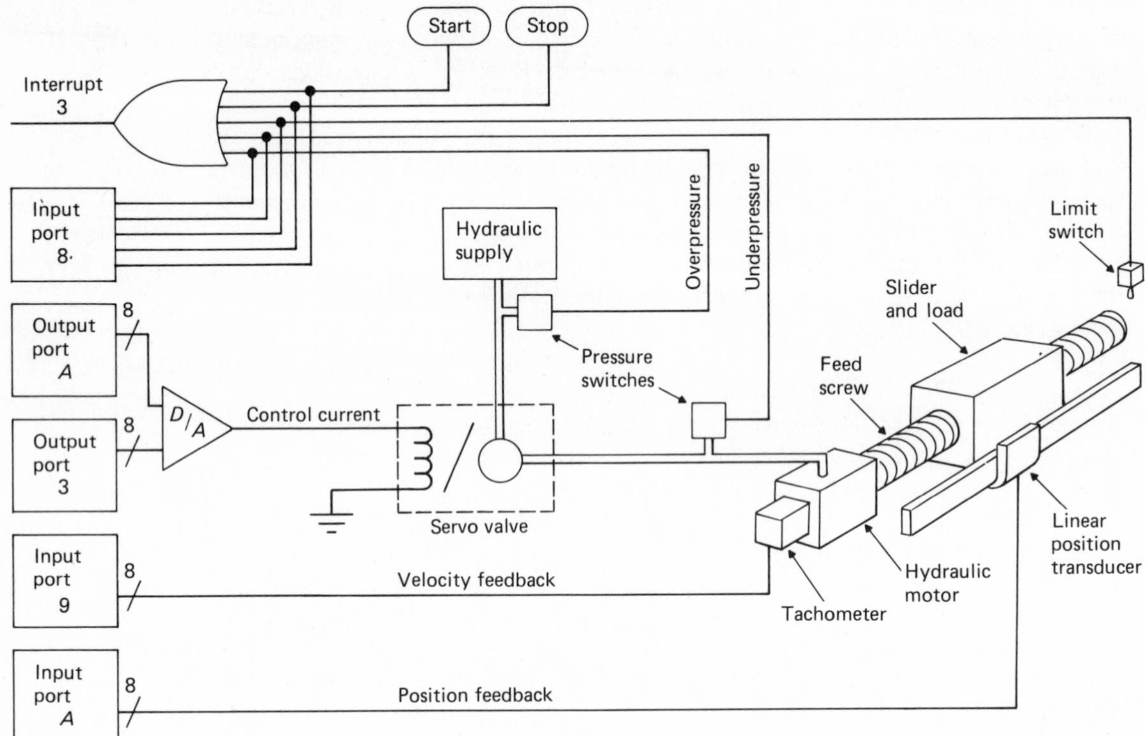

Fig. 8.8. Rough schematic of a numerically controlled machine tool.

The application is as sketched in Fig. 8.8. A cutting tool is mounted on a feed mechanism. A servo valve and hydraulic motor drive the tool, and a linear position transducer tells where it is positioned. The simple version of the device that we shall consider drives the tool in only one direction. We assume that the operator positions the tool, sets the desired feed rate, and presses the start button. The program then uses a real-time clock to determine where the tool should be (from the specified feed rate and the elapsed time), compares this with its actual position, and from these values computes the control current to the servo motor from the formulas:

$$P_d = P_0 + F * t$$
$$\text{Current} = K_p * (P_d - P_a)$$

where

P_d = Desired position,
P_0 = Initial position,
F = Feedrate, set by operator,
t = Elapsed time since start,
K_p = Position coefficient,
P_a = Actual position.

The program will use interrupt 1 to count the time with a real-time clock that, we shall assume for simplicity, produces pulses at a 1-kHz rate. In the program we shall use the Intellec clock, which is slightly faster than that, but the difference is unimportant for our purposes.

Interrupt 3 will be used to signal the presence of any of five conditions in the machine tool. In decreasing order of priority these are:

1. The stop button,
2. Overpressure in the hydraulic supply,
3. A limit switch on the travel of the tool,
4. Underpressure in the hydraulic supply,
5. The start button.

As Fig. 8.8 shows, these five signals are ORed together to produce the interrupt; individually they are available at an input port. Accordingly, in the interrupt service routine we begin by reading that input port to find out what actually caused the interrupt, and then take appropriate action.

For the first three conditions we are required to set an alarm, shut down the hydraulic pump, and send the elapsed time (since pressing the start button) to a recorder. For the underpressure condition, we simply set an alarm and record the time. For the last condition, the start button, we get the time from the real-time clock, read the desired feed rate, and read the initial position of the tool. We also start the process of continuously reading the actual position and computing the control current required to close the gap between the desired position and the actual position. This, of course, is the essence of a servomechanism.

PSEUDOCODE OF THE PROGRAM SKELETON

We begin the program development process with a pseudocode of the bare essentials of the top level of the program. The bare essentials in this case involve the interactions between the main-program loop, two interrupt service routines, and a routine that is called both by an interrupt service routine and by a procedure that is in the main-program loop. At this stage of program development, we give no attention to the details of what is done with the numerical control data. That is, of course, crucial, but we choose to focus attention on one level of detail at a time, and the level we wish to concentrate on first is the top level.

```
NUMERICAL$CONTROL:
DO;
   DECLARE . . .

TIME$IN$TENTHS$PROCEDURE:
   PROCEDURE ADDRESS REENTRANT;
   Convert time in ms to time in tenths of a second.
END TIME$IN$TENTHS$PROCEDURE;

CLOCK:
   PROCEDURE INTERRUPT 1;
   Add to counter each time interrupted by real-time clock.
END CLOCK;

INTERRUPT$PROCESSOR:
   PROCEDURE INTERRUPT 3;
   Establish what caused interrupt and take appropriate action,
   usually including a call of TIME$IN$TENTHS$PROCEDURE.
END INTERRUPT$PROCESSOR;

SETUP:
   PROCEDURE;
   Carry out various initializing operations.
END SETUP;

COMPUTE$CONTROL$CURRENT:
   PROCEDURE;
   Compute control current and write it.  Call TIME$IN$TENTHS$PROCEDURE.
END COMPUTE$CONTROL$CURRENT;

/* main program */
   CALL SETUP;
   Initialize for Intellec interrupt operations.

   DO FOREVER;
      IF GO$FLAG THEN
         CALL COMPUTE$CONTROL$CURRENT;
   END;

WRAPUP:
   Carry out abort operations required for Intellec checkout version.

END NUMERICAL$CONTROL;
```

Fig. 8.9. Top-level pseudocode of a program for the numerical control of a machine tool.

A pseudocode is shown in Fig. 8.9. As usual, the main program provides a top-level view of what the program is about. It begins with initializing operations, does some things needed to get the interrupt process started correctly, and goes into a DO FOREVER loop that carries out the required processing. A WRAPUP section will be entered by GO TO statements when abort conditions arise in the developmental versions of the program.

The setup operations do not interest us at this stage, nor does the computation of the control current except to note that it involves calling a routine named TIMEINTENTHS$PROCEDURE. The processing of interrupts on level 3 is reasonably straightforward. The very simple clock routine counts milliseconds. In the full-scale program it would involve two variables having a total of 24 or 32 bits, allowing it to hold times, in milliseconds, as long as some hours. In the developmental version it will be an ADDRESS variable of 16 bits, which allows us to count a time of about 65 seconds. The procedure named TIMEINTENTHS$-PROCEDURE converts from a time in milliseconds to a time in tenths of a second. In the developmental version this is a simple matter of dividing by 100, but in the full-scale version it would be rather more complicated because of the necessity to do a double-precision division.

The crucial thing to note is that TIMEINTENTHS$PROCEDURE is called both by the COMPUTE$CONTROL$CURRENT routine, which is in the main-program loop, and by the routine named INTERRUPT$PROCESSOR; TIME$IN$-TENTHS$PROCEDURE must therefore be reentrant. Furthermore, neither of the interrupt routines—nor any routine they call—may invoke any ISIS functions, since these are not reentrant.

THE CASE STUDY PROGRAM

With the main outlines of the program worked out in pseudocode, the program in Fig. 8.10 is not as complex as a first glance at its length might suggest. Let us study it in the order in which functions will be invoked by the main program.

We wish to develop and test this program using an Intellec Microcomputer Development System, which means that the reading of the numerical control values must be simulated in some way. The way chosen here is to set up two files of these values on diskette, one for the values coming from the ORed interrupt port and another for the values coming from the position transducer port. These files can be set up in advance to provide values for testing the program. Since reading the values from the diskette involves calls to ISIS, we must read these files into Intellec memory in a preliminary operation. This is the main function of the procedure named SETUP. Before reading these files, however, it is necessary to OPEN them, along with a scratch file used for line editing. A null line at the end of each file, which places a carriage-return character into the first position of the buffer, is used to terminate reading of the file. Sentinels of all 1 bits are placed at the end of the arrays into which the simulated input values are placed in memory, so that the

```
PL/M-80 COMPILER    FIG. 8.10                                                      PAGE   1

          $NOINTVECTOR
          /*****************************************************************************/
          /* A NUMERICAL CONTROL PROGRAM, PRESENTED HERE IN AN EARLY DEVELOPMENTAL      */
          /* VERSION THAT EMPHASIZES INTERRUPT AND REENTRANCY CONSIDERATIONS.           */
          /*                                                                           */
          /* THIS VERSION USES INPUT TAKEN FROM DISK, SET UP FOR CHECKOUT PURPOSES,     */
          /* AND WRITES ITS OUTPUT EITHER TO THE LINE PRINTER OR TO DISK.               */
          /*****************************************************************************/
          /*
          GLOBAL VARIABLES:
             TIME$MS             TIME IN MILLISECONDS
             TIME$TENTHS         TIME IN TENTHS OF A SECOND
             TIME$ZERO$TENTHS    TIME AT WHICH START BUTTON WAS PRESSED
             FEEDRATE            INPUT VALUE: RATE AT WHICH TOOL IS TO MOVE
             POSITION$ZERO       INITIAL POSITION OF TOOL WHEN START BUTTON IS PRESSED
             GO$FLAG             FLAG INDICATING THAT START BUTTON HAS BEEN PRESSED
             ECHO$AFTN           AFTN = 'ACTIVE FILE TABLE NUMBER' FOR FILE NEEDED BY ISIS
                                    PROCESSING OF SIMULATED INPUT
             DISK$1$AFTN         AFTN OF DISK FILE OF SIMULATED INPUT: INTERRUPT IDENTIFIERS
             DISK$2$AFTN         AFTN FOR INPUT: ALL OTHER
             LP$AFTN             AFTN FOR OUTPUT: SIMPLE CHANGE IN PROGRAM SENDS OUTPUT TO DISK
          */
          NUMERICAL$CONTROL:
          DO;
             DECLARE (TIME$MS, TIME$TENTHS, TIME$ZERO$TENTHS) ADDRESS INITIAL(0, 0, 0);
             DECLARE (FEED$RATE, POSITION$ZERO) ADDRESS;
             DECLARE GO$FLAG BYTE;
             DECLARE (ECHO$AFTN, DISK$1$AFTN, DISK$2$AFTN, LP$AFTN) ADDRESS;
             DECLARE TRUE LITERALLY '0FFH';
             DECLARE FALSE LITERALLY '0';
             DECLARE FOREVER LITERALLY 'WHILE 1';
             DECLARE LOC$8 BYTE AT(8);
             DECLARE LOC$9 ADDRESS AT (9);
             DECLARE LOC$9$SAVE ADDRESS;
             DECLARE LOC$24 BYTE AT(24);
             DECLARE LOC$25 ADDRESS AT(25);
             DECLARE INPUT$1(50) BYTE;          /* STORAGE FOR PART OF SIMULATED INPUT */
             DECLARE INPUT$2(200) ADDRESS;      /* DITTO */
             DECLARE OUTPUT$A(250) BYTE;        /* STORAGE FOR PART OF SIMULATED OUTPUT */
             DECLARE OUTPUT$B(250) ADDRESS;     /* DITTO */
             DECLARE (INDEX$1, INDEX$2, OUTDEX, OUTDEX$FINAL) ADDRESS;
             DECLARE BUFFER(128) BYTE;
             DECLARE (BUFFPTR, COUNT, STATUS) ADDRESS;

          $INCLUDE(:F1:INOUT.SRC)
        = $NOLIST
```

routines that use the simulated data can know when to stop. After the completion of all these operations, three indexes that point to the simulated input and output files are set to zero, and GO$FLAG, which specifies whether the start button has been pressed, is set to FALSE.

The next function in the main program is to initialize the interrupts, which is done in essentially the same fashion as in the programs earlier in the chapter. We

```
PL/M-80 COMPILER    FIG. 8.10                                    PAGE   2

                 $EJECT
      1          TIME$IN$TENTHS$PROCEDURE:
                 PROCEDURE ADDRESS REENTRANT;
      2             DECLARE TEMPORARY ADDRESS;

      2             DISABLE;  /* CRITICAL REGION: TIME$MS ALSO PROCESSED BY INTERRUPT ROUTINE */
      2             TEMPORARY = TIME$MS / 100;
      2             ENABLE;
      2             RETURN TEMPORARY;

                 /* IN FULL-SCALE PROGRAM, TIME$MS WOULD BE 24 OR 32 BITS, REQUIRING A MORE
                    ELABORATE PROCESSING ROUTINE HERE */

      2          END TIME$IN$TENTHS$PROCEDURE;

      1          CLOCK:
                 PROCEDURE INTERRUPT 1;
      2             TIME$MS = TIME$MS + 1;
    | 2             OUTPUT(0FFH) = 2;      /* ENABLE REAL-TIME CLOCK */
    | 2             OUTPUT(0FDH) = 20H;    /* RESTORE INTELLEC INTERRUPT LOGIC */

                 /* IN FULL-SCALE PROGRAM, TIME$MS WOULD BE 24 OR 32 BITS, REQUIRING A MORE
                    ELABORATE PROCESSING ROUTINE HERE */

      2          END CLOCK;
```

now come to the DO FOREVER loop with GO$FLAG having been set to FALSE. This loop will simply repeat at a very fast rate, waiting for interrupt 3 to occur.

When it does, in our case as a result of the appropriate button on the Intellec console having been pressed, we enter the interrupt service routine for interrupt 3. This may possibly involve a slight wait while interrupt service routine 1 finishes its operations if it was under way when interrupt 3 occurred. Even though we enable interrupts at the beginning of the service routine for interrupt 3, interrupt 3 would still have to wait, since it has a lower priority.

When interrupt 3 occurs, the service routine named INTERRUPT$PROCESSOR does a simulated input operation to get a value from the array of values read earlier from diskette. Observe that the various possible causes of the interrupt are checked in a priority sequence: Overpressure is a more urgent matter than the start button, so the former is tested first. This program is not designed to deal with simultaneous occurrences of interrupts, but such programs can be written. This suggests a way, in other words, of implementing a priority interrupt scheme with just one level of interrupts.

The functions carried out by INTERRUPT$PROCESSOR are as sketched in the description of the application. We note that one of the results of detecting pressing of the start button is to set GO$FLAG to TRUE.

```
PL/M-80 COMPILER    FIG. 8.10                                                    PAGE   3


              $EJECT
 53   1       INTERRUPT$PROCESSOR:
              PROCEDURE INTERRUPT 3;
 54   2          DECLARE INTERRUPT$IDENTIFIERS BYTE;

 55   2          ENABLE;     /* ALLOW THIS INTERRUPT SERVICE ROUTINE TO BE INTERRUPTED */

                 /* SIMULATE INPUT OF INTERRUPT INDENTIFIER */
 56   2          IF INPUT$1(INDEX$1) = 0FFH THEN    /* SENTINEL: END OF SIMULATED INPUT */
 57   2             GO TO WRAPUP;
                 ELSE
 58   2             INTERRUPT$IDENTIFIERS = INPUT$1(INDEX$1);
 59   2          INDEX$1 = INDEX$1 + 1;

 60   2          IF     (INTERRUPT$IDENTIFIERS = 00000001B)     /* STOP SIGNAL */
                    OR (INTERRUPT$IDENTIFIERS = 00000010B)     /* OVER-PRESSURE */
                    OR (INTERRUPT$IDENTIFIERS = 00000100B)     /* LIMIT SWITCH */
                 THEN
 61   2          DO;
 62   3             OUTPUT$A(OUTDEX) = 11000000B;      /* ALARM AND SHUT DOWN */
 63   3             OUTPUT$B(OUTDEX) = TIME$IN$TENTHS$PROCEDURE - TIME$ZERO$TENTHS;
 64   3             OUTDEX = OUTDEX + 1;
 65   3             GO$FLAG = FALSE;
 66   3          END;

 67   2          IF INTERRUPT$IDENTIFIERS = 00001000B THEN      /* UNDER-PRESSURE */
 68   2          DO;
 69   3             OUTPUT$A(OUTDEX) = 10000000B;          /* ALARM */
 70   3             OUTPUT$B(OUTDEX) = TIME$IN$TENTHS$PROCEDURE - TIME$ZERO$TENTHS;
 71   3             OUTDEX = OUTDEX + 1;
 72   3          END;

 73   2          IF INTERRUPT$IDENTIFIERS = 00010000B THEN      /* START BUTTON */
 74   2          DO;
 75   3             TIME$ZERO$TENTHS = TIME$IN$TENTHS$PROCEDURE;
 76   3             FEED$RATE = 4;       /* REPLACE WITH INPUT OPERATIONS LATER */
 77   3             POSITION$ZERO = 20; /* DITTO */
 78   3             GO$FLAG = TRUE;
 79   3          END;

 80   2          DISABLE;  /* MUST DISABLE INTERRUPTS BEFORE RESTORING INTELLEC INTERRUPT LOGIC */
 81   2          OUTPUT(0FDH) = 20H;     /* RESTORE INTELLEC INTERRUPT LOGIC */

 82   2       END INTERRUPT$PROCESSOR;
```

With GO$FLAG TRUE, the main program loop will now invoke COMPUTE$-CONTROL$CURRENT. This routine is required to determine the actual position of the tool, in our case with simulated input, and compute the control current. For our purposes, at this stage of program development, we are not really interested in the details of this processing, which would involve multiple-precision arithmetic, shifting operations to scale fractional quantities, etc. In the full-scale program it would almost certainly involve a more elaborate control formula, perhaps taking

```
PL/M-80 COMPILER    FIG. 8.10                                              PAGE   4

          $EJECT
          SETUP:
          PROCEDURE;

             CALL OPEN(.ECHO$AFTN, .(':F1:SCRTCH '), 2, 0, .STATUS);
             CALL OPEN(.DISK$1$AFTN, .(':F1:8NC1.DAT '), 1, ECHO$AFTN, .STATUS);
             CALL OPEN(.DISK$2$AFTN, .(':F1:8NC2.DAT '), 1, ECHO$AFTN, .STATUS);
             CALL OPEN(.LP$AFTN, .(':LP: '), 2, 0, .STATUS);

             /* READ DISK FILES TO GET SIMULATED DATA INTO MAIN MEMORY.  CANNOT BE DONE
                WITH ISIS CALLS WITHIN INTERRUPT SERVICE ROUTINES, BECAUSE ISIS ROUTINES
                ARE NOT REENTRANT. */

             INDEX$1 = 0;
             DO WHILE INDEX$1 < 50;
                CALL READ(DISK$1$AFTN, .BUFFER, 20, .COUNT, .STATUS);
                IF BUFFER(0) = 0DH THEN   /* IMPLIES NULL LINE MARKING END OF INPUT */
                DO;
                   INPUT$1(INDEX$1) = 0FFH;    /* SENTINEL: END OF SIMULATED INPUT */
                   INDEX$1 = 50;            /* GET OUT OF LOOP */
                END;
                ELSE
                DO;
                   BUFFPTR = .BUFFER;
                   INPUT$1(INDEX$1) = NUMIN(.BUFFPTR);
                   INDEX$1 = INDEX$1 + 1;
                END;
             END;

             INDEX$2 = 0;
             DO WHILE INDEX$2 < 200;
                CALL READ(DISK$2$AFTN, .BUFFER, 20, .COUNT, .STATUS);
                IF BUFFER(0) = 0DH THEN
                DO;
                   INPUT$2(INDEX$2) = 0FFFFH;    /* SENTINEL: END OF SIMULATED INPUT */
                   INDEX$2 = 200;
                END;
                ELSE
                DO;
                   BUFFPTR = .BUFFER;
                   INPUT$2(INDEX$2) = NUMIN(.BUFFPTR);
                   INDEX$2 = INDEX$2 + 1;
                END;
             END;

             INDEX$1, INDEX$2, OUTDEX = 0;     /* SET UP FOR SIMULATED INPUT AND OUTPUT */
             GO$FLAG = FALSE;

          END SETUP;
```

into account the velocity of the tool; and it would surely have to account for the possibility of overshoot, meaning that the tool had moved past its desired position. If this happens within the program as written, the values produced will be meaningless since no test has been made to detect this fact and handle it properly. Also,

```
PL/M-80 COMPILER    FIG. 8.10                                                   PAGE   5


               $EJECT
        1      COMPUTE$CONTROL$CURRENT:
               PROCEDURE;
        2        DECLARE (PRESENT$POSITION, DESIRED$POSITION, CURRENT) ADDRESS;
        2        DECLARE POSITION$COEFFICIENT ADDRESS DATA(3);
        2        DECLARE ELAPSED$TIME ADDRESS;
        2        DECLARE TIME$INDEX BYTE;

                 /* SIMULATE INPUT OF TOOL POSITION */
        2        IF INPUT$2(INDEX$2) = 0FFFFH THEN   /* SENTINEL: END OF SIMULATED INPUT */
        2          GO TO WRAPUP;
                 ELSE
        2          PRESENT$POSITION = INPUT$2(INDEX$2);
        2        INDEX$2 = INDEX$2 + 1;

        2        ELAPSED$TIME = TIME$IN$TENTHS$PROCEDURE - TIME$ZERO$TENTHS;
        2        DESIRED$POSITION = POSITION$ZERO + FEED$RATE * ELAPSED$TIME;
        2        CURRENT = POSITION$COEFFICIENT * (DESIRED$POSITION - PRESENT$POSITION);
        2        OUTPUT$A(OUTDEX) = 1;    /* IDENTIFIES COLUMN 2 AS CURRENT */
        2        OUTPUT$B(OUTDEX) = CURRENT;
        2        OUTDEX = OUTDEX + 1;
        2        OUTPUT$A(OUTDEX) = 2;    /* IDENTIFIES COLUMN 2 AS TIME */
        2        OUTPUT$B(OUTDEX) = TIME$IN$TENTHS$PROCEDURE - TIME$ZERO$TENTHS;
        2        OUTDEX = OUTDEX + 1;

        2        DO TIME$INDEX = 0 TO 9;     /* WASTE SOME TIME, SO SIMULATED INPUT */
        3          CALL TIME(170);           /* DOESN'T RUN TOO FAR AHEAD OF REALTIME CLOCK */
        3        END;

        2      END COMPUTE$CONTROL$CURRENT;
```

the illustrative numerically controlled machine has no way to drive the tool in more than one direction.

Throughout all of this the routine named CLOCK has been counting milliseconds—except, of course, during any moments when INTERRUPT$PROCESSOR might have interrupts disabled. Since, in the program as written, these latter operations would take well under a millisecond, the clock would not be thrown off even if interrupts were disabled throughout the routine. However, to allow for the more general possibility that these operations could take considerably longer than a millisecond, we enable interrupts at the beginning of this routine. Now interrupts at level 1 can break into the servicing of interrupts at level 3 and the clock keeps correct time.

If both of these routines called some other routine, that other routine would have to be reentrant.

Eventually all of the data in one of the two files simulating input will have been read, which is the abort condition in this developmental program. This is the condition we have earlier (Chapter 7) described as being the one legitimate use of

```
PL/M-80 COMPILER    FIG. 8.10                                    PAGE   6


                  $EJECT
                  /*       MAIN PROGRAM     */

141   1              CALL SETUP;

142   1              DISABLE;
143   1              OUTPUT(0FDH) = 12H;      /* INITIALIZE INTELLEC INTERRUPT LOGIC */
144   1              OUTPUT(0FCH) = 0;        /* DITTO */
145   1              OUTPUT(0FCH) = 0F0H;     /* ACCEPT INTERRUPTS 0, 1, 2 AND 3 */
146   1              OUTPUT(0FFH) = 2;        /* ENABLE REAL-TIME CLOCK */

147   1              LOC$9$SAVE = LOC$9;      /* SAVE ADDRESS OF ISIS INTERRUPT 1 ROUTINE */
148   1              LOC$8 = 0C3H;            /* SET UP JUMP TO INTERRUPT 1 SERVICE ROUTINE */
149   1              LOC$9 = .CLOCK;          /* DITTO */
150   1              LOC$24 = 0C3H;           /* SET UP JUMP TO INTERRUPT 3 SERVICE ROUTINE */
151   1              LOC$25 = .INTERRUPT$PROCESSOR;    /* DITTO */

152   1              ENABLE;

153   1              DO FOREVER;
154   2                 IF GO$FLAG THEN
155   2                    CALL COMPUTE$CONTROL$CURRENT;
156   2              END;

157   1           WRAPUP:
                     OUTDEX$FINAL = OUTDEX - 1;
158   1              DO OUTDEX = 0 TO OUTDEX$FINAL;
159   2                 CALL NUMOUT(OUTPUT$A(OUTDEX), 2, '0', .BUFFER, 8);
160   2                 CALL NUMOUT(OUTPUT$B(OUTDEX), 10, ' ', .BUFFER + 8, 8);
161   2                 BUFFER(16) = 0DH;
162   2                 BUFFER(17) = 0AH;
163   2                 CALL WRITE(LP$AFTN, .BUFFER, 18, .STATUS);
164   2              END;

165   1              LOC$9 = LOC$9$SAVE;    /* RESTORE ADDRESS OF ISIS INTERRUPT 1 ROUTINE */

166   1              CALL CLOSE(ECHO$AFTN, .STATUS);
167   1              CALL CLOSE(DISK$1$AFTN, .STATUS);
168   1              CALL CLOSE(DISK$2$AFTN, .STATUS);
169   1              CALL CLOSE(LP$AFTN, .STATUS);
170   1              CALL EXIT;

171   1           END NUMERICAL$CONTROL;
```

a GO TO. The GO TO exits to a wrapup paragraph that writes the simulated output, closes the files, and executes a CALL EXIT to return control to ISIS. It may be noted that, because of the ENABLE at the beginning of INTERRUPT$PROCESSOR, we will be returning to ISIS with interrupts enabled. In order to make the CALL EXIT work, we must restore the address in location 9 to its value as needed by ISIS.

1	2	3		4	
20	00010000B	00000001	0	00000001	0
23	00001000B	00000010	0	00000010	0
29	00001000B	00000001	27	00000001	15
37	00000001B	00000010	3	00000010	2
43	00010000B	00000001	33	00000001	21
50	00000010B	00000010	5	00000010	4
58	00010000B	00000001	33	10000000	6
61	00000100B	00000010	7	00000001	21
70	00010000B	00000001	39	00000010	6
85	00000001B	00000010	9	00000001	27
97		00000001	42	00000010	8
112		00000010	11	00000001	30
119		00000001	42	00000010	10
125		00000010	13	00000001	30
		00000001	57	00000010	12
		00000010	15	00000001	45
		00000001	54	00000010	14
		00000010	17	10000000	15
		00000001	33	00000001	42
		00000010	19	00000010	16
		00000001	21	11000000	18
		00000010	21	00000001	65341
		00000001	0	00000010	0
		00000010	23	00000001	65329
		00000001	3	00000010	2
		00000010	25	00000001	65308
		00000001	9	00000010	4
		00000010	27	11000000	6
				00000001	65239
				00000010	0
				00000001	65245
				00000010	2
				11000000	2

Fig. 8.11. First column: simulated input positions for the numerical control program. Second column: simulated values for the signals that can cause interrupts. Third column: program output when the process was interrupted once, so that operation was terminated by running out of position input. Fourth column: program output when the process was interrupted repeatedly. The large values of the current in the last entries of the fourth column are the complements of negative values; when the simulated start button is read, the simulated positions then read are beyond the starting position, and the program makes no provision for moving the tool backward.

Figure 8.11 shows two sample files of simulated input and the output produced when the program was run using them. It is inherent in the nature of programs involving real time and interrupts that it would be essentially impossible to exactly duplicate this output since it depends on the exact timing with which the button for interrupt 3 was pressed during program execution.

EXERCISES

1. Write an interrupt routine to accept characters from a paper tape reader. Assume that a BYTE variable named READING is zero if a read operation has not been initiated, and one if so. If the interrupt occurs with READING equal to zero, READING should be set to one. The next arrival of this interrupt signals the presence of the first character on port 3; place that character in the first element of an array named TEXT. On subsequent interrupts, place succeeding characters in succeeding elements of TEXT, until an end-of-transmission character (04H) is detected; do not store this character, and set READING to zero.

2. Write a program to compute the speed of an automobile, assuming an interrupt that denotes one revolution of a wheel of known radius and the availability of another interrupt from a 1-kHz clock.

3. Suppose that an automobile computer is furnished engine-speed data in the form of an interrupt every other revolution. A clock provides another interrupt every 10 ms. Each interrupt is unlatched and lasts 50 μs. Write a routine that places in RPS the engine speed in revolutions per second (rps), and updates the value every second. At each update, the program should place in ACCEL a zero if the engine speed has not changed by more than 3 rps in the last second, a one if it has increased by more than 3 rps, and a 2 if it has decreased by more than 3 rps.

4. Write a program to implement the functions of an electronic stopwatch in "pause–accumulate" mode, as follows: A 0.1-second clock is available at location 8000H by *direct memory access* (DMA). This means that the clock value is placed in that location by external circuitry that "steals" enough processor time to update the clock value every tenth of a second. During the approximately 1 μs that the update requires, the processor is unable to access that location, so there is no danger of trying to read the value while it is changing and therefore unreliable. The program can change the value, such as by setting it to zero.

   One input to the stopwatch means to reset it to zero; this is given to the program as an interrupt. A second interrupt means either to start timing (the first, third, fifth, . . .) time it is pressed, or to stop timing (the second, fourth, sixth, . . . time it is pressed). This is the function of a stopwatch that is being used, for example, to time a sports event except during time-outs.

   The output, five digits giving minutes, seconds, and tenths of seconds, goes to five DMA locations that drive the displays.

CHAPTER 9

LINKAGE, LOCATION, AND OTHER ISIS-II FEATURES

INTRODUCTION

The writing and development of programs is materially simplified by the availability of a variety of service programs. A number of these are combined in the Intel Systems Implementation Supervisor, ISIS-II.

We have already worked with a number of these features, especially when we have used the READ and WRITE routines. There are a number of others, however, that we shall now explore to a greater or lesser degree, depending on how closely they tie in with PL/M programming. From this standpoint the most important of the added features are *linkage* and *location*. We shall give less emphasis to general file management and the text editor. Debugging features will be considered in a final section.

FILE MANAGEMENT

The ISIS-II operating system deals with *files*. Examples of files include:

- A PL/M source program;
- An object program, which is the output of the compiler;
- A program, ready to be loaded and executed;

- Data;
- A stored sequence of ISIS commands for automatic execution using the SUBMIT command.

Each file is known to the system by a *file name*. A diskette file has a three-part file name made up as follows (curly braces mean that the item is optional):

{:device:} name {.extension}

where

- *:device:* might be :F0:, :F1:, :F2:, or :F3:, to indicate a diskette drive. (If omitted, :F0: is assumed.)
- *name* is from one to six letters or digits and must be present.
- *extension* is from one to three letters or digits. If omitted the file name is identified simply by *name*. If present, it must be separated from *name* by a period.

OPENING AND CLOSING FILES

Before a file can be accessed by ISIS-II it must be opened. Opening a file puts information about the file into system tables and allocates input and/or output (I/O) buffers as needed. When a file is *closed,* entries for it are removed from the system tables and, in the case of a diskette file, directory information is written in the diskette directory.

When a file is accessed by ISIS-II in response to a console command, such as COPY, ISIS-II takes care of opening and closing the file. When a file is accessed by an applications program, the program must open and close the file by using the OPEN and CLOSE system calls.

FILE NAMES FOR STANDARD DEVICES

A number of devices can be connected to an Intellec system, such as a teletypewriter keyboard, teletypewriter tape reader and punch, cathode-ray tube, high-speed papertape reader and punch, and a line printer. All have standard names. The only one we shall have occasion to use is the line printer, which has the name :LP:. Two other names are used a good deal: :CI: and :CO: stand for the console input and output devices, where the console can be either a CRT device or a teletypewriter. Each time the Intellec system is turned on, it is informed of what the console device is so that, for example, :CI: stands for either the CRT keyboard *or* the teletypewriter keyboard. The :CI: and :CO: files are always open and thus do not require an OPEN operation before they can be used.

ISIS-II FILE CONTROL COMMANDS

About a dozen commands having to do with diskette files can be executed from the Intellec console. All of these are fully explained in appropriate manuals, and here we simply give the briefest sketch to indicate what some of the functions are.

The COPY command copies an existing file or files to another file. For example, we could say

```
COPY :F1:4SORT2.SRC TO 4SORT2.SRC
```

With the destination having been given no device name, :FO: is assumed. The effect is to copy the file from diskette 1 to diskette 0. SRC is the extension normally used for a *source* file. Another COPY command operation is illustrated by

```
COPY :F1:4SORT2.LST TO :LP:
```

which copies the file named to the line printer. LST is the extension for a *listing* file.

The DIR command (for directory) provides a listing of the directory of the diskette in a specified disk drive. If not specified otherwise, the directory is sent to the console output device, but it can also be sent to the line printer or to another diskette file.

The DELETE command removes a file from diskette.

The RENAME command changes the name of a diskette file.

Several additional ISIS-II console commands are described in the ISIS manuals.

THE SUBMIT COMMAND

It is possible, using the SUBMIT command, to carry out a sequence of commands automatically, picking them up from a diskette file where they have been placed in advance. Furthermore, substitutions can be made in the prewritten file of commands to make them apply to specific parameters. Let us see, through an example, how the command works.

Suppose that we frequently have occasion to compile a program, write the listing file from the compilation to the line printer, then carry out LINK and LOCATE operations (discussed later in this chapter). We prepare a file having a name of our choosing, an extension of CSD, and containing the following commands:

```
PLM80 :F1:%0.SRC DEBUG DATE(%1)
COPY :F1:%0.LST TO :LP:
LINK :F1:%0.OBJ,PLM80.LIB TO :F1:%0.LNK
LOCATE :F1:%0.LNK MAP PRINT(:LP:)
```

PLM80 is the command to carry out a PL/M compilation. Anywhere the percent sign appears, it indicates a parameter that will be supplied when the set of commands is invoked with a SUBMIT. %0 refers to the *first* parameter written in the SUBMIT, %1 to the *second* parameter, etc. All other items written in a SUBMIT file represent themselves; for example, :F1:, SRC, OBJ, etc. We assume that our source files always have the extension SRC; this is not necessary, and could be changed if desired. The extension could also be made a parameter.

When we wish to carry out this sequence of commands on a file, we type in a command such as:

```
SUBMIT :F1:PLM(8NC3, '20 FEB 77')
```

Where we have written 8NC3, those characters will be substituted in the three skeleton commands where there is a %0. '20 FEB 77' will be substituted where the %1 appears. The net effect of the SUBMIT shown is exactly as if we had typed in the individual commands

```
PLM80 :F1:8NC3.SRC DEBUG DATE('20 FEB 77')
COPY :F1:8NC3.LST TO :LP:
LINK :F1:8NC3.OBJ,PLM80.LIB TO :F1:8NC3.LNK
LOCATE :F1:8NC3.LNK MAP PRINT(:LP:)
```

Quite elaborate sequences of commands can be set up using this powerful feature of the ISIS system.

THE ISIS-II TEXT EDITOR

Using the ISIS-II text editor, it is possible to create a file at the Intellec console and then—or at a later time—modify and correct it in a variety of ways, before writing it back to the diskette.

During the creation of the file, simple typing errors can be corrected by "rubbing out" preceding characters with a special key or by deleting the entire line. After a file has been created, a variety of facilities are available for making modifications and changes. New lines can be inserted anywhere in the file, or existing lines can be deleted. Additional characters can be added anywhere in a line, or characters may be deleted. The file can be searched for a specified string of characters. For example, we might say "find the first instance of the word DISABLE." One of the most useful features is the ability to substitute one string of characters for another. We might say, for example, "substitute LINE$COUNTER for CTR." Furthermore, and very powerfully, we can say (in effect) "substitute LINE$COUNTER for *all* instances of CTR anywhere in the entire file."

A number of additional text-editing commands perform necessary functions such as moving the pointer specifying which line we are currently looking at forward or backward or to the beginning or the ending of the file. All of these commands as well as the others are fully described in appropriate manuals.

LINKAGE AND LOCATION: THE NUMERICAL-CONTROL PROGRAM AGAIN

The important subject of linkage and location can best be approached for our purposes here through a case study. An investigation of the requirements of the program development process will put our sketch of the new concepts into context.

MODULARIZATION FOR BETTER PROGRAMMING

Consider again the program at the end of the previous chapter for the numerical control of a machine tool. We realize that the program shown is little more than a skeleton of the complete application program, since we omitted a number of essential process-control features such as driving the tool in both directions, and since there are major simplifications in the program itself, such as restricting the millisecond counter to 16 bits. It is clear that, as development proceeds, the program will become very much larger, leading at least to very long compilation times. This is almost the least of the considerations arguing for modularization, but it *is* an annoyance to have to wait 20 minutes for recompilation of a very large program when only a few statements are changed.

More importantly, it is often necessary to have more than one programmer working on a large job, making it highly desirable for them to be able to work somewhat independently on well-defined separate functions in the program. This is one motivation for wishing to be able to compile—and to some degree check out—portions of a complete program separately.

Perhaps most important of all is the problem of maintaining program stability as parts of the program have to be changed. It routinely happens that program specifications change, for a wide variety of good and bad reasons, and that as a result some part of the program has to be modified. It is urgent that programs be designed in such a way that one function of the program can be modified with some reasonable hope that the modification will not have unexpected and undesired repercussions elsewhere in the program. In other words, we like to group program functions so that each section of the program carries out just one set of closely related operations. This means that when something does have to be changed, the impact of the change will tend to be localized and not have a ripple effect throughout the entire program.

The answer to all of these considerations is good program *modularization*. We have already spoken of this indirectly in discussing procedures in Chapters 5 and 6, where, for example, we discussed localizing functions by minimization of global variables. In that context we thought of a procedure as a section of a program carrying out closely related functions. That emphasis is still valid, but in this chapter we now move on to a more encompassing level of program organization, the *module*.

A module in PL/M is any compilable program, which is a simple DO block having a label and not enclosed in any other block. If the module contains any executable statements at the module level—that is to say, any statements other than DECLAREs and PROCEDURE statements that are not inside a procedure—then the module is said to be a *main-program module*. All of the programs from Chapter 5 up to this point have been main-program modules containing one or more procedures as well as executable statements at the module level. Now we will work with a program organization in which there is one main-program module as well as a number of other modules containing only procedures.

In the case of the numerical-control program it would be convenient to have five modules, as follows:

- A main program module containing the main program as before plus the procedure named SETUP.
- A module containing the interrupt service routine for the real-time clock and the procedure that converts from milliseconds to tenths of a second. Both of these procedures depend heavily on the data structure for milliseconds (16, 24, or 32 bits), so that they constitute a set of closely related functions. When either of these procedures changes, the other would have to be changed, too.
- The service routine for interrupt level 3. This puts in one place all of the functions having to do with interrupts coming from the machine-tool system.
- A module to compute the control current.
- A module containing NUMIN and NUMOUT.

We must emphasize that each of these modules can be written and compiled independently. Naturally they have to be able to communicate with each other, which is an issue to which we shall devote attention later; but, if necessary, several different people could be working on the major modules independently. Once the basic program skeleton modularized in this fashion is running, the person working on the module that computes the current could revise that program, recompile it, and combine it with the other modules to check it out. The other modules would not have to be recompiled.

THE PUBLIC AND EXTERNAL ATTRIBUTES

Working with separately compiled modules requires communication between modules. For example, when the main program says CALL COMPUTE$CONTROL$CURRENT and the main program no longer contains that procedure, what is the compiler supposed to do? Or what happens when the procedure named INTERRUPT$PROCESSOR says GO TO WRAPUP, but WRAPUP is now in a different module altogether? The answer is the combination of the PUBLIC and EXTERNAL attributes.

Any time a procedure, variable, or label is to be defined in one module and referred to in other modules, its declaration in the module where it is defined must be made with the PUBLIC attribute. For instance, we might have statements like these:

```
PROCEDURE (ARGUMENT) ADDRESS PUBLIC;
DECLARE INDEX$2 ADDRESS PUBLIC;
DECLARE WRAPUP LABEL PUBLIC;
```

Three simple restrictions apply to the PUBLIC attribute: First, within all the modules to be linked together to form a complete program, the same object cannot be declared PUBLIC more than once. Second, based variables may not be declared PUBLIC. Third, a PUBLIC declaration must be at the module level.

The EXTERNAL attribute can also be applied to procedures, variables, and labels. When an object is declared to be EXTERNAL it means that the object is used in this module but defined elsewhere with a PUBLIC declaration. Thus, although a given object cannot be declared PUBLIC more than once, it can be declared EXTERNAL many times. However, an object cannot be declared PUBLIC and EXTERNAL in the same module, for that would make no sense. Also, since it is the PUBLIC appearance that defines an object, the EXTERNAL attribute may not be used in combination with the AT attribute, which is involved in allocating space, or with initialization by the INITIAL or DATA statements. Like PUBLIC, EXTERNAL may not be used with a based variable and must be at the module level. Furthermore, for rather different reasons, EXTERNAL may not be used in combination with INTERRUPT or REENTRANT.

All of this will make more sense in the context of a complete program, so let us return to the numerical-control application.

THE MAIN PROGRAM AS A SEPARATE MODULE

The main-program module in this organization of the program is shown in Fig. 9.1. The executable statements at the end are as before. The procedure SETUP, which is still contained in the main-program module, is also as before. All of the other procedures have been removed to modules of their own, so the main-program module is, of course, shorter, but the declarations have changed somewhat and there are a number of new declarations associated with the procedures that are no longer part of this program. Let us look at these latter aspects.

Looking first at the DECLARE statements, we see that the attribute PUBLIC has been added to most of them. The only variables that are not PUBLIC are those that are used only in this module, such as BUFFER and a few others. We see in line 21 the declaration of a label to be PUBLIC. It is only in this kind of situation that we have any occasion to declare a label.

All of the procedures used by this program, with the exception of SETUP, are now in other modules, so we must somehow inform the compiler of that fact by declaring them here as being EXTERNAL. This is the function of all of the procedure declarations on the second page of Fig. 9.1, all of which contain the EXTERNAL attribute in their PROCEDURE statements. When this is done, the procedure must contain nothing but declarations of the formal parameters. It would obviously make no sense for a procedure that is declared to be EXTERNAL to contain executable statements or declarations of any other kinds of variables except procedure parameters.

We said earlier that the same *object* cannot be declared to *be* both EXTERNAL and PUBLIC in the same module. As we see in this module, however, it is quite acceptable for the same module to *contain* PUBLIC and EXTERNAL declarations—of different objects, naturally.

```
PL/M-80 COMPILER    FIG. 9.1                                                    PAGE   1

            /***************************************************************************/
            /* A NUMERICAL CONTROL PROGRAM, PRESENTED HERE IN AN EARLY DEVELOPMENTAL    */
            /* VERSION THAT EMPHASIZES INTERRUPT AND REENTRANCY CONSIDERATIONS.         */
            /* THIS VERSION USES INPUT TAKEN FROM DISK, SET UP FOR CHECKOUT PURPOSES    */
            /* AND WRITES ITS OUTPUT EITHER TO THE LINE PRINTER OR TO DISK.             */
            /*                                                                          */
            /* THIS REVISED VERSION PLACES MOST PROCEDURES INTO SEPARATELY-COMPILED     */
            /* MODULES, FOR IMPROVED PROGRAM DEVELOPMENT.                               */
            /***************************************************************************/
            /*
            GLOBAL VARIABLES:
               TIME$MS           TIME IN MILLISECONDS
               TIME$TENTHS       TIME IN TENTHS OF A SECOND
               TIME$ZERO$TENTHS  TIME AT WHICH START BUTTON WAS PRESSED
               FEEDRATE          INPUT VALUE: RATE AT WHICH TOOL IS TO MOVE
               POSITION$ZERO     INITIAL POSITION OF TOOL WHEN START BUTTON IS PRESSED
               GO$FLAG           FLAG INDICATING THAT START BUTTON HAS BEEN PRESSED
               ECHO$AFTN         AFTN = 'ACTIVE FILE TABLE NUMBER' FOR FILE NEEDED BY ISIS
                                    PROCESSING OF SIMULATED INPUT
               DISK$1$AFTN       AFTN OF DISK FILE OF SIMULATED INPUT: INTERRUPT IDENTIFIERS
               DISK$2$AFTN       AFTN FOR INPUT: ALL OTHER
               LP$AFTN           AFTN FOR OUTPUT: SIMPLE CHANGE IN PROGRAM SENDS OUTPUT TO DISK
            */

            NUMERICAL$CONTROL$3:
            DO;
               DECLARE (TIME$MS, TIME$TENTHS, TIME$ZERO$TENTHS) ADDRESS PUBLIC;
               DECLARE (FEED$RATE, POSITION$ZERO) ADDRESS PUBLIC;
               DECLARE GO$FLAG BYTE PUBLIC;
               DECLARE (ECHO$AFTN, DISK$1$AFTN, DISK$2$AFTN, LP$AFTN) ADDRESS PUBLIC;
               DECLARE TRUE LITERALLY '0FFH';
               DECLARE FALSE LITERALLY '0';
               DECLARE FOREVER LITERALLY 'WHILE 1';
               DECLARE LOC$8 BYTE AT(8);
               DECLARE LOC$9 ADDRESS AT(9);
               DECLARE LOC$9$SAVE ADDRESS;
               DECLARE LOC$24 BYTE AT(24);
               DECLARE LOC$25 ADDRESS AT(25);
               DECLARE INPUT$1(50) BYTE PUBLIC;        /* STORAGE FOR PART OF SIMULATED INPUT */
               DECLARE INPUT$2(200) ADDRESS PUBLIC;    /* DITTO */
               DECLARE OUTPUT$A(250) BYTE PUBLIC;      /* STORAGE FOR PART OF SIMULATED OUTPUT */
               DECLARE OUTPUT$B(250) ADDRESS PUBLIC;   /* DITTO */
               DECLARE (INDEX$1, INDEX$2, OUTDEX, OUTDEX$FINAL) ADDRESS PUBLIC;
               DECLARE BUFFER(128) BYTE;
               DECLARE (BUFFPTR, COUNT, STATUS) ADDRESS;
               DECLARE WRAPUP LABEL PUBLIC;
```

```
PL/M-80 COMPILER    FIG. 9.1                                          PAGE   2


                  $EJECT
 22    1          OPEN:
                  PROCEDURE (AFT, FILE, ACCESS, MODE, STATUS) EXTERNAL;
 23    2             DECLARE (AFT, FILE, ACCESS, MODE, STATUS) ADDRESS;
 24    2          END OPEN;

 25    1          CLOSE:
                  PROCEDURE (AFT, STATUS) EXTERNAL;
 26    2             DECLARE (AFT, STATUS) ADDRESS;
 27    2          END CLOSE;

 28    1          EXIT:
                  PROCEDURE EXTERNAL;
 29    2          END EXIT;

 30    1          READ:
                  PROCEDURE (AFT, BUFFER, COUNT, ACTUAL, STATUS) EXTERNAL;
 31    2             DECLARE (AFT, BUFFER, COUNT, ACTUAL, STATUS) ADDRESS;
 32    2          END READ;

 33    1          WRITE:
                  PROCEDURE (AFT, BUFFER, COUNT, STATUS) EXTERNAL;
 34    2             DECLARE (AFT, BUFFER, COUNT, STATUS) ADDRESS;
 35    2          END WRITE;

 36    1          NUMIN:
                  PROCEDURE (POINTER) ADDRESS EXTERNAL;
 37    2             DECLARE POINTER ADDRESS;
 38    2          END NUMIN;

 39    1          NUMOUT:
                  PROCEDURE (VALUE, BASE, LC, BUFFADR, WIDTH) EXTERNAL;
 40    2             DECLARE (VALUE, BASE, LC, BUFFADR, WIDTH) ADDRESS;
 41    2          END NUMOUT;

 42    1          TIME$IN$TENTHS$PROCEDURE:
                  PROCEDURE ADDRESS EXTERNAL;    /* NOTE THAT REENTRANT ATTRIBUTE DOES NOT APPEAR HERE */
 43    2          END TIME$IN$TENTHS$PROCEDURE;

 44    1          CLOCK:
                  PROCEDURE EXTERNAL;    /* NOTE THAT INTERRUPT ATTRIBUTE DOES NOT APPEAR HERE */
 45    2          END CLOCK;

 46    1          INTERRUPT$PROCESSOR:
                  PROCEDURE EXTERNAL;
 47    2          END INTERRUPT$PROCESSOR;

 48    1          COMPUTE$CONTROL$CURRENT:
                  PROCEDURE EXTERNAL;
 49    2          END COMPUTE$CONTROL$CURRENT;
```

```
PL/M-80 COMPILER    FIG. 9.1                                                                        PAGE   3


         $EJECT
50   1   SETUP:
         PROCEDURE;

51   2      CALL OPEN(.ECHO$AFTN, .(':F1:SCRTCH '), 2, 0, .STATUS);
52   2      CALL OPEN(.DISK$1$AFTN, .(':F1:8NC1.DAT '), 1, ECHO$AFTN, .STATUS);
53   2      CALL OPEN(.DISK$2$AFTN, .(':F1:8NC2.DAT '), 1, ECHO$AFTN, .STATUS);
54   2      CALL OPEN(.LP$AFTN, .(':LP: '), 2, 0, .STATUS);

            /* READ DISK FILES TO GET SIMULATED DATA INTO MAIN MEMORY.  CANNOT BE DONE
               WITH ISIS CALLS WITHIN INTERRUPT SERVICE ROUTINES, BECAUSE ISIS ROUTINES
               ARE NOT REENTRANT. */

55   2      INDEX$1 = 0;
56   2      DO WHILE INDEX$1 < 50;
57   3         CALL READ(DISK$1$AFTN, .BUFFER, 20, .COUNT, .STATUS);
58   3         IF BUFFER(0) = 0DH THEN   /* IMPLIES NULL LINE MARKING END OF INPUT */
59   3         DO;
60   4            INPUT$1(INDEX$1) = 0FFH;    /* SENTINEL: END OF SIMULATED INPUT */
61   4            INDEX$1 = 50;              /* GET OUT OF LOOP */
62   4         END;
               ELSE
63   3         DO;
64   4            BUFFPTR = .BUFFER;
65   4            INPUT$1(INDEX$1) = NUMIN(.BUFFPTR);
66   4            INDEX$1 = INDEX$1 + 1;
67   4         END;
68   3      END;

69   2      INDEX$2 = 0;
70   2      DO WHILE INDEX$2 < 200;
71   3         CALL READ(DISK$2$AFTN, .BUFFER, 20, .COUNT, .STATUS);
72   3         IF BUFFER(0) = 0DH THEN
73   3         DO;
74   4            INPUT$2(INDEX$2) = 0FFFFH;    /* SENTINEL: END OF SIMULATED INPUT */
75   4            INDEX$2 = 200;
76   4         END;
               ELSE
77   3         DO;
78   4            BUFFPTR = .BUFFER;
79   4            INPUT$2(INDEX$2) = NUMIN(.BUFFPTR);
80   4            INDEX$2 = INDEX$2 + 1;
81   4         END;
82   3      END;

83   2      INDEX$1, INDEX$2, OUTDEX = 0;     /* SET UP FOR SIMULATED INPUT AND OUTPUT */
84   2      TIME$MS, TIME$TENTHS, TIME$ZERO$TENTHS = 0; /* CANNOT COMBINE INITIAL AND PUBLIC ATTRIBUTES */
85   2      GO$FLAG = FALSE;

86   2   END SETUP;
```

```
PL/M-80 COMPILER    FIG. 9.1                                         PAGE   4

            $EJECT
            /*      MAIN PROGRAM    */

 87   1        CALL SETUP;

 88   1        DISABLE;
 89   1        OUTPUT(0FDH) = 12H;      /* INITIALIZE INTELLEC INTERRUPT LOGIC */
 90   1        OUTPUT(0FCH) = 0;        /* DITTO */
 91   1        OUTPUT(0FCH) = 0F0H;     /* ACCEPT INTERRUPTS 0, 1, 2 AND 3 */
 92   1        OUTPUT(0FFH) = 2;        /* ENABLE REAL-TIME CLOCK */

 93   1        LOC$9$SAVE = LOC$9;      /* SAVE ADDRESS OF ISIS INTERRUPT 1 ROUTINE */
 94   1        LOC$8 = 0C3H;            /* SET UP JUMP TO INTERRUPT 1 SERVICE ROUTINE */
 95   1        LOC$9 = .CLOCK;          /* DITTO */
 96   1        LOC$24 = 0C3H;           /* SET UP JUMP TO INTERRUPT 3 SERVICE ROUTINE */
 97   1        LOC$25 = .INTERRUPT$PROCESSOR;    /* DITTO */

 98   1        ENABLE;

 99   1        DO FOREVER;
100   2           IF GO$FLAG THEN
101   2              CALL COMPUTE$CONTROL$CURRENT;
102   2        END;

103   1     WRAPUP:
               OUTDEX$FINAL = OUTDEX - 1;
104   1        DO OUTDEX = 0 TO OUTDEX$FINAL;
105   2           CALL NUMOUT(OUTPUT$A(OUTDEX), 2, '0', .BUFFER, 8);
106   2           CALL NUMOUT(OUTPUT$B(OUTDEX), 10, ' ', .BUFFER + 8, 8);
107   2           BUFFER(16) = 0DH;
108   2           BUFFER(17) = 0AH;
109   2           CALL WRITE(LP$AFTN, .BUFFER, 18, .STATUS);
110   2        END;

111   1        DISABLE;
112   1        OUTPUT(0FFH) = 1;  /* DISABLE REAL-TIME CLOCK */
113   1        LOC$9 = LOC$9$SAVE;  /* RESTORE ADDRESS OF ISIS INTERRUPT 1 ROUTINE */
114   1        ENABLE;

115   1        CALL CLOSE(ECHO$AFTN, .STATUS);
116   1        CALL CLOSE(DISK$1$AFTN, .STATUS);
117   1        CALL CLOSE(DISK$2$AFTN, .STATUS);
118   1        CALL CLOSE(LP$AFTN, .STATUS);
119   1        CALL EXIT;

120   1     END NUMERICAL$CONTROL$3;
```

Figure 9.2 shows the module containing the procedure COMPUTE$CONTROL$CURRENT. We see that the procedure has been made part of a compilable module by enclosing it in a DO block that has a label. This label has been made descriptive by adding the word MODULE, but this is not required. We see that all

```
PL/M-80 COMPILER    FIG. 9.2                                              PAGE   1

/******************************************************************************/
/* NUMERICAL CONTROL PROGRAM: MODULE TO COMPUTE CURRENT                       */
/******************************************************************************/

COMPUTE$CONTROL$CURRENT$MODULE:
DO;
   DECLARE INPUT$2(200) ADDRESS EXTERNAL;
   DECLARE OUTPUT$A(250) BYTE EXTERNAL;
   DECLARE OUTPUT$B(250) ADDRESS EXTERNAL;
   DECLARE (INDEX$2, OUTDEX) ADDRESS EXTERNAL;
   DECLARE WRAPUP LABEL EXTERNAL;
   DECLARE (TIME$ZERO$TENTHS, POSITION$ZERO, FEED$RATE) ADDRESS EXTERNAL;

TIME$IN$TENTHS$PROCEDURE:
   PROCEDURE ADDRESS EXTERNAL;
END TIME$IN$TENTHS$PROCEDURE;

COMPUTE$CONTROL$CURRENT:
PROCEDURE PUBLIC;
   DECLARE (PRESENT$POSITION, DESIRED$POSITION, CURRENT) ADDRESS;
   DECLARE POSITION$COEFFICIENT ADDRESS DATA(3);
   DECLARE ELAPSED$TIME ADDRESS;
   DECLARE TIME$INDEX BYTE;

   /* SIMULATE INPUT OF TOOL POSITION */
   IF INPUT$2(INDEX$2) = 0FFFFH THEN   /* SENTINEL: END OF SIMULATED INPUT */
      GO TO WRAPUP;
   ELSE
      PRESENT$POSITION = INPUT$2(INDEX$2);
   INDEX$2 = INDEX$2 + 1;

   ELAPSED$TIME = TIME$IN$TENTHS$PROCEDURE - TIME$ZERO$TENTHS;
   DESIRED$POSITION = POSITION$ZERO + FEED$RATE * ELAPSED$TIME;
   CURRENT = POSITION$COEFFICIENT * (DESIRED$POSITION - PRESENT$POSITION);
   OUTPUT$A(OUTDEX) = 1;    /* IDENTIFIES COLUMN 2 AS CURRENT */
   OUTPUT$B(OUTDEX) = CURRENT;
   OUTDEX = OUTDEX + 1;
   OUTPUT$A(OUTDEX) = 2;    /* IDENTIFIES COLUMN 2 AS TIME */
   OUTPUT$B(OUTDEX) = TIME$IN$TENTHS$PROCEDURE - TIME$ZERO$TENTHS;
   OUTDEX = OUTDEX + 1;

   DO TIME$INDEX = 0 TO 9;     /* WASTE SOME TIME, SO SIMULATED INPUT */
      CALL TIME(170);          /* DOESN'T RUN TOO FAR AHEAD OF REALTIME CLOCK */
   END;

END COMPUTE$CONTROL$CURRENT;

END COMPUTE$CONTROL$CURRENT$MODULE;
```

of the variables that, in the Chapter 8 version of this program, were global to this procedure have been declared here to be EXTERNAL. For example, a variable like INPUT$2 was declared once in the earlier version, at the beginning of the combined program. Now it is declared with the PUBLIC attribute in the main program module, where it is defined, and as an EXTERNAL in any other module in which it is used. We note that WRAPUP is declared here to be EXTERNAL. We note that TIME$-IN$TENTHS$PROCEDURE is declared in this module to be EXTERNAL just as it was in the main-program module; both of these modules need to refer to this procedure, which is defined elsewhere. The one procedure contained in this module, COMPUTE$CONTROL$CURRENT, is declared to be PUBLIC so that its name will be known in any module where its name is declared to be EXTERNAL.

Figure 9.3 shows a module named CLOCKS that contains two procedures.

```
PL/M-80 COMPILER    FIG. 9.3                                        PAGE   1


             $NOINTVECTOR

             /*****************************************************************************/
             /* NUMERICAL CONTROL PROGRAM: CLOCKS MODULE                                  */
             /*****************************************************************************/

  1          CLOCKS:
             DO;
  2   1         DECLARE TIME$MS ADDRESS EXTERNAL;

  3   1      CLOCK:
             PROCEDURE INTERRUPT 1 PUBLIC;
  4   2         TIME$MS = TIME$MS + 1;
  5   2         OUTPUT(0FFH) = 2;      /* ENABLE REAL-TIME CLOCK */
  6   2         OUTPUT(0FDH) = 20H;    /* RESTORE INTELLEC INTERRUPT LOGIC */

             /* IN FULL-SCALE PROGRAM, TIME$MS WOULD BE 24 OR 32 BITS, REQUIRING A MORE
                ELABORATE PROCESSING ROUTINE HERE */

  7   2      END CLOCK;

  8   1      TIME$IN$TENTHS$PROCEDURE:
             PROCEDURE ADDRESS REENTRANT PUBLIC;
  9   2         DECLARE TEMPORARY ADDRESS;

 10   2         DISABLE;  /* CRITICAL REGION: TIME$MS ALSO PROCESSED BY INTERRUPT ROUTINE */
 11   2         TEMPORARY = TIME$MS / 100;
 12   2         ENABLE;
 13   2         RETURN TEMPORARY;

             /* IN FULL-SCALE PROGRAM, TIME$MS WOULD BE 24 OR 32 BITS, REQUIRING A MORE
                ELABORATE PROCESSING ROUTINE HERE */

 14   2      END TIME$IN$TENTHS$PROCEDURE;

 15   1      END CLOCKS;
```

Both procedures refer to TIME$MS, which is defined to be PUBLIC in the main-program module. This EXTERNAL declaration, at the module level, is global to both procedures in the module. We see that the procedure CLOCK is declared here with the attributes INTERRUPT 1 and PUBLIC.

Figure 9.4 shows the module containing the procedure named INTERRUPT$-PROCESSOR. This involves no new concepts.

Figure 9.5 shows a module containing NUMIN and NUMOUT. These are exactly as we have seen and used them before except that the PUBLIC attribute has been added to their PROCEDURE statements. We do see here one feature that is not present in any of the other procedures defined elsewhere in this program and that is the presence of parameters. We observe that formal parameters are not declared as either EXTERNAL or PUBLIC, since they are within procedures.

THE OUTPUT OF COMPILATION

When a PL/M source program is compiled, the compiler produces two output files. The first is a listing of the type we have used to display programs throughout the book. The second file contains what is called *object code*. This is in the general form of machine-language instructions for the computer on which the object program will be run, but it is not quite ready to be loaded and executed. The main feature of the object code produced by the compiler is that it is *relocatable,* which means that, in a separate operation carried out by the ISIS program named LOCATE, it can be set up to be loaded in any desired part of microcomputer memory. We shall consider this operation at the end of the chapter.

The object code from the compilation of a module is also incomplete in that any objects that were declared in the source program to be EXTERNAL are specially marked with that information and of course do not contain final addresses or contents. The next project in getting the program running is to link the different modules together.

THE ISIS LINK PROGRAM

The ISIS program named LINK combines two or more modules of object code into one module and also combines information from PUBLIC objects with all the places the objects were declared EXTERNAL. This is called *satisfying the external references.* The output of the linkage operation is one module of object code. Everything has been linked together, in other words. The final program takes no more memory than if it had been written as one big program with a single compilation.

THE PL/M-80 LIBRARY

Quite a number of compiler-generated procedures are used in compiling a PL/M program. Such things as multiplication, division, and the addition of ADDRESS vari-

```
PL/M-80 COMPILER    FIG. 9.4                                          PAGE   1

             /****************************************************************************/
             /* NUMERICAL CONTROL PROGRAM: INTERRUPT PROCESSOR MODULE                   */
             /****************************************************************************/

  1          INTERRUPT$PROCESSOR$MODULE:
             DO;
  2    1        DECLARE INPUT$1(50) BYTE EXTERNAL;
  3    1        DECLARE INPUT$2(200) ADDRESS EXTERNAL;
  4    1        DECLARE (INDEX$1, INDEX$2, OUTDEX) ADDRESS EXTERNAL;
  5    1        DECLARE WRAPUP LABEL EXTERNAL;
  6    1        DECLARE OUTPUT$A(250) BYTE EXTERNAL;
  7    1        DECLARE OUTPUT$B(250) ADDRESS EXTERNAL;
  8    1        DECLARE GO$FLAG BYTE EXTERNAL;
  9    1        DECLARE (TIME$ZERO$TENTHS, FEED$RATE, POSITION$ZERO) ADDRESS EXTERNAL;
 10    1        DECLARE TRUE LITERALLY '0FFH', FALSE LITERALLY '0';

 11    1     TIME$IN$TENTHS$PROCEDURE:
                PROCEDURE ADDRESS EXTERNAL;
 12    2     END TIME$IN$TENTHS$PROCEDURE;

 13    1     INTERRUPT$PROCESSOR:
             PROCEDURE INTERRUPT 3 PUBLIC;
 14    2        DECLARE INTERRUPT$IDENTIFIERS BYTE;

 15    2        ENABLE;     /* ALLOW THIS INTERRUPT SERVICE ROUTINE TO BE INTERRUPTED */

                /* SIMULATE INPUT OF INTERRUPT INDENTIFIER */
 16    2        IF INPUT$1(INDEX$1) = 0FFH THEN    /* SENTINEL: END OF SIMULATED INPUT */
 17    2           GO TO WRAPUP;
                ELSE
 18    2           INTERRUPT$IDENTIFIERS = INPUT$1(INDEX$1);
 19    2        INDEX$1 = INDEX$1 + 1;

 20    2        IF    (INTERRUPT$IDENTIFIERS = 00000001B)   /* STOP SIGNAL */
                   OR (INTERRUPT$IDENTIFIERS = 00000010B)   /* OVER-PRESSURE */
                   OR (INTERRUPT$IDENTIFIERS = 00000100B)   /* LIMIT SWITCH */
                THEN
 21    2        DO;
 22    3           OUTPUT$A(OUTDEX) = 11000000B;     /* ALARM AND SHUT DOWN */
 23    3           OUTPUT$B(OUTDEX) = TIME$IN$TENTHS$PROCEDURE - TIME$ZERO$TENTHS;
 24    3           OUTDEX = OUTDEX + 1;
 25    3           GO$FLAG = FALSE;
 26    3        END;

 27    2        IF INTERRUPT$IDENTIFIERS = 00001000B THEN      /* UNDER-PRESSURE */
 28    2        DO;
 29    3           OUTPUT$A(OUTDEX) = 10000000B;        /* ALARM */
 30    3           OUTPUT$B(OUTDEX) = TIME$IN$TENTHS$PROCEDURE - TIME$ZERO$TENTHS;
 31    3           OUTDEX = OUTDEX + 1;
 32    3        END;
 33    2        IF INTERRUPT$IDENTIFIERS = 00010000B THEN      /* START BUTTON */
 34    2        DO;
 35    3           TIME$ZERO$TENTHS = TIME$IN$TENTHS$PROCEDURE;
 36    3           FEED$RATE = 202;       /* REPLACE WITH INPUT OPERATIONS LATER */
 37    3           POSITION$ZERO = 20; /* DITTO */
 38    3           GO$FLAG = TRUE;
 39    3        END;

 40    2        DISABLE;  /* MUST DISABLE INTERRUPTS BEFORE RESTORING INTELLEC INTERRUPT LOGIC */
 41    2        OUTPUT(0FDH) = 20H;     /* RESTORE INTELLEC INTERRUPT LOGIC */

 42    2     END INTERRUPT$PROCESSOR;

 43    1     END INTERRUPT$PROCESSOR$MODULE;
```

```
            /*****************************************************************************/
            /* NUMERICAL CONTROL PROGRAM: MODULE CONTAINING NUMIN AND NUMOUT            */
            /*****************************************************************************/

  1         ASCII$IN$AND$OUT:
            DO;

  2    1    NUMIN:
            PROCEDURE(POINTER) ADDRESS PUBLIC;
  3    2       DECLARE (POINTER, CHAR$PTR, BASE2, BASE8, BASE10, BASE16) ADDRESS,
                       POINTER$REF BASED POINTER ADDRESS,
                       (CURRENT$CHAR BASED CHAR$PTR, I) BYTE,
                       MORE$STRING BYTE;
  4    2       DECLARE DIGITS (*) BYTE DATA ('0123456789ABCDEF');
  5    2       DECLARE TRUE  LITERALLY '0FFH',
                       FALSE LITERALLY '0';

  6    2       BASE2, BASE8, BASE10, BASE16 = 0;
  7    2       CHAR$PTR = POINTER$REF;
  8    2       DO WHILE CURRENT$CHAR = ' ';
  9    3          CHAR$PTR = CHAR$PTR + 1;
 10    3       END;
 11    2       MORE$STRING = TRUE;
 12    2       DO WHILE MORE$STRING;
 13    3          MORE$STRING = FALSE;
 14    3          DO I = 0 TO LAST(DIGITS);
 15    4             IF CURRENT$CHAR = DIGITS(I) THEN
 16    4             DO;
 17    5                IF I < 2 THEN
 18    5                   BASE2 = BASE2 + BASE2 + I;
 19    5                BASE8 = SHL(BASE8, 3) + I;
 20    5                IF I < 10 THEN
 21    5                   BASE10 = BASE10 * 10 + I;
 22    5                BASE16 = SHL(BASE16, 4) + I;
 23    5                CHAR$PTR = CHAR$PTR + 1;
 24    5                MORE$STRING = TRUE;
 25    5             END;
 26    4          END;
 27    3       END;
 28    2       POINTER$REF = CHAR$PTR + 1;
 29    2       IF CURRENT$CHAR = 'H' THEN
 30    2          RETURN BASE16;
 31    2       IF CURRENT$CHAR = 'O' OR CURRENT$CHAR = 'Q' THEN
 32    2          RETURN BASE8;
 33    2       POINTER$REF = CHAR$PTR;
 34    2       CHAR$PTR = CHAR$PTR - 1;
 35    2       IF CURRENT$CHAR = 'B' THEN
 36    2          RETURN BASE2;
 37    2       RETURN BASE10;
 38    2    END NUMIN;
 39    1    NUMOUT:
            PROCEDURE(VALUE, BASE, LC, BUFADR, WIDTH) PUBLIC;
 40    2       DECLARE (VALUE, BUFADR) ADDRESS;
 41    2       DECLARE (BASE, LC, WIDTH, I) BYTE;
 42    2       DECLARE (CHARS BASED BUFADR) (1) BYTE;
 43    2       DECLARE DIGITS(*) BYTE DATA('0123456789ABCDEF');

 44    2       DO I = 1 TO WIDTH;
 45    3          CHARS(WIDTH - I) = DIGITS(VALUE MOD BASE);
 46    3          VALUE = VALUE / BASE;
 47    3       END;
 48    2       I = 0;
 49    2       DO WHILE CHARS(I) = '0' AND I < WIDTH - 1;
 50    3          CHARS(I) = LC;
 51    3          I = I + 1;
 52    3       END;
 53    2    END NUMOUT;

 54    1    END ASCII$IN$AND$OUT;
```

ables, for example, which are not directly available in the 8080 instruction set, must be done by procedure calls. In many cases these procedures are compiled into the program automatically and the programmer need hardly be aware that it is being done. However, any time the compiler sees the attribute EXTERNAL in a compilation, it does not automatically emit these procedures, on the theory that they may very well be called for in other modules as well and that there is no point in having multiple copies of them. Therefore, when we link modules together, we must also specify a library where any needed procedures of this type may be obtained. This library has the name PLM80.LIB. These procedures do not have to be declared.

Another library named SYSTEM.LIB contains object-code procedures that implement the various ISIS system calls such as READ, WRITE, OPEN, etc., and should also be specified in the linkage operation whenever these functions are used. These procedures must be declared as EXTERNAL.

The actual linkage operation is a simple matter of typing the command LINK at the console followed by the names of all the modules to be included, followed by the names of any libraries to be searched in satisfying external references, and naming the module to contain the linked program. The few necessary details can readily be found in appropriate manuals. For the modules involved in our situation, the LINK command is as follows:

```
LINK :F1:8NC3.OBJ, :F1:INOUTM.OBJ, :F1:CLOCKS.OBJ, :F1:INTPR3.OBJ, &
:F1:COMPUT.OBJ, SYSTEM.LIB, PLM80.LIB TO :F1:8NC3.LNK
```

The ampersand (&) at the end of the first line is an indication that the command is continued on the next line.

THE LOCATE COMMAND

The final operation before running the program is to LOCATE it. This is a matter of converting the addresses from relative form to absolute locations, producing absolute object code that can actually be loaded into memory, executed, and run. Alternatively, the output of the LOCATE operation can be used to program PROMs or used for in-circuit emulation.

If we don't care where the program and its data are located in memory, the command can be as simple as

```
LOCATE :F1:8NC3.LNK
```

The output is a file having the same name as that named in the LOCATE command but no extension. This file contains a program ready to be loaded and run. This is done simply by typing the name of the file.

The LOCATE command has a number of other features, however, of which we may note some of the more commonly used.

There are four parts to a program produced by the compiler and combined by the linker. These are:

Code the actual machine instructions and constants,

Data the part containing variable data and storage for I/O buffers,

The program stack area used for a variety of special purposes,

Memory which is anything not in the first three groups; sometimes used for direct memory access.

It is common for these different parts of the program to be physically stored in different kinds of memory. For example, the code, which never has to be modified, can be placed in ROM or PROM, although it can also be placed in RAM if desired. The other three parts of the program must all be in RAM, but even then it is sometimes desirable to be able to specify exact locations to make these segments correspond with physical devices. For these reasons the LOCATE command permits us to specify exactly where these four parts of the program are to be allocated. To do this, it is necessary to know how long each segment is; this information is easily obtained by doing the LOCATE operation once with no segment locations specified. One of the outputs of this operation is a map, which for our program is as follows:

```
MEMORY MAP OF MODULE 8NC3,
READ FROM FILE :F1:8NC3.LNK,
WRITTEN TO FILE :F1:8NC3,
START ADDRESS OF 36AAH.

ADDRESS LENGTH  SEGMENT

0018H   0003H   ABSOLUTE
3680H   06FDH   CODE
3D7DH   0044H   STACK
3DC1H   0595H   DATA
4356H   B36AH   MEMORY
```

Now suppose we wish to place the code starting in 4000H and all the rest of the program starting in 8000H. This is all that has to be done:

```
LOCATE :F1:9NC3.LNK CODE(4000H) DATA(8000H)
```

The LOCATE command also permits us to produce a listing of the absolute locations corresponding to symbols and the beginnings of lines in the original source program. In order for this to be possible, the compilation must have been done with a variation of the compiler command containing the word DEBUG, so that the necessary information can be carried along with the object program for use in this way. The listing of lines and symbols then makes it possible, using the ISIS DEBUG command, to inspect and control the operation of the absolute object program from the Intellec console. We shall consider this operation briefly below.

THE LIB COMMAND

Programs can be combined into libraries. For an example, suppose that the numerical-control program is under development, and that the programmer is working exclusively at one stage on the module that computes the control current. As the module is revised and recompiled, it will be necessary each time to link it with all the other modules that make up the complete program. Here, there are only four other modules; in a complete applications program there could conceivably be dozens. The time and effort of typing all these names correctly in a LINK command is an avoidable burden, using the LIB facility.

The technique is to place all of the object modules (compiler output modules), except the one under active development, into a library, having a name such as :F1:NUMCON.LIB, perhaps. The mechanics of doing so are quite simple. Now, when we wish to link a new version of the current computation module with all the others, we can simply write:

```
LINK :F1:COMPUT.OBJ, :F1:NUMCON.LIB, SYSTEM.LIB, PLM80.LIB TO :F1:8NC3.LNK
```

PROGRAM DEBUGGING

Programs as originally written unfortunately usually contain errors. These can have causes ranging from mistyping and other simple carelessness, to misunderstanding of the language, incorrect program logic, misunderstanding of the specifications, or failure of communication between programmers writing different modules. When a program has been written, it is always necessary to try to establish that it works correctly.

Some errors will result in a syntactically wrong program such that the compiler can report a problem. Other errors lead to a program that is syntactically correct, but still does not produce correct results. An essential part of the testing of any program is to compare its output with hand-calculated answers.

We can get a brief indication of some of these operations by studying a final version of the module to compute the current.

COMPILER DIAGNOSTICS

The module shown before in Fig. 9.2 was modified to introduce some deliberate errors. One of the changes was to reverse the test of the simulated input against the sentinel. The other changes were designed to illustrate various aspects of the diagnostic work of the compiler. The modified source program is shown in Fig. 9.6. How many errors can you find?

The listing from compiling this program is shown in Fig. 9.7. The first report of an error is after statement 15 where the diagnostic message is perfectly clear and is placed immediately after the offending statement. The message after statement 21 takes a little more detective work, since the problem actually occurred earlier. In

```
/*************************************************************************/
/* NUMERICAL CONTROL PROGRAM: MODULE TO COMPUTE CURRENT                 */
/*                                                                       */
/* CHECKOUT VERSION 1                                                    */
/* THIS VERSION CONTAINS A NUMBER OF DELIBERATE ERRORS                  */
/* ---- ------- -------- - ------ -- ---------- ------                   */
/*                                                                       */
/*************************************************************************/

COMPUTE$CONTROL$CURRENT$MODULE:
DO;
   DECLARE INPUT$2(200) ADDRESS EXTERNAL;
   DECLARE OUTPUT$A(250) BYTE EXTERNAL;
   DECLARE OUTPUT$B(250) ADDRESS EXTERNAL;
   DECLARE (INDEX$2, OUTDEX) ADDRESS EXTERNAL;
   DECLARE WRAPUP LABEL;
   DECLARE (TIME$ZERO$TENTHS, POSITION$ZERO, FEED$RATE) ADDRESS EXTERNAL;

TIME$IN$TENTHS$PROCEDURE:
   PROCEDURE ADDRESS EXTERNAL;
END TIME$IN$TENTHS$PROCEDURE;

COMPUTE$CONTROL$CURRENT:
PROCEDURE PUBLIC;
   DECLARE (PRESENT$POSITION, DESIRED$POSITION, CURRENT) ADDRESS;
   DECLARE POSITION$COEFFICIENT ADDRESS DATA(3);
   DECLARE ELAPSED$TIME ADDRESS;
   DECLARE TIME$INDEX BYTE;
   DECLARE CURRENT ADDRESS;

   /* SIMULATE INPUT OF TOOL POSITION */
   IF INPUT$2(INDEX$2) = 0FFH THEN;   /* SENTINEL: END OF SIMULATED INPUT */
   DO;
      GO TO WRAPUP;
   END;
   ELSE
   DO;
      PRESENT$POSITION = INPUT$2(INDEX$2);
   INDEX$2 = INDEX$2 + 1;

   ELAPSED$TIME = TIME$IN$TENTHS$PROCEDURE - TIME$ZERO$TENTHS;
   DESIRED$POSITION = POSITION$ZERO + FEED$RATE * ELAPSED$TIME;
   CURRENT = POSITION$COEFFICIENT * (DESIRED$POSITION - PRESENT$POSITION);
   OUTPUT$A(OUTDEX) = 1;    /* IDENTIFIES COLUMN 2 AS CURRENT
   OUTPUT$B(OUTDEX) = CURRENT
   OUTDEX = OUTDEX + 1;
   OUTPUT$A(OUTDEX) = 2;    /* IDENTIFIES COLUMN 2 AS TIME */
   OUTPUT$B(OUTDEX) = TIME$IN$TENTHS$PROCEDURE - TIME$ZERO$TENTHS;
   OUTDEX = OUTDEX + 1

   DO TIME$INDEX = 0 TO 9;     /* WASTE SOME TIME, SO SIMULATED INPUT */
      CALL TIME(170);          /* DOESN'T RUN TOO FAR AHEAD OF REALTIME CLOCK */
   END;

END COMPUTE$CONTROL$CURRENT;


END COMPUTE$CONTROL$CURRENT$MODULE;
```

Fig. 9.6. Source listing of a modified version of the module shown in Fig. 9.2, with a number of deliberate errors introduced.

```
             /****************************************************************************/
             /* NUMERICAL CONTROL PROGRAM: MODULE TO COMPUTE CURRENT                    */
             /*                                                                          */
             /* CHECKOUT VERSION 1                                                       */
             /* THIS VERSION CONTAINS A NUMBER OF DELIBERATE ERRORS                     */
             /* ---- ------- -------- - ------ -- ---------- ------                       */
             /*                                                                          */
             /****************************************************************************/

   1         COMPUTE$CONTROL$CURRENT$MODULE:
             DO;
   2    1       DECLARE INPUT$2(200) ADDRESS EXTERNAL;
   3    1       DECLARE OUTPUT$A(250) BYTE EXTERNAL;
   4    1       DECLARE OUTPUT$B(250) ADDRESS EXTERNAL;
   5    1       DECLARE (INDEX$2, OUTDEX) ADDRESS EXTERNAL;
   6    1       DECLARE WRAPUP LABEL;
   7    1       DECLARE (TIME$ZERO$TENTHS, POSITION$ZERO, FEED$RATE) ADDRESS EXTERNAL;

   8    1    TIME$IN$TENTHS$PROCEDURE:
                PROCEDURE ADDRESS EXTERNAL;
   9    2    END TIME$IN$TENTHS$PROCEDURE;

  10    1    COMPUTE$CONTROL$CURRENT:
             PROCEDURE PUBLIC;
  11    2       DECLARE (PRESENT$POSITION, DESIRED$POSITION, CURRENT) ADDRESS;
  12    2       DECLARE POSITION$COEFFICIENT ADDRESS DATA(3);
  13    2       DECLARE ELAPSED$TIME ADDRESS;
  14    2       DECLARE TIME$INDEX BYTE;
  15    2       DECLARE CURRENT ADDRESS;
*** ERROR #78, STATEMENT #15, NEAR 'CURRENT',   DUPLICATE DECLARATION

                /* SIMULATE INPUT OF TOOL POSITION */
  16    2       IF INPUT$2(INDEX$2) = 0FFH THEN;   /* SENTINEL: END OF SIMULATED INPUT */
  18    2       DO;
  19    3          GO TO WRAPUP;
*** ERROR #105, STATEMENT #19, NEAR 'WRAPUP',   UNDECLARED IDENTIFIER
  20    3       END;
  21    2       ELSE
*** ERROR #29, STATEMENT #21, NEAR 'ELSE',   ILLEGAL STATEMENT
                DO;
  22    2          PRESENT$POSITION = INPUT$2(INDEX$2);
  23    2       INDEX$2 = INDEX$2 + 1;

  24    2       ELAPSED$TIME = TIME$IN$TENTHS$PROCEDURE - TIME$ZERO$TENTHS;
  25    2       DESIRED$POSITION = POSITION$ZERO + FEED$RATE * ELAPSED$TIME;
  26    2       CURRENT = POSITION$COEFFICIENT * (DESIRED$POSITION - PRESENT$POSITION);
  27    2       OUTPUT$A(OUTDEX) = 1;   /* IDENTIFIES COLUMN 2 AS CURRENT
                OUTPUT$B(OUTDEX) = CURRENT
                OUTDEX = OUTDEX + 1;
                OUTPUT$A(OUTDEX) = 2;   /* IDENTIFIES COLUMN 2 AS TIME */
  28    2       OUTPUT$B(OUTDEX) = TIME$IN$TENTHS$PROCEDURE - TIME$ZERO$TENTHS;
  29    2       OUTDEX = OUTDEX + 1

*** ERROR #32, STATEMENT #29, NEAR 'DO',   INVALID SYNTAX, TEXT IGNORED UNTIL ';'
                DO TIME$INDEX = 0 TO 9;     /* WASTE SOME TIME, SO SIMULATED INPUT */
  30    2          CALL TIME(170);          /* DOESN'T RUN TOO FAR AHEAD OF REALTIME CLOCK */
  31    2       END;

  32    1     END COMPUTE$CONTROL$CURRENT;
*** ERROR #20, STATEMENT #32, NEAR 'COMPUTECONTROLCURRENT', MISMATCHED IDENTIFIER AT END OF BLOCK


*** ERROR #93, STATEMENT #32,   MISSING 'DO' FOR 'END', 'END' IGNORED
              END COMPUTE$CONTROL$CURRENT$MODULE;
*** ERROR #172, NEAR 'WRAPUP',   INVALID LABEL: UNDEFINED
```

seeking the cause, one might notice that there seems to be no statement 17; this actually is true, since the semicolon after the THEN in statement 16 produces a null statement. Statement 16 as written is not incorrect; it simply never does anything. Statements 18–20 are also correct; statement 19 would be carried out unconditionally. Statement 21, therefore, is in fact the first one that is syntactically wrong. Bear in mind that statement 21 containing the DO is ignored.

The next diagnostic message is even farther from the source of the trouble, which is the missing EXTERNAL attribute on statement 6. The assertion that WRAPUP is undeclared relates to this procedure.

The message after statement 29 is caused by the missing semicolon. Note again that, because of this error, what should have been a separate statement on the next line is also ignored.

The error message after statement 32 tells us that the END statement does not match a DO having the label given. The problem has to do with the DO statements in 21 and 29 that were ignored because of other errors. Eventually, if not sooner, we will also notice there is a missing END after statement 22.

The last two error messages give us further reports of things we already knew.

These are all the syntactic errors in this program but they are not the only serious typographical errors. Observe that statement 27 covers four lines! The problem is the missing */ at the end of the first line, which caused the next three statements to be treated as part of the comment. This also means that the missing semicolon in the second line of the statement could not be detected.

We now correct these errors and recompile, leading to the program shown in Fig. 9.8. The compiler reports no program errors and yet there is one rather serious error, which careful reading should reveal. Can you find it?

This module was linked with the other four, without recompiling the others. The output module from linkage was located and the program was run. It went into an infinite loop and produced no output. At this stage we must engage in detective work to establish what happened. There are software tools for trying to track down the trouble, but before using them it usually pays to think about the symptoms a bit. In this case it would be reasonable to ask something like "What is the main difference between this program and the one that ran correctly before?" The answer is the reversal of the condition in line 15 of Fig. 9.8. If we look at this section of the program, we will now see that the END statement in line 22, which was missing in the earlier version, has been misplaced; lines 21 and 22 should be reversed. The fact that the program as shown here has incorrect indentation is not a syntactic error, since the compiler derives no meaning from indentation.

This illustrates the principle that the correction of one error can frequently be the cause of others.

THE DEBUG CONTROL

This error was corrected and the LINK and LOCATE operations repeated, after which the program produced answers, but now the answers are very much too large.

```
PL/M-80 COMPILER    FIG. 9.8                                    PAGE   1

             /***********************************************************************/
             /* NUMERICAL CONTROL PROGRAM: MODULE TO COMPUTE CURRENT                */
             /*                                                                     */
             /* CHECKOUT VERSION 2                                                  */
             /* THIS VERSION CONTAINS A NUMBER OF DELIBERATE ERRORS                 */
             /* ---- ------- -------- - ------ -- ---------- ------                 */
             /*                                                                     */
             /***********************************************************************/

  1          COMPUTE$CONTROL$CURRENT$MODULE:
             DO;
  2   1         DECLARE INPUT$2(200) ADDRESS EXTERNAL;
  3   1         DECLARE OUTPUT$A(250) BYTE EXTERNAL;
  4   1         DECLARE OUTPUT$B(250) ADDRESS EXTERNAL;
  5   1         DECLARE (INDEX$2, OUTDEX) ADDRESS EXTERNAL;
  6   1         DECLARE WRAPUP LABEL EXTERNAL;
  7   1         DECLARE (TIME$ZERO$TENTHS, POSITION$ZERO, FEED$RATE) ADDRESS EXTERNAL;

  8   1      TIME$IN$TENTHS$PROCEDURE:
                PROCEDURE ADDRESS EXTERNAL;
  9   2      END TIME$IN$TENTHS$PROCEDURE;

 10   1      COMPUTE$CONTROL$CURRENT:
             PROCEDURE PUBLIC;
 11   2         DECLARE (PRESENT$POSITION, DESIRED$POSITION, CURRENT) ADDRESS;
 12   2         DECLARE POSITION$COEFFICIENT ADDRESS DATA(3);
 13   2         DECLARE ELAPSED$TIME ADDRESS;
 14   2         DECLARE TIME$INDEX BYTE;

                /* SIMULATE INPUT OF TOOL POSITION */
 15   2         IF INPUT$2(INDEX$2) = 0FFH THEN   /* SENTINEL: END OF SIMULATED INPUT */
 16   2         DO;
 17   3            GO TO WRAPUP;
 18   3         END;
                ELSE
 19   2         DO;
 20   3            PRESENT$POSITION = INPUT$2(INDEX$2);
 21   3         INDEX$2 = INDEX$2 + 1;
 22   3         END;

 23   2         ELAPSED$TIME = TIME$IN$TENTHS$PROCEDURE - TIME$ZERO$TENTHS;
 24   2         DESIRED$POSITION = POSITION$ZERO + FEED$RATE * ELAPSED$TIME;
 25   2         CURRENT = POSITION$COEFFICIENT * (DESIRED$POSITION - PRESENT$POSITION);
 26   2         OUTPUT$A(OUTDEX) = 1;   /* IDENTIFIES COLUMN 2 AS CURRENT */
 27   2         OUTPUT$B(OUTDEX) = CURRENT;
 28   2         OUTDEX = OUTDEX + 1;
 29   2         OUTPUT$A(OUTDEX) = 2;   /* IDENTIFIES COLUMN 2 AS TIME */
 30   2         OUTPUT$B(OUTDEX) = TIME$IN$TENTHS$PROCEDURE - TIME$ZERO$TENTHS;
 31   2         OUTDEX = OUTDEX + 1;

 32   2         DO TIME$INDEX = 0 TO 9;     /* WASTE SOME TIME, SO SIMULATED INPUT */
 33   3            CALL TIME(170);          /* DOESN'T RUN TOO FAR AHEAD OF REALTIME CLOCK */
 34   3         END;

 35   2      END COMPUTE$CONTROL$CURRENT;


 36   1      END COMPUTE$CONTROL$CURRENT$MODULE;
```

Nothing about the actual computation was changed, so we have more detective work to do.

This time there are no obvious blunders so it is necessary to find out exactly what the program used for data at each stage of the computation of the current. In order to do this we recompile this module and the main-program module, in each case adding the compiler control DEBUG when the modules are compiled. This directs the compiler to place in the object modules information about all the symbols and all the lines in each source module. The modules were linked in the usual way. In the LOCATE operation, however, we add the diagnostic controls LINES, SYMBOLS, and PRINT(:LP:). As a result of these controls, we obtain the listing shown in Fig. 9.9 (Here the listing has been put into three columns to save space in the book.) This gives us the absolute memory location for each symbol and each line in both of these modules. (It does not give the same information for the other three modules because when they were compiled the DEBUG control was not used.) This says, for instance, looking at the last column, that CURRENT is in absolute memory location 431A and that the object program statements for line 23 in this module begin in 390E.

Now we type in the command:

```
DEBUG :F1:9NC4
```

The program is loaded but execution does not begin. At this point we can type in any of a variety of commands from the repertory of the debug system, which is part of the *monitor* program of the Intellec system. We can ask to see the contents of memory locations or of the 8080 machine registers; we can change the contents of memory; we can set *breakpoints*.

Setting a breakpoint means to direct the program to stop if it ever reaches the location specified in the breakpoint command. What we wish to do here is set a breakpoint at the location corresponding to the beginning of statement 26 in Fig. 9.8 and tell the program to begin execution. When this point is reached, all of the tables of simulated input should have been set up and the value of current corresponding to the first simulated position should have been computed. We can now inspect the actual contents of memory locations corresponding to all the variables involved in the computation of CURRENT, see if they are as expected, and check that the computation has been done properly. If we wish, we could give any of these variables new values and direct the monitor to repeat that part of the program again, stopping wherever we might wish.

In our simulated checkout exercise, we would discover at this point that the programmer working on the INTERRUPT$PROCESSOR module changed the value of the feedrate to a larger number, which was intended to have four binary places. Somehow we didn't get the word! Obviously this is a contrived example, but such problems are a major consideration in the management of programming. Effective communication between programmers working on different sections of a

```
ISIS-II OBJECT LOCATER, V1.3
INVOKED BY:
-LOCATE :F1:9NC4.LNK LINES SYMBOLS MAP PRINT(:TO:)

SYMBOL TABLE OF MODULE 9NC4,
READ FROM FILE :F1:9NC4.LNK,
WRITTEN TO FILE :F1:9NC4.

VALUE TYPE SYMBOL

      MOD  NUMERICALCONTROL3
4358H SYM  MEMORY
3DC3H SYM  TIMEMS
3DC5H SYM  TIMETENTHS
3DC7H SYM  TIMEZEROTENTHS
3DC9H SYM  FEEDRATE
3DCBH SYM  POSITIONZERO
3DCDH SYM  GOFLAG
3DCEH SYM  ECHOAFTN
3DD0H SYM  DISK1AFTN
3DD2H SYM  DISK2AFTN
3DD4H SYM  LPAFTN
0008H SYM  LOC8
0009H SYM  LOC9
3DD6H SYM  LOC9SAVE
0018H SYM  LOC24
0019H SYM  LOC25
3DD8H SYM  INPUT1
3E0AH SYM  INPUT2
3F9AH SYM  OUTPUTA
4094H SYM  OUTPUTB
4288H SYM  INDEX1
428AH SYM  INDEX2
428CH SYM  OUTDEX
428EH SYM  OUTDEXFINAL
4290H SYM  BUFFER
4310H SYM  BUFFPTR
4312H SYM  COUNT
4314H SYM  STATUS
36EDH SYM  WRAPUP
37A5H SYM  SETUP
37A5H LIN     50
37A5H LIN     51
37BAH LIN     52
37D1H LIN     53
37E8H LIN     54
37FDH LIN     55
3803H LIN     56
380EH LIN     57
3823H LIN     58
382BH LIN     60
3834H LIN     61
383AH LIN     62
383DH LIN     64
3843H LIN     65
3853H LIN     66
385AH LIN     67
385AH LIN     68
385DH LIN     69
3863H LIN     70
386EH LIN     71
3883H LIN     72
388BH LIN     74
3899H LIN     75
389FH LIN     76
38A2H LIN     78
38A8H LIN     79
38BBH LIN     80
38C2H LIN     81
38C2H LIN     82
38C5H LIN     83
38D1H LIN     84
38DAH LIN     85
38DEH LIN     86
36AAH LIN     87
36B0H LIN     88
36B1H LIN     89
36B5H LIN     90
36B9H LIN     91
36BDH LIN     92
36C1H LIN     93
36C7H LIN     94
36CCH LIN     95
36D3H LIN     96
36D8H LIN     97
36DFH LIN     98
36E0H LIN     99
36E0H LIN    100
36E7H LIN    101
36EAH LIN    102
36EDH LIN    103
36F7H LIN    104
3709H LIN    105
3725H LIN    106
3742H LIN    107
3747H LIN    108
374AH LIN    109
375BH LIN    110
3768H LIN    111
3769H LIN    112
376DH LIN    113
3773H LIN    114
3774H LIN    115
377FH LIN    116
378AH LIN    117
3795H LIN    118
37A0H LIN    119
37A3H LIN    120
      MOD  COMPUTECONTROLCURRENTMODULE
4358H SYM  MEMORY
38E1H SYM  COMPUTECONTROLCURRENT
4316H SYM  PRESENTPOSITION
4318H SYM  DESIREDPOSITION
431AH SYM  CURRENT
38DFH SYM  POSITIONCOEFFICIENT
431CH SYM  ELAPSEDTIME
431EH SYM  TIMEINDEX
38E1H LIN     10
38E1H LIN     15
38F2H LIN     17
3901H LIN     18
3904H LIN     20
3907H LIN     21
3907H LIN     22
390EH LIN     23
391BH LIN     24
392DH LIN     25
393EH LIN     26
3947H LIN     27
3958H LIN     28
395FH LIN     29
3965H LIN     30
397CH LIN     31
3983H LIN     32
3991H LIN     33
3996H LIN     34
399DH LIN     35

MEMORY MAP OF MODULE 9NC4,
READ FROM FILE :F1:9NC4.LNK,
WRITTEN TO FILE :F1:9NC4,
START ADDRESS OF 36AAH.

ADDRESS LENGTH  SEGMENT

0018H    0003H   ABSOLUTE
3680H    06FFH   CODE
3D7FH    0044H   STACK
3DC3H    0595H   DATA
4358H    B368H   MEMORY
```

Fig. 9.9. Output from the LOCATE command when LINES and SYMBOLS were requested.

```
PL/M-80 COMPILER    FIG. 9.10                                          PAGE   1

              /*************************************************************************/
              /* NUMERICAL CONTROL PROGRAM: MODULE TO COMPUTE CURRENT                  */
              /*                                                                       */
              /* THE FINAL, CORRECT, VERSION                                           */
              /*                                                                       */
              /*************************************************************************/

              COMPUTE$CONTROL$CURRENT$MODULE:
              DO;
       1         DECLARE INPUT$2(200) ADDRESS EXTERNAL;
       1         DECLARE OUTPUT$A(250) BYTE EXTERNAL;
       1         DECLARE OUTPUT$B(250) ADDRESS EXTERNAL;
       1         DECLARE (INDEX$2, OUTDEX) ADDRESS EXTERNAL;
       1         DECLARE WRAPUP LABEL EXTERNAL;
       1         DECLARE (TIME$ZERO$TENTHS, POSITION$ZERO, FEED$RATE) ADDRESS EXTERNAL;

       1      TIME$IN$TENTHS$PROCEDURE:
                 PROCEDURE ADDRESS EXTERNAL;
       2      END TIME$IN$TENTHS$PROCEDURE;

       1      COMPUTE$CONTROL$CURRENT:
              PROCEDURE PUBLIC;
       2         DECLARE (PRESENT$POSITION, DESIRED$POSITION, CURRENT) ADDRESS;
       2         DECLARE POSITION$COEFFICIENT ADDRESS DATA(3);
       2         DECLARE ELAPSED$TIME ADDRESS;
       2         DECLARE TIME$INDEX BYTE;

                 /* SIMULATE INPUT OF TOOL POSITION */
       2         IF INPUT$2(INDEX$2) <> 0FFH THEN   /* SENTINEL: END OF SIMULATED INPUT */
       2         DO;
       3            PRESENT$POSITION = INPUT$2(INDEX$2);
       3         END;
                 ELSE
       2         DO;
       3            GO TO WRAPUP;
       3         END;
       2         INDEX$2 = INDEX$2 + 1;

       2         ELAPSED$TIME = TIME$IN$TENTHS$PROCEDURE - TIME$ZERO$TENTHS;
       2         DESIRED$POSITION = POSITION$ZERO + FEED$RATE * ELAPSED$TIME;
       2         CURRENT = POSITION$COEFFICIENT * (DESIRED$POSITION - PRESENT$POSITION);
       2         OUTPUT$A(OUTDEX) = 1;   /* IDENTIFIES COLUMN 2 AS CURRENT */
       2         OUTPUT$B(OUTDEX) = CURRENT;
       2         OUTDEX = OUTDEX + 1;
       2         OUTPUT$A(OUTDEX) = 2;   /* IDENTIFIES COLUMN 2 AS TIME */
       2         OUTPUT$B(OUTDEX) = TIME$IN$TENTHS$PROCEDURE - TIME$ZERO$TENTHS;
       2         OUTDEX = OUTDEX + 1;

       2         DO TIME$INDEX = 0 TO 9;     /* WASTE SOME TIME, SO SIMULATED INPUT */
       3            CALL TIME(170);          /* DOESN'T RUN TOO FAR AHEAD OF REALTIME CLOCK */
       3         END;
```

large program is one of the most crucial elements in a successful project and one that must be systematized and given the attention that it deserves.

Correcting this error leads to the program shown in Fig. 9.10, which runs correctly. Or perhaps it would be judicious to say "which—so far as the author and reviewers can determine—runs correctly."

SUMMARY

This completes our sketch of the facilities provided by the ISIS system. There are other capabilities not discussed in this book and we have made no attempt even to cover all of the details of those features that have been discussed. It is hoped that this much of an introduction will at least whet the reader's appetite to learn the full power of the system and use it for faster and more effective program development.

ANSWERS TO SELECTED EXERCISES

Chapter 2

1. Acceptable: Q, Q13, ENDOFTEXT, ENDOFTEXT, PROCESS$12, FIFTY$PERCENT, FIFTY$, DO$CASE.
   Unacceptable: 13Q (does not begin with a letter)
   END-OF-TEXT (hyphens not permitted)
   PROCESS 12 (blank not permitted; PROCESS by itself acceptable)
   'VARIABLE' (quotes not permitted)
   SECTION501(C)3 (parentheses not permitted)
   FIFTY% (percent sign not permitted)
   50 (does not begin with a letter)
   CASE (reserved word)
   DO CASE (both reserved words; blank not permitted)
3. 7 and 7Q are equivalent
   7D and 7H are equivalent
   1101$1000$0001B and 1101100000001 would be equivalent if the second number were followed by a 'B' to indicate binary.
   23.0 is not a legal constant: decimal points not permitted
   —3 is not a legal constant: minus signs not permitted
   2FH and 37Q are equivalent
   BAH and 186D would be equivalent if the first number were written 0BAH, with the required leading digit.

39Q and 39O *are* equivalent—that's the letter "oh" in the second one, although it's very difficult to tell with the typeface used. That's why the Q form is provided for octal.

19 and 13H are equivalent.

5. 469 could not be the value of a BYTE variable, which can hold a number no larger than 255.

6. 212 could be the value of an ADDRESS variable; the high-order eight bits would be zeros.

7. No problem. Describing a variable as being of type "ADDRESS" means simply that it contains 16 bits. This terminology relates to the number of bits required to represent an address in the Intel 8080 architecture, but the contents of an ADDRESS variable does not depend on the memory configuration of a particular system.

8. 46.7 is illegal because of the decimal point
−12 is illegal because of the minus sign
65547 is too large
46P is illegal because the P is not permitted
123HEX is illegal because the EX is not permitted

9. a) Legal
b) Legal
c) Legal
d) Illegal because of the decimal point in the constant
e) Legal
f) Illegal because of the two asterisks; there is no exponentiation in PL/M.
g) Legal

11. a) 47
b) 4; result cannot be contained in the eight bits of a BYTE variable.
c) 260
d) Zero, perhaps; the product exceeds 16 bits, and the result is not guaranteed.
e) 1
f) 12 to all three
g) Zero; 1 bit is shifted out of range of BYTE variable.
h) 256
i) 41
j) 41

13. a) Equivalent
b) Not equivalent; without parentheses, multiplication is done before addition.
c) Not equivalent; 12X is not a legal identifier, and there is no implied multiplication in PL/M.
d) Not equivalent: X * 12 calls for a multiplication, whereas X12 is an identifier.
e) Equivalent, since operations at same hierarchy level are carried out from left to right in absence of parentheses. Not equivalent if carried out from right to left.
f) Equivalent mathematically, for operations on real numbers of unlimited precision, but two considerations could make them not equivalent in a computer dealing with integers of finite length: doing the addition before the division could

cause loss of significance if the sum exceeds number capacity; if both numbers are odd, doing the addition first will lead to a result one larger than if the divisions are done first.

15. a) `INITIAL$PRESSURE = 0;`

b) `B = A + 12;`

c) `ITERATIONS = ITERATIONS + 1;`

d) `XSQUARED = X * X;`

e) `MEAN$TEMP = (TEMP$1 + TEMP$2 + TEMP$3) / 3;`

f) `DIGIT$1 = SHR(INPORT$1, 4);`

g) `Y = A / (B + C);`

h) `NEXT$DIGIT = VALUE MOD BASE;`

i) `HALF$VALUE = SHR(VALUE, 1);`

j) `ROUNDED$HALF$VALUE = SHR(VALUE+1, 1);`

k) `TOTAL$1, TOTAL$2 = 0;`

17. a) `01000001B`

b) `10010000B`

c) `10001010B`

d) `11111011B`

e) `01110011B`

19. Yes.

Chapter 3

1. a)
```
IF AGE >= 18 THEN
    LEGAL$ADULT = LEGAL$ADULT + 1;
```

b)
```
IF SIZE$A > 800 THEN
    BIG = BIG + 1;
ELSE
    LITTLE = LITTLE + 1;
```

c)
```
IF VAR$1 > VAR$2 THEN
    TEMPORARY = VAR$1;
ELSE
    TEMPORARY = VAR$2;
```

d)
```
IF HOURS$WORKED <> 40 THEN
   NON$STANDARD = 1;
```

e)
```
IF (DIGIT >= 30H) AND (DIGIT <= 39H) THEN
   GOOD = 1;
ELSE
   GOOD = 0;
```

3.
```
IF (GRADE$1 + GRADE$2 + GRADE$3) / 3 >= 65 THEN
   PASS = 1;
ELSE
   PASS = 0;
```

5. All three versions place the larger of A and B in BIG.

8. No. In the second version, the ELSE clause is invoked only if A = B and C = D but E ≠ F, whereas in the first version the ELSE clause is invoked if any of the three tests fails. Compare with the examples in Exercise 9.

10.
```
IF ANNUAL$EARNINGS <= 2000 THEN
   TAX = 0;
ELSE IF ANNUAL$EARNINGS <= 5000 THEN
   TAX = 2 * (ANNUAL$EARNINGS - 2000) / 100;
ELSE
   TAX = 60 + 5 * (ANNUAL$EARNINGS - 5000) / 100;
```

12. Send the squares of the integers from 12 down to 1, in succession, to output port 1.

14.
```
DECLARE (COUNT, N) BYTE;

COUNT = 0;
DO WHILE COUNT < 60;
   OUTPUT(16) = COUNT;
   N = 0
   DO WHILE N < 50;
      CALL TIME(200);
      N = N + 1;
   END;
   COUNT = COUNT + 1;
END;
```

17.
```
IF N  <= 3 THEN
DO CASE N;
   P = 1;
   P = X;
   P = (3*X*X - 1) / 2;
   P = (5*X*X*X - 3*X) / 2;
END;
ELSE
   P = 0;
```

19.
```
DECLARE (I, N) BYTE;
DECLARE SUM ADDRESS;

I, SUM = 0;
DO WHILE I < 100;
   SUM = SUM + INPUT(1);
   N = 0;
   DO WHILE N < 5;
      CALL TIME(200);
      N = N + 1;
   END;
   I = I + 1;
END;

OUTPUT(2) = SUM / 100;
```

Chapter 4

1. a)
```
ABC = (B(1) + B(2)) / B(3);
```

b)
```
B(16), B(17), B(18), B(19) = 0;
```

c)
```
IF B(9) > TEST THEN
   B(9) = (B(8) + B(10)) / 2;
```

d)
```
DO I = 0 TO LAST(B);
   B(I) = B(I) + 1;
END;
```

3. a) This is the FORTRAN format. Must use TO and BY.
   b) No negative numbers in PL/M; cannot decrement the index. Can be done with a DO–WHILE loop.
   c) Cannot combine the iterative DO with a DO–WHILE.

5. Send the odd integers from 1 to 15 to output port 1 and their squares to output port 2.

7. Yes, and the addition of the array elements is carried out in the same order.

9.
```
DO I = 0 TO 48;
   DX(I) = X(I+1) - X(I);
END;
```

11.
```
DECLARE (COUNT, N) BYTE;

DO COUNT = 0 TO 59;
   OUTPUT(16) = COUNT;
   DO N = 0 TO 49
      CALL TIME(200);
   END;
END;
```

14.
```
DECLARE SAMPLE(100) BYTE;
DECLARE (I, N) BYTE;

DO I = 0 TO 99;
    SAMPLE(I) = INPUT(8);
    DO N = 0 TO 4;
       CALL TIME(200);
    END;
END;
```

19. a) No error.
b) Not possible to factor out the array declaration.
c) No error.

Chapter 5

1.
```
RATE$1 = 12;
RATE$2 = INPUT(24);
RATE$3 = SHR(INPUT(25), 4);
RATE$4 = INPUT(26) AND 0FH;
CALL MEAN$PROCEDURE$1;
```

3.
```
MAX3:
PROCEDURE (ARG$1, ARG$2, ARG$3) ADDRESS;
   DECLARE (ARG$1, ARG$2, ARG$3, TEMP) ADDRESS;

   IF ARG$1 > ARG$2 THEN
      TEMP = ARG$1;
   ELSE
      TEMP = ARG$2;
   IF TEMP < ARG$3 THEN
      TEMP = ARG$3;
   RETURN TEMP;
END MAX3;
```

5.
```
SUMSQ3:
PROCEDURE (A1, A2, A3) ADDRESS;
   DECLARE (A1, A2, A3) BYTE;

   RETURN A1*A1 + A2*A2 + A3*A3;

END SUMSQ3;
```

7.
```
IF X$IN < X(0) OR X$IN > X(LAST(X)) THEN
DO;
   OUT$OF$RANGE = 0;
   RETURN;
END;
```

10. With RANDOM$NUMBER declared in RANDOM$PROC, there would be no way to communicate the *seed* (the starting number to the procedure) except to make it an argument. One would then need to determine whether it is legal for a RETURN statement to give a value to an argument; if not, the RETURN would have to name a second variable, and then the calling program would have to transfer the new value to RANDOM$NUMBER.

12. No, because none of the procedures call each other. All of them, of course, must precede the main program.

Chapter 6

1. a) The base must be an ADDRESS variable.
   b) The word BASED must immediately follow the name of the based variable.
   c) Same comment as (b); use two declarations. (It *is* legal for two variables to have the same base.)
   d) No type given for the based variable.

2. a) ARRAY(0) gives the *value* of the first element of the array; .ARRAY(0) gives the *location* of the first element of the array.
   b) Give the mean of the first ten elements of SECOND$ARRAY to MEAN$3.
   c) No difference.
   d) Compute the mean of the ten numbers starting with the one in ARRAY(9) and continuing with whatever follows. As it happens in the program as written, that *could* be the first nine elements of SECOND$ARRAY, but we are given no guarantees about how the compiler will allocate storage with the statements as written.

4. It would make no difference whatever; no storage is allocated to a based variable.

5. No good. An INITIAL value is given to a variable only when it is loaded into RAM. The program would work correctly for the first invocation, but thereafter the starting value of TEMP would be what the previous invocation left there.

12. Chaos! The first two arguments, which should have been location references, would instead send values. The procedure would take its arguments from the locations corresponding to those values. Worse, the third argument is a location reference, which would probably be some large number, leading to a long loop in executing the procedure.

Chapter 7

1. The inclusive extent is statements 69–192. The exclusive extent is statements 69–75 and 184–192.

2. The inclusive extent is statements 76–151. The exclusive extent is statements 76–83.

4. The scope of the variable I declared in statement 7 is statements 60–73, the main program, since the scope of this variable is interrupted by the variable of the same name declared in statement 33. (This was not intentional!) The scope of MEAN$1 is the entire program.

6. The scope is the entire program.

INDEX